Digital Education and Learning

Series Editors
Michael Thomas
University of Central Lancashire
Preston, UK

John Palfrey
Phillips Academy
Andover, MA, USA

Mark Warschauer
University of California
Irvine, USA

Much has been written during the first decade of the new millennium about the potential of digital technologies to produce a transformation of education. Digital technologies are portrayed as tools that will enhance learner collaboration and motivation and develop new multimodal literacy skills. Accompanying this has been the move from understanding literacy on the cognitive level to an appreciation of the sociocultural forces shaping learner development. Responding to these claims, the Digital Education and Learning Series explores the pedagogical potential and realities of digital technologies in a wide range of disciplinary contexts across the educational spectrum both in and outside of class. Focusing on local and global perspectives, the series responds to the shifting landscape of education, the way digital technologies are being used in different educational and cultural contexts, and examines the differences that lie behind the generalizations of the digital age. Incorporating cutting edge volumes with theoretical perspectives and case studies (single authored and edited collections), the series provides an accessible and valuable resource for academic researchers, teacher trainers, administrators and students interested in interdisciplinary studies of education and new and emerging technologies.

More information about this series at
http://www.palgrave.com/gp/series/14952

Matthew Barr

Graduate Skills and Game-Based Learning

Using Video Games for Employability in Higher Education

palgrave
macmillan

Matthew Barr
Centre for Computing Science Education
University of Glasgow
Glasgow, UK

Digital Education and Learning
ISBN 978-3-030-27785-7   ISBN 978-3-030-27786-4   (eBook)
https://doi.org/10.1007/978-3-030-27786-4

This Palgrave Macmillan imprint is published by the registered company Springer Nature Switzerland AG
The registered company address is: Gewerbestrasse 11, 6330 Cham, Switzerland

To Eva

Acknowledgements

This book couldn't exist without all those who contributed in various ways to its creation. First, I must thank my student participants, including those of you who took part in the initial pilot study, the main experimental study, and the subsequent interviews. There are too many of you to mention, but you know who you are! For those of you who ended up in any of my lectures, I apologise.

Thank you to the inspiring (and inspired) educators who took the time to tell me about the exciting ways in which you are using video games in higher education, even if it has meant sneaking them into the curriculum. I also want to thank the incredibly talented game developers who talked to me about the wonderful games they make, many of which featured in the experimental study. On any of the work I've done with the games industry, I am constantly amazed by the generosity of time and quality of insight that you folks offer to wretched academics.

Speaking of which, a number of academic colleagues also deserve thanks, especially Dr Steve Draper and Dr Susan Stuart, for their encouragement, insight, and support. Several of Steve's pearls of wisdom have made their way into this book, although I have begrudgingly given him credit. For the most part. Thank you also to Professor Richard Bartle and Professor Frank Coton, who examined the PhD on which a portion of this book is based. They say that time heals all wounds, and I expect that the psychological scars left by the viva experience will fade, eventually.

Thanks also to my colleagues in the College of Arts IT Support team, Chris, Raymond, Louise, and Mike, for their help in setting up the game lab, and to Ann Gow for letting me get away with having a game lab in the first place.

Thank you to Dr David Barr for his enormous help with the statistical analysis and advice on experimental design which, when I didn't ignore it, only improved the quality of the study. And thanks to Gee Whitley for supplying the Nintendo Entertainment System that sparked my interest in games and allowed me to repeatedly demonstrate my game-playing superiority over (the other) Dr Barr. Finally, thank you to Suzanne Daly for putting up with all of my nonsense.

Praise for *Graduate Skills and Game-Based Learning*

"*Graduate Skills and Game-Based Learning* offers us a new tool for the heart and soul of graduate education, a tool for experimentation, risk-taking, creativity, and using failure as a form of learning. These are just the bits where we need the most help."
—James Paul Gee, *Mary Lou Fulton Presidential Professor of Literacy Studies and Regents' Professor, Arizona State University, USA*

"A compelling read for any faculty member who is considering whether and how to use games in their teaching. This book provides practical recommendations and robust research evidence about how students can learn important transferrable skills through gaming."
—Professor Judy Robertson, *Chair in Digital Learning, University of Edinburgh, UK*

"This book provides a much needed foundation for games in learning, linking them explicitly to graduate attributes and pedagogic theory. Moving beyond potential and advocacy, Barr grounds the application in empirical research, while also clearly setting out the perspectives of educators and students. It provides a very insightful account of how games can be used effectively in higher education, and also the issues involved."
—Martin Weller, *Professor of Educational Technology at the Open University, UK and President of the Association for Learning Technology (ALT)*

"This work provides key insights to using games as pedagogical tools in graduate education, positioning games in the classroom, and understanding the views and opinions of graduate students in engaging with such efforts. It explores the themes of games as tools for inquiry and experiential learning in ways that are both grounded in relevant theory and wonderfully concrete for practicing educators. I have no doubt that this will prove to be an important work for those in the field."
—Andrew Phelps, *Professor at the Human Interface Technologies Laboratory, University of Canterbury, New Zealand and Professor and Director, American University Game Lab*

Contents

About the Author

Matthew Barr is a lecturer at the University of Glasgow, UK, where he established the university's first game studies course and was the founding editor of the peer-reviewed student game studies journal, *Press Start*. He is currently based in the Centre for Computing Science Education, where he leads the Graduate Apprenticeship in Software Engineering programme. Barr has also taught on the games development programme at Glasgow Caledonian University, leading modules including game content design and game narrative. His research, which has attracted significant media attention, examines how video games may be used to develop skills and competencies such as critical thinking, adaptability, and communication skill. Barr serves as Vice Chair of British DiGRA (the Digital Games Research Association) and sits on the Board of Directors for the Scottish Game Developers Association. His *Super Mario Kart* skills are superior to those of his brother, David.

List of Figures

List of Tables

1

Video Games and Learning

Respected academic and businessperson, John Seely Brown, has stated that he'd rather hire a high-level *World of Warcraft* (*WoW*) player than an MBA from Harvard (Brown 2012). Brown cites the collaborative learning and strategic thinking required to succeed in *WoW* (Blizzard Entertainment 2004), suggesting that the game-based self-organisation and strategy ideation compare favourably to the corporate world. Indeed, many commercial video games require players to collaborate and communicate if they are to progress; they must also exercise a range of skills and competencies, including adaptability and resourcefulness, to overcome in-game challenges. As it happens, these are the very same skills that employers look for when hiring graduates, the skills that higher education is expected to develop in students.

As discussed in the chapter that follows, Brown is not alone in suggesting video games may offer significant potential for learning; but, to date, the empirical evidence for the efficacy of using games to develop skills in higher education has been slight. Previous work has largely focused on younger learners and has not always embraced the most rigorous of research methods. At the heart of this book, however, is a robust, new experimental study that provides compelling quantitative and qualitative

© The Author(s) 2019
M. Barr, *Graduate Skills and Game-Based Learning*, Digital Education and Learning,
https://doi.org/10.1007/978-3-030-27786-4_1

data in support of the idea that games can be used to develop useful graduate skills. Specifically, the study employed a randomised controlled trial design to measure any gains in students' skills acquisition over a relatively short period of campus-based game play. The results were remarkably convincing, with statistically significant gains in communication skill, resourcefulness, and adaptability observed in the game-playing intervention group. Based on a belief that statistics present only one view of the picture, however, interviews with students involved in the study were carried out, to better understand how and why the games might have helped develop these skills. In addition, new interviews with leading educators and game developers that illuminate the discussion from alternative perspectives are included.

The work described here is situated within the broad context of game-based learning, and thus requires an understanding of the existing research in this area. It also requires an appreciation of the existing pedagogical theory that underpins learning from video games. The remainder of this chapter sets out to provide the necessary context.

The Learning Potential of Video Games

The alleged ill-effects of video games have been the subject of much consternation, from the APA's inclusion of 'Internet Gaming Disorder' in the classification of mental and behavioural disorders as a condition for further study (American Psychiatric Association 2013) to the WHO's addition of 'gaming disorder' to the 11th edition of the *International Classification of Diseases* (World Health Organization 2019). However, not only are such classifications open to criticism ("Scholars' Open Letter to the APA Task Force on Violent Media Opposing APA Policy Statements on Violent Media" 2013), there exists a body of literature that suggests video games can be a force for good in peoples' lives. Authors such as McGonigal (2011) and Johnson (2005) argue vociferously for the beneficial effects of gaming, claiming that good video games provide clues to improving our 'real' lives. Aside from the obvious pleasure afforded by gaming, games have been used in a variety of other contexts, for example, to aid rehabilitation of stroke victims (Merians et al. 2011), to increase quality of life in the elderly (Basak et al. 2008), and to help young people cope with their cancer treatment (Lee 2006). Granic et al. (2014) offer an overview of the cognitive, social, and emotional benefits that games have been shown to produce and suggest that games offer untapped potential for mental health care. The learning potential of games has already received considerable attention, as has the design and development of bespoke educational titles, which generally fall under the purview of 'serious games'. Authors including Gee (2005b), Squire (2003), and Steinkuehler (2004) have been particularly influential in establishing the pedagogical value of video games, and it is on their work that those who follow must build.

However, with some notable exceptions, such as the work of Kurt Squire (2004), Derek Robertson (Robertson and Miller 2009), and Valerie Shute (Shute et al. 2015), the potential to learn from commercially released games—those designed to entertain, rather than educate—has not been fully explored. In addition, much of the existing research has pertained to school-age children using video games in, or alongside, their regular classes. Perhaps this is to be expected: it is widely accepted that humans and other animals learn through play, and structured play forms an important part of primary-level education (Bruce 1987; Moyles 1989). If video games, which many incorrectly assume are played mostly by children, are simply toys with educational potential then it follows that much of the initial work in this area has concerned minors.

Squire (2011, p. 5) suggests that we can learn 'academic' content through games, including the in-game terminology, a range of strategies, and "the emergent properties of the game as a system". That video games can help develop systemic understanding—analysing the game world, as opposed to simply learning facts—is an idea echoed by James Paul Gee (2005b, p. 82), who states that what gamers learn is "empathy for a complex system". Both Squire and Gee note that the best-designed games typically comprise a series of coinciding or intersecting goals, with short-, medium-, and long-term conclusions. They suggest that this arrangement of goals, which permits the student to progress on a number of fronts simultaneously—even when one goal is seemingly out of reach—has significant advantages for student engagement because those struggling with one task can choose to make headway on another, rather than disengaging altogether. Such overlapping goals are familiar to anyone who has played BioWare's RPGs (role-playing games), or the later *Grand Theft Auto* games from Rockstar. However, they are perhaps more difficult to implement in a structured, often didactic, educational environment such as a school or university, where curricula may not offer the flexibility to allow different students to be working on many different problems at the same time.

The remainder of this chapter aims to provide an overview of the educational and learning theory most relevant to games, beginning with a brief discussion of how learning is conceptualised and quantified.

Taxonomies of Learning

One area of learning theory is that concerned with how learning is measured or quantified and, ultimately, assessed. Course objectives and intended learning outcomes are terms familiar to most twenty-first-century educators and such outcomes generally relate directly to the material being taught. More generally applicable taxonomies of learning may, however, be used to describe pedagogical attainment in a wide variety of educational settings. Bloom's Taxonomy (Bloom et al. 1956) is perhaps the most prevalent such classification. It comprises three domains: cognitive (related to knowledge), affective (attitudes and values), and psychomotor (skills), and was originally conceived as a means of making assessment more systematic (Draper 2005). The first of these domains—cognitive—is by far the most widely cited in the educational literature, although Bloom did not actually complete his work on the psychomotor domain. Bloom's affective domain model (Bloom et al. 1956), while less frequently cited and perhaps less readily understood, is also relevant to learning from video games, and is discussed briefly below.

While Bloom's model of the cognitive domain is concerned primarily with knowledge, the ability to recall or recite knowledge is merely the first level in the hierarchy. From this starting point, the learner may move on to comprehend (make inferences from, or reconstruct) acquired knowledge and ultimately be able to apply it in scenarios other than those in which the material was originally presented. Beyond this point, they begin to analyse and organise information, synthesise and reorganise it and, ultimately, evaluate and critique what they know (Fig. 1.1).

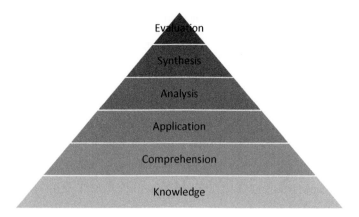

Fig. 1.1 Bloom's Taxonomy—cognitive domain (adapted from Bloom et al. 1956)

Bloom's mapping of the affective domain (Bloom et al. 1956) deals with what the authors refer to as 'values', or emotional responses and attitudes. It starts at the lowest level, 'Receiving', wherein the learner is no more than aware of the issues being put forward or the phenomena experienced. As the learner moves up the hierarchy through 'Responding' and 'Valuing', they become better able to place a value on the issues at hand and begin to categorise and group these values into a system (Fig. 1.2). In gaming terms, the affective model seems to correspond most closely with social aspects of multiplayer games, wherein players become more adept at playing in teams and prioritising interactions with other players as they ascend the hierarchy. Aside from their engagement with other players, the affective domain might also be used to describe how players deal with the ethical and social issues presented by more complex games' content and their interactions with NPCs (non-player characters).

Anderson et al. (2001) updated Bloom's model of the cognitive domain to place greater emphasis on the creation of new knowledge (see Fig. 1.3). In addition to the six levels of cognition, Anderson et al. introduced an additional dimension in the form of four types of cognitive process (factual, conceptual, procedural, and metacognitive). While it is not always presented as a hierarchy, the taxonomy suggested by Anderson et al. can be mapped to the Bloom hierarchy on which it is based, with 'Creating' replacing 'Evaluation' at its pinnacle. Aside from this change in emphasis,

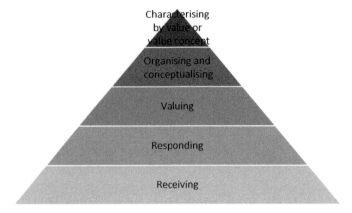

Fig. 1.2 Bloom's Taxonomy—affective domain (adapted from Bloom et al. 1956)

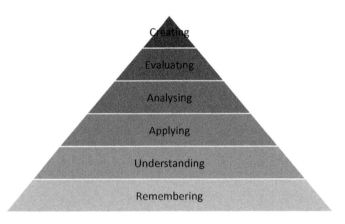

Fig. 1.3 Anderson and Krathwohl's revision of Bloom's Taxonomy (adapted from Anderson et al. 2001)

and the addition of a 'types' dimension, the most significant difference between the two taxonomies is perhaps the shift to using verbs to describe each of the levels. Bloom's 'Application' has, for example, become 'Applying'. This focus on action seems to suggest that the later taxonomy aligns more closely with constructivist theories of learning and is, arguably, more readily applied to the active learning that video games are said (by Gee, and others) to support.

One might express Anderson and Krathwohl's taxonomy in terms of engagement with video games as follows, beginning with the lowest level (Table 1.1).

While such a taxonomy of learning was not intended to describe a player's engagement with a game, it is clear that playing video games involves a sort of progression from understanding to application and, for some players, on to evaluation and creation. When such a learning taxonomy is applied to games in this way, a hierarchy of a particular form is suggested. One cannot get to the point of actually playing the game until one has reached the third level of cognition and it seems likely that a relatively small proportion of players will ever attain the top two levels, meaning the majority of those who play must sit in the middle of the hierarchy. Further, the application of the taxonomy above focuses on what the player learns about the game itself, not what they can learn from the game that might be applicable elsewhere. However, the further up the taxonomy the player moves, the more widely applicable their learning becomes. Being able to recall which buttons to press in a particular game is of no utility in a wider context, but as the player moves towards the top of the hierarchy, they begin to develop analytical and critical skills that might conceivably become relevant in other situations. Certainly, by the time a player is writing about a game, or modifying it in some way, they are honing transferable skills.

Table 1.1 Anderson and Krathwohl's taxonomy of learning applied to video games

Level	Application
Remembering	Recall of control scheme and basic premise, setting and genre.
Understanding	Comprehension of game mechanics and required player interactions.
Applying	Ability to use knowledge of the game to progress.
Analysing	Recognition of patterns in enemy or NPC (non-player character) behaviour. Self-determination of appropriate goals.
Evaluating	Identifying flaws (such as bias or imbalance) in the game. Comparing the game with others in the same genre.
Creating	Writing about the game (reviews or guides to playing the game). Building new levels or modifications.

Theories of Learning

This section provides an overview of the educational theories that are most relevant to learning from video games. It draws on theories of education (i.e. how pedagogic content is delivered or otherwise received, or the practice of teaching), which seem more prevalent in earlier works, and on theories of learning (how pedagogic content is understood, or how we learn), which gain greater prominence in later literature.

Initially, it may be helpful to divide the literature into two broad categories: instructivist and constructivist. The instructivist model presents learning as the acquisition of knowledge and is probably the form of learning—or, at least, of teaching—that anyone who has been to school, college, or university has experienced most often. It is typified by the didactic image of the teacher or lecturer at the front of the class, transmitting knowledge to their students. From Pavlov's behavioural conditioning (extrapolated to great effect in Aldous Huxley's 1932 novel, *Brave New World*) to Skinner's ideas about self-instruction and reinforcement (Holland and Skinner 1961) through to work that followed (see Carroll 1968; Carroll 1989; Merrill 2002), there is seemingly no great, unifying theory of instruction. Perhaps what binds together these ideas is their pervasiveness and the fact that—where formal education is concerned, at least—the instructivist approach dominates.

There are certainly those who have written extensively about models of instruction, even if no single name is particularly associated with instructivism. Gagné (1977) identified five main types of learning: verbal information, intellectual skills, cognitive strategies, motor skills, and attitudes. In order to meet his "conditions for learning", Gagné suggested that each of these types must be addressed by a particular form of instruction. These 'instructional events' included activities such as informing learners of the objective, providing learning guidance, providing feedback, and assessing performance. Gagné, together with Briggs (1974), identified conditions, internal and external to the learner, that need to be met for each type of learning to occur. For example, learning of the type referred to as 'cognitive strategies' might require the internal recall of relevant concepts, while the corresponding external condition might involve the learner demonstrating a solution based on those concepts. Similarly, motor skills require both an internal memorisation of component chains and an external practice to hone those skills. Intellectual skills are treated somewhat differently, as Gagné and Briggs break these skills into subcategories, each with its own type of 'performance'; for example, understanding of a rule can be demonstrated by applying that rule. So, while the model of instruction offered by Gagné and Briggs was intended for use in a teacher-learner environment and, as such, is not immediately promising for the apparently more constructivist learning that games may support, there are comparisons to be made if the teacher or learning environment is supplanted by a video game. Understanding and applying rules, memorising, and using motor components (game controls), or applying a solution to an in-game problem based on recall of similar problems and associated strategies are all phenomena familiar to those who play video games. It is striking, perhaps, that most games—certainly the better-designed titles—feature very limited instruction. Many games begin with a tutorial level that introduces the player to the mechanics and goals of the game. However, it is considered jarring, at least by modern game design standards, to have the game stop and explain to the player how something works, perhaps by means of an on-screen message. Skilful writing and design can get around this problem by having, for example, a narrative reason for the player to be told what to do. Often the familiar trope of memory loss is used to justify why a friendly NPC must explain the workings of aspects of the game world that should be routinely familiar to the player character, for instance. The *Dark Souls* series (FromSoftware 2011) is infamous for providing little or no instruction to the player: aside from a few cryptic messages scattered around the beginning of the games, the player is forced to construct their own understanding of the game world. Other, apparently more simplistic, games such as *Super Mario Bros.* (Nintendo Creative Department 1985) and *Super Meat Boy* (Team Meat 2010) use skilful level design to introduce concepts to players, such that they effectively discover these concepts for themselves.

Laurillard (2002b) offers a dialogic model of instruction, termed the 'Conversational Framework', which identifies the activities necessary to complete a learning task in a formal education environment. Her model characterises the teaching-learning process as an 'iterative conversation'. This basic concept, as Laurillard herself notes, is not new: there are echoes of dialogic instruction throughout modern learning theory (e.g. Vygotsky) and the idea dates back to at least Socrates. Laurillard states that her Conversational Framework is "not normally applicable to learning through experience, nor to 'everyday' learning" (Laurillard 2002a p. 87) but in the second edition of *Rethinking University Teaching* (2002a), the author includes educational video games as a form of adaptive media—alongside virtual environments and simulations—which may be modelled using the Framework. Figure 1.4 shows how Laurillard interpreted the Conversational Framework for a geology simulation designed to teach students about rock formations. As an example of adaptive media, not so far removed from a game, this interpretation offers an indication of how the Framework might be applied to an educational game, although, as Laurillard concedes, this simulation-based interpretation is not tremendously discursive.

The geology simulation above is able to adapt the feedback given to a student based on their activities, but this feedback is limited to the regurgitation of the same canned text that may have introduced the topic. It is tailored to the student's actions, to a degree, but it is not especially dynamic. This is one area in which video games can excel, as commercial

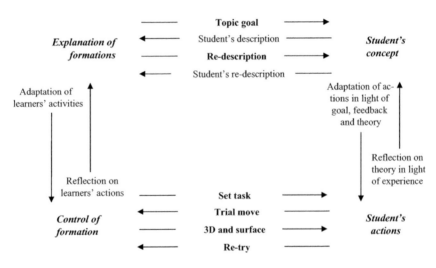

Fig. 1.4 Interpretation of Laurillard's Conversational Framework for a geology simulation (Laurillard 2002a)

titles are already capable of dynamically adjusting game difficulty in response to player performance (Hunicke and Chapman 2004; Andrade et al. 2005). Games can also offer assistance to players after detecting a series of failed attempts to traverse an area, as in the *New Super Mario Bros.* releases from Nintendo.

While Laurillard is broadly optimistic about the use of video games in formal education, her focus is on educational titles rather than commercial games, noting that their strengths include "intrinsic feedback" (2002a p. 143), and the "real-time nature of the interaction, because this requires close attention and responsiveness from the user, whether it is a combative game, or an environment that changes over time". Laurillard also notes multiplayer games' potential for use as interactive, social environments, and that goals can be programme-defined (i.e. set by the game), or player-defined, as in certain open-world titles or construction simulations. It is worth noting, however, that the first edition of Laurillard's book talked about intelligent tutoring systems with similar expectation. Here, she cautions that educational games might be 'another chimera', unlikely to live up to their pedagogic potential as a result of market forces; that is, there is very little money in educational games, compared to the multi-million-dollar blockbusters produced by large commercial game studios. This is a common concern. While games backed by the US military, such as the recruitment and training-focused *America's Army* (United States Army 2002), can match the production values of *Call of Duty* (Activision 2003) and games of that calibre, the more fertile ground for educational titles is perhaps in the web or mobile space, where effective games can be developed on much more modest budgets. The other possibility, of course, is to appropriate existing commercial games for educational purposes (see Squire 2004; Miller and Robertson 2011) and harness the big games publishers' budgets for pedagogic benefit.

Returning to theories of learning, the constructivist model broadly suggests that learning should be more self-directed, with the learner more actively assembling or constructing knowledge rather than receiving it from the teacher, by completing tasks and thinking for themselves. The teacher primarily is a facilitator whose role is to administer tasks through which the learner may construct their own meaning, and, in this sense, constructivism might be considered a more individualistic approach to learning than its instructive counterpart might. However, it begins to become apparent that the convenient classification of the literature into instructivist and constructivist camps is not entirely appropriate. Skinner, for example, also stated that "to acquire behaviour, the student must engage in behaviour" (Holland and Skinner 1961, p. 389) which sounds rather more like an active process of learning than the passive picture that his broadly instructivist views suggest. Also, while there must be some instructional element to learning from video games (as discussed above), constructivism and its related concepts are more relevant to the development of graduate skills discussed in this book. Herein lies another issue encountered when trying to divide the literature into two crude categories: the term 'constructivism' does not *necessarily* incorporate ideas of 'learning by doing' or 'discovery learning', which seem relevant to games and certainly do not fall within the instructivist purview. Further, constructivism comes in many flavours, a point illustrated by the comparison of Piaget and Papert that follows. There are also learning theories and paradigms that do not readily fall into a single school of thought, and numerous other attempts to group and categorise views on learning.

Mayes and de Freitas (2006), for example, highlight three "perspectives on the nature of learning itself", based on the views of educational design identified by Greeno et al. (1996), which considered each view in terms of designing learning environments, formulating curricula, and constructing assessments. Mayes and de Freitas present these three views as follows:

- The associationist/empiricist perspective (learning as activity)
- The cognitive perspective (learning as achieving understanding)
- The situative perspective (learning as social practice)

From the *associationist* perspective, the focus is on "routines of activity for effective transmission of knowledge" (Greeno et al. 1996), aligning such views with instructionists such as Gagné. However, the associationist approach is not at odds with constructivism. Clear goals, feedback, and reinforcement are all thought to be advantageous or, as Mayes and de Freitas phrase it, "learning is the formation, strengthening, and adjustment of associations, particularly through the reinforcement of particular connections through feedback". Where this perspective can seem out-dated is in its assumption that learning must take place in a 'bottom-up' fashion, with small, less complex units of knowledge or understanding eventually, and sequentially, building towards an understanding of a more complex whole. However, as Mayes and de Freitas note, this is exactly the approach taken in the majority of today's e-learning resources.

The *cognitive* perspective, also referred to as the *rationalist* view by Greeno et al., relies upon the development of an understanding of the learned material, drawing on cognitive tools such as memory, reasoning, and problem-solving ability. According to Mayes and de Freitas, the "underlying theme for learning is to model the processes of interpreting and constructing meaning", such that knowledge acquisition may be viewed as the "outcome of an interaction between new experiences and the structures for understanding that have already been created".

The *situative* view, which Greeno et al. originally termed the *situative/pragmatist-sociohistoric* view, introduced social aspects of learning, acknowledging the influence of "the social and cultural setting in which the learning occurs, which will also define at least partly the learning outcomes" (Mayes and de Freitas). This perspective sees the learner develop their own personal identity within a group, or community of practice, while engaging in learning activities that focus not only on the subject matter at hand (which might be a video game) but also on cooperation and communication. One of the most significant facets of the situative view is the "importance of context-dependent learning in informal settings"; as well as social interaction, the situative view is dependent on an authentic context in which to carry out the practice of learning. One such context might be a multiplayer video game, where learning to cooperate and communicate is central to the experience.

Constructivism

Constructivism refers to the active process through which learners may themselves construct new knowledge, by applying existing knowledge to new problems. Describing what he terms "radical constructivism", Glasersfeld (1995, p. 18) states that "knowledge, no matter how it be defined, is in the heads of persons [...] the thinking subject has no alternative but to construct what he or she knows on the basis of his or her own experience". Bruner (1960, p. 17) states that prior learning "renders later performance more efficient" through "what is conveniently called nonspecific transfer or, more accurately, the transfer of principles and attitudes". In this way, Bruner argues, such learning "consists of learning initially not a skill but a general idea, which can then be used as a basis for recognizing subsequent problems as special cases of the idea originally mastered".

Savery and Duffy (1995) offer a number of instructional principles that support what they term the 'philosophy' of constructivism:

1. Understanding is *in* our interactions with the environment
2. Cognitive conflict or puzzlement is the stimulus for learning and determines the organisation and nature of what is learned
3. Knowledge evolves through social negotiation and through the evaluation of the viability of individual understandings

Savery and Duffy consider the first of these propositions to be the core concept of constructivism (their emphasis on the 'in'). Indeed, this seems a neat summation of the idea, but the second and third components are also useful, and serve to illustrate constructivism's close coupling with the sort of learning games can stimulate. What is a game without some "cognitive conflict or puzzlement", after all? Related to this point, Savery and Duffy also note that "it is the goal of the learner that is central in considering what is learned", which aligns with another aspect of video games: that they—to varying degrees—often permit the player to set their own goals or, at least, attempt to tackle the game's challenges at their own pace. In their third proposition, it is interesting to note the importance that the authors place on social aspects of learning—these are discussed in relation to games below.

As noted, 'constructivism' is not a clearly delineated concept, and nor can it be attributed to a single scholar. Alongside Dewey (1938) and Montessori (1949), Piaget (1956) and Papert (1980) are two of the names most closely associated with constructivism in the literature. However, their ideas about constructivism are not identical. Papert suggests the modified term 'constructionism' which, like the constructivism described by Piaget, characterises the concept of learning as "building knowledge structures" while also adding "the idea that this happens especially felicitously in a context where the learner is consciously engaged in constructing a public entity, whether it's a sandcastle on the beach or a theory of the universe" (Papert and Harel 1991). Piaget and Papert are both constructivists, then, but Papert is also something else and it might be problematic to assume that 'constructivism' carries the same meaning for all when applying it to video games, or any other pursuit. A further issue associated with some of the seminal work produced on constructivism—especially that described by Piaget and Papert—is its focus on children; it is mostly applied to adults only by extrapolation. This book is concerned primarily with video games' effects on adult learners, and so it should also be noted that Piaget's theories have been successfully adapted and applied to tertiary-level education (e.g. see Wankat and Oreovicz 1993).

In gaming terms, one could see constructivism taking on multiple meanings. First, it might refer to the learning that occurs as a player turns their attention to the process of developing their own game, or perhaps more commonly, creating their own modification or extension of a game, or using built-in tools to construct new levels or in-game items. While the player here is undoubtedly drawing on their existing experience of playing video games—they must possess some understanding of the form and conventions associated with games before they may construct their own—this is a highly literal application of the constructivist concept, more akin to Papert's notion of constructionism. A stronger interpretation might acknowledge the process of learning to play a game based on previous gaming experience, and on real-world experience: games are conceived and designed in the real world, even if their settings or themes are otherworldly. Thus, our understanding of the world around us may also be used to inform our play. This idea may be taken further, and reversed: in learning about the world around us, may we not, in constructivist terms, draw upon experiences gained through video games? Interactions with other players, for example, may serve as an analogue for effective communication in the real world.

If learning through constructivist means relies upon prior experience, then the recollection, or retrieval, of memories associated with such experience is an important factor. Karpicke and Blunt (2011) state that "because each act of retrieval changes the memory, the act of reconstructing knowledge must be considered essential to the process of learning", demonstrating that "retrieval practice is a powerful way to promote meaningful learning of complex concepts". In showing that practicing retrieval is as effective, or more so, than elaborative learning techniques (such as the drawing of concept maps while studying source material) Karpicke and Blunt's work suggests that the act of recalling what we have learned is as important as how we store this information in the first place. It is conceivable that, at a low level, video games may also excel at providing players with reason to practice such retrieval, leveraging the same effects that Karpicke and Blunt elucidate, in order to teach players how to play. When a new game concept is introduced—for example, a new skill or ability that one's player character obtains—this new knowledge is not typically intended to be stored away for later use, to be examined by means of an in-game test at some point in the possibly distant future. Instead, the player is usually expected to start retrieving this knowledge almost immediately, and often repeatedly, until it becomes second nature. The player may have constructed their own knowledge by observing the mechanics of the new game concept—it is not necessarily spelled out for them—but it is in the repeated act of retrieval that they truly understand how to apply it.

Experiential Learning

Confucius is mistakenly assumed to have coined the following phrase which, aside from its dubious origins (a version may originate with fellow Chinese philosopher, Xun-zi), neatly summarises experiential learning:

> *Tell me and I will forget,*
> *Show me and I may remember,*
> *Involve me and I will understand.*

Dewey has been credited as the "modern father of experiential education" (Neill 2005). Dewey was among the earliest modern writers to consider the conflict between what he considered the two extremes of education: the traditional, didactic, teacher-led approach versus the more progressive, less structured student-led approach (Dewey 1938). For

Dewey, good educational design took into consideration the learner's place in society, how they might contribute to it, and how they—as an individual—experience it. Every learner's experience will be different, and the best learning environments (and teachers) should be able to adapt to these differences. Dewey's followers and the experiential learning cycles they developed have perhaps been more influential still. Kolb's (1983) learning cycle and associated model of learning (Fig. 1.5) is the most widely cited of these, and relates directly to Dewey's work (and to that by Piaget):

At the ends of both continuums are stages in the learning cycle, which the learner may enter at any point. Using video games as an example, the cycle might be illustrated as follows:

- Active experimentation (doing): Picking up a controller or mouse and simply playing the game.
- Concrete experience (feeling): Playing through portions of the game, following specific guidance such as in-game prompts.
- Reflective observation (watching): Thinking about what happened as you played the game, having observed what occurred in response to your input.
- Abstract conceptualisation (thinking): Formulating possible strategies for playing the game.

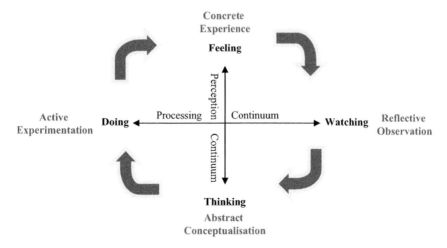

Fig. 1.5 Kolb's experiential learning model and cycle (adapted from Kolb 1983)

For effective learning to occur, Kolb states that a balance must be struck between the opposing ends of both continuums, for example, between active experimentation (having a go at playing the game) and reflective observation (thinking about what happened as you played).

Social Learning

Like many theories of social learning, Lave and Wenger's (1991) communities of practice (which have a great deal in common with Gee's affinity spaces—see below) are also somewhat rooted in the constructivist camp. Wenger (2006) defines communities of practice as "groups of people who share a concern or a passion for something they do and learn how to do it better as they interact regularly", that is, a manifestation of social learning. Such communities comprise three elements: a domain of knowledge, a community of people, and some notion of shared practice. The domain might be anything—including video games—but the individuals involved must share an interest in that domain, and the shared practice must be appropriate to the domain at hand. Of particular relevance to this book is the idea that the community of practice need not have formed with the intention of learning about a particular domain: any learning that does take place can be entirely incidental.

Related to how Dewey places such emphasis on the learner's previous experience, Vygotsky (1930) suggests that how we learn is also dependent on earlier learning and on the cultural norms to which we are exposed. Moreover, Vygotsky sees learning as an inherently social process, dependent on interaction with teachers (or adults more generally—much of Vygotsky's work is concerned with learning in children) and peers. His suggested "zone of proximal development" is defined as "the distance between the actual developmental level as determined by independent problem solving and the level of potential development as determined through problem solving under adult guidance, or in collaboration with more capable peers" (1930, p. 86). The learner's zone of proximal development will evolve over time as they internalise and understand more complex ideas and, as such, one can see how this concept may be applied to adults—learning something new or more complicated than they have previously known—as well as children (Fig. 1.6).

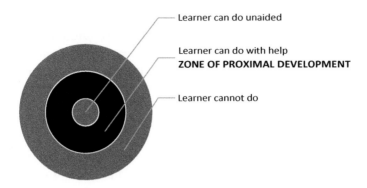

Learner can do unaided

Learner can do with help
ZONE OF PROXIMAL DEVELOPMENT

Learner cannot do

Fig. 1.6   Vygotsky's zone of proximal development (adapted from Vygotsky 1930)

In gaming terms, these social interactions might be with a more experienced player in the same room, a group of peers playing online, or, perhaps, an NPC providing instruction within the game. Indeed, when games fail to take into account the player's zone of proximal development, such in-game instruction can quickly become tiresome. Navi, the player's in-game companion and guide throughout the otherwise venerable *The Legend of Zelda: Ocarina of Time* (Nintendo EAD 1998), is one example of a game's designers arguably intruding on the player's zone of proximal development, providing guidance where it is unwanted.

Scaffolding

Vygotsky's zone of proximal development leads naturally to the concept of 'scaffolding', a concept attributed to Bruner, who describes the need to ask a pupil 'medium questions' which are answerable, based on the pupil's current level of understanding, but which point to the next, more difficult concept (1960, p. 44). Scaffolding—sometimes referred to as 'instructional scaffolding'—has been defined as a "process that enables a child or novice to solve a problem, carry out a task, or achieve a goal which would be beyond his unassisted efforts" (Wood et al. 1976). Interestingly, Bruner elsewhere uses the example of a game—albeit one played between an infant and their parent—to illustrate the concept:

The game consists of an initial contact, the establishment of joint attention, disappearance, reappearance, and acknowledgement of renewed contact. These obligatory features or the "syntax" of the game occur together with optional features, such as vocalizations to sustain the infant's interest, responses to the infant's attempts to uncover the mother's face, etc. These "non-rule bound" parts of the game are an instance of the mother providing a "scaffold" for the child. (Bruner and Sherwood 1976, p. 280)

The presence of scaffolding is clearly discernible in video games. Wouters and van Oostendorp (2013), for example, found that instructional support in game-based learning facilitates the acquisition of skills and knowledge, where 'instructional support' includes the scaffolding provided in-game (e.g. "system-generated hints and suggestions to focus attention") and that which is afforded by collaboration with others (e.g. "discussion often aiming at the explication of implicit knowledge").

The scaffolding metaphor also implies that as successful completion of the task nears, the scaffolds are gradually removed and the learner—as with a new building—is left to stand alone. In video games, the tutor may take many forms, from the occasionally irritating NPC that guides the player through fundamental concepts, to more subtle clues and direction peppered throughout the game by its designers. However, the scaffolding is plainly there to see for anyone who seeks it out. It might be argued that the scaffolding in a good video game *should*, in fact, be all but invisible to the player.

Mastery Learning

Mastery learning or 'learning for mastery' is a concept most widely attributed to Bloom (1968), who was critical of conventional schooling and its apparent failure to cope with differing levels of ability within a single class (see also Illich's *Deschooling Society* (1971)). So, while Bloom estimated that over 90% of students had the potential to master a given topic, in reality a much smaller proportion of the class will fulfil this potential: "the problem of developing a strategy for mastery learning is one of determining how individual differences in learners can be related to the learning and teaching process" (Bloom 1968). Learning for mastery has much in common with the concept of instructional scaffolding, in that learners are provided with adequate assistance as they work towards mastering a topic. Mastery learning acknowledges that individual learners will require more or less time on each topic but, as Bloom suggests, the vast majority of learners can achieve mastery, should they be granted sufficient time and opportunity to do so. Everyone in a class is working towards achieving the same goal, but the instruction afforded to each individual (or groups of individuals) is varied as required. Other key aspects of mastery learning are frequent assessment (Slavin 1987) and prompt formative feedback (Guskey 2007). While learners must demonstrate a certain level of mastery in the assessment associated with one topic before moving onto the next, each assessment results in useful, prescriptive feedback that the learner can use to improve their understanding and advance towards mastery.

The parallels between mastery learning and video game design are quite obvious here. Most video games are designed to appeal to a wide range of players and must therefore take into account an equally wide range of abilities. Therefore, with top-selling games being sold to many millions of players it is reasonable to assume that the range of abilities for which games must cater is larger than any classroom. Further, a typical game requires the player to master a level before advancing to the next, and this quest for mastery is aided by almost constant feedback on the player's actions. This feedback may simply take the form of one's on-screen avatar falling to their death due to the misappropriation of some in-game tool or a badly judged leap, or it may be delivered by means more akin to a spreadsheet that details every aspect of the player's performance. Regardless of the form that this feedback takes, it is abundant, promptly delivered, and generally designed to help the player master the game.

Surface and Deep Learning

Marton and Säljö (1976) identified *surface-level* or *deep-level* processing as the two categories of conception by which students learned from reading passages of prose. This distinction between surface and deep approaches to learning has since been elaborated upon; for example, both Entwistle (1987) and Biggs (1987) identified a third 'strategic' approach, wherein the learner may switch between surface and deep modes as appropriate. These approaches to learning extend beyond the mere memorisation of facts and it is for this reason that the concept of surface and deep learning may be relevant when considering the acquisition of graduate skills and competencies. Marton and Säljö (1997) identify six conceptions of learning that may be split into those related to surface learning and those related to deep learning. The conceptions that Marton and Säljö associate with deep learning (the abstraction of meaning, understanding reality in a different way, and developing as a person) may also be related to the ideas about student development that are encapsulated in graduate attributes. The implication is that deep learning may be required to develop an individual's critical thinking, adaptability, ethical and social awareness, and so on: to develop as a person. Furthermore, deep learning is often associated with the active learning which is thought (by Gee, and others) to be supported by games. There are also echoes of Bloom's Taxonomy of learning (and Anderson and Krathwohl's revision thereof) in Marton and Säljö's spectrum of learning conceptions: the memorisation of knowledge is, broadly speaking, at the lower level of both theoretical frameworks, for example. If video games may offer a means of enhancing graduate attributes—developing students as people—then the educational literature would suggest that it is games' capacity to support deep, active learning which makes this possible.

Gee's Learning Principles

James Paul Gee is an inspiration for the work described in this book. In *What Video Games Have to Teach Us About Learning and Literacy* (2007), Gee describes what he terms 'semiotic domains' as a means of ascribing meaning to anything from images and sounds to objects and other humans. He defines a semiotic domain more precisely as "any set of practices that recruits one or more modalities (e.g. oral or written language, images, equations, symbols, sounds, gestures, graphs, artifacts, etc.) to communicate distinctive types of meanings" (2007, p. 19). Among his examples, he includes Roman Catholic theology, cellular biology, and first-person shooter video games. If the reader is uncomfortable with the word 'semiotic', Gee offers an alternative interpretation: "an area or set of activities where people think, act, and value in certain ways" with one such area being video games. He argues that to be literate merely in terms of reading and writing is insufficient in the modern day: we must be literate in a variety of semiotic domains other than those associated with the printed word. So, Gee argues, one can be literate in one or more video game semiotic domains (whether it be first-person shooter, real-time strategy, or platformer) and this literacy is developed according to 36 learning principles, which modern video games have the potential to exploit. The most pertinent of these principles are discussed here, but the complete list of 36 principles described in Gee's seminal book is essential reading for anyone interested in game-based learning.

While Gee presents his principles in no particular order of importance, the first idea (the Active, Critical Learning Principle) highlights a key aspect of Gee's thinking: that learning should be active, not passive. As discussed under 'Theories of learning' above, the utility of active learning is a widely observed phenomenon: from the constructivism of Piaget (1956) to the experiential learning espoused by Kolb (1983), and Moy's (1999) assertion that graduate attribute-like skills can only be developed through active engagement. Video games are designed to engage the player in active learning—increasingly so in the era of the disappearing player manual—in such a way that they grasp the games' concepts and conventions by interacting with them. The critical aspect of this learning Gee grounds in the notion of 'situated cognition': the player assigns meaning to objects, characters, and events in terms of how they manifest within the context of the game.

Gee's semiotic domains, and, in particular, the affinity groups with which they are associated also have clear links with established learning theory such as Lave and Wenger's (1991) situated learning and communities of practice (see Gee 2005a) and Vygotsky's (1930) semiotic mediation. The emphasis Gee places on mastering such domains—even if they have been constructed around a video game—also suggests links with Bloom's (1968) learning for mastery. As discussed, video games certainly employ some version of mastery learning in their design. The player must generally master a level or area of the game before moving on to the next, but they may achieve mastery at their own pace: more able players can progress through the game more quickly, while less advanced players benefit from the constant feedback that the game provides, so that they can ultimately master it. Indeed, mastery learning is closely related to a number of Gee's principles, for example, the Ongoing Learning Principle and associated 'Regime of Competence' Principle, which states that "the learner gets ample opportunity to operate within, but at the outer edge of, his or her resources, so that at those points things are felt as challenging but not 'undoable'".

As noted above, there are echoes of Bruner's scaffolding, Bloom's mastery learning, and Vygotsky's zone of proximal development (ZPD) in these principles. Gee's regime of competence, at the edges of which the learner/player should be found, is largely synonymous with Vygotsky's ZPD. While Vygotsky's intended learning environment comprised a more traditional classroom with a teacher helping students to navigate their ZPD, Gee is suggesting that video games can (and do) fulfil this role, at least in terms of learning about the game itself. When the designers of a mainstream game ignore the regime of competence principle, they threaten to derail the whole endeavour: an excellent example is *Deus Ex: Human Revolution* (Eidos Montréal 2011). The game permitted—and often encouraged—the player to play by stealthy means, avoiding direct conflict, and honing a very particular set of skills that did not involve big guns. It would then abruptly throw the player into a ballistic gun fight with an end-of-level boss where stealth was meaningless and big guns were a fundamental requirement if the player was to progress. So, rather than building on skills and competencies developed through previous interactions, the player's regime of competence was all but ignored, requiring them instead to master skills to which many players had hitherto not been exposed. The reviews for the otherwise well-received *Deus Ex* uniformly—and justifiably—lambasted these incongruous battles, and the issue subsequently addressed in later versions of the game.

As relatively risk-free environments where "learners can take risks in a space where real-world consequences are lowered" (the 'Psychosocial Moratorium' Principle), Gee notes that video games allow players to experiment and develop not only an understanding of the game system but also the skills required to probe and hypothesise about the real world. These ideas are encapsulated in his Probing Principle and Discovery Principle. Several writers have made this connection between games' apparent reliance on—and players' application of—the scientific method. Intuitively, it is easy to see how this idea makes sense, as a player formulates strategies to progress, tries them out, and refines them as necessary. In fact, Steinkuehler and Duncan (2008) produced empirical evidence of games' ability to foster what they term "scientific habits of mind".

Several of Gee's principles (e.g. the Committed Learning Principle and Practice Principle), it may be argued, are concerned with how and why video games command so much of players' attention and effort. Motivation is often cited as a reason for considering games as learning tools, but more so than the remainder of Gee's 36 principles, this subset might require some qualification. What these principles assume is that the learner enjoys being a player, too—if video games are not for them, then these principles aren't merely irrelevant, they can be counterproductive. Place someone, who has not played games before, in front of a title that requires quick reflexes and a mastery of somewhat abstract controls, perhaps something as 'universal' as *Super Mario Bros.*, and they will not feel that for a little input they are getting a lot of output (as suggested by the Amplification of Input Principle). It is not thought that Gee is asserting that all these principles hold true for all games and all people; rather, he is presenting a list of principles that *may* be observed in games and how players learn from them.

Gee's Identity Principle and Self-Knowledge Principle seem to suggest that learners can discover something about themselves, by reflection or by projection on to their in-game identity. These ideas become all the more compelling when considered in conjunction with later principles (such as the Cultural Models about the World Principle) which concern the learner/player thinking "consciously and reflectively" about a number of cultural models, as presented in the game. These may be models about the world, models about the player's own learning, or models about the semiotic domain(s) in which they operate. Gee states that learners/players enjoy a certain freedom in thinking about these models, because they can do so using any combination of their "tripartite play of identities" without "denigration" of their own identity or social background.

All of Gee's principles deserve attention: this list is an attempt to draw out those that seem most relevant to the work described in subsequent chapters. This overview concludes with two related principles: the Affinity Group Principle and the Insider Principle. The first of these principles seems to draw on established notions of communities of practice and social learning. It is an aspect of video games that is often overlooked—certainly by those who do not habitually play them—but such groups do exist and now thrive as online forums, guilds, and wikis (see Barr 2014), where they might once have been confined to the office or playground. In this way, the Affinity Group Principle is linked to the Insider Principle: the learner/player is also an active producer, not simply a passive consumer, creating content in and around the game, often in collaboration with other members of their affinity group. It may be argued that these two principles represent some of the most powerful learning potential in video games and might offer a clue as to games' suitability as a framework for developing sought-after generic skills and attributes.

Summary

This chapter has explored how many established theories of education and learning are applicable to commercial video games, with an emphasis on those theories that relate to constructivism. As discussed, the links between video games and learning have already been documented, most notably by James Paul Gee, whose learning principles form the basis of much of the work on game-based learning. In the following chapter, connections between Gee's learning principles and higher education are considered, as part of a wider discussion of games' relevance to student development.

References

American Psychiatric Association. (2013). *Diagnostic and Statistical Manual of Mental Disorders* (5th ed.). American Psychiatric Association. https://doi.org/10.1176/appi.books.9780890425596.

Anderson, L. W., Krathwohl, D. R., Airasian, P. W., Cruikshank, K. A., Mayer, R. E., Pintrich, P. R., et al. (2001). *A Taxonomy for Learning, Teaching, and*

Assessing: A Revision of Bloom's Taxonomy of Educational Objectives (1st ed.). New York: Pearson.

Andrade, G., Ramalho, G., & Santana, H. (2005). Extending Reinforcement Learning to Provide Dynamic Game Balancing. In *Proceedings of the 2005 IJCAI Workshop on Reasoning, Representation, and Learning in Computer Games*, Edinburgh, Scotland. Retrieved December 31, 2012.

Barr, M. (2014). Learning Through Collaboration: Video Game Wikis. *International Journal of Social Media and Interactive Learning Environments*, 2(2), 119–133.

Basak, C., Boot, W. R., Voss, M. W., & Kramer, A. F. (2008). Can Training in a Real-Time Strategy Video Game Attenuate Cognitive Decline in Older Adults? *Psychology and Aging, 23*(4), 765–777. https://doi.org/10.1037/a0013494.

Biggs, J. B. (1987). *Student Approaches to Learning and Studying*. Australian Council for Educational Research Ltd., Radford House, Frederick St., Hawthorn 3122, Australia. Retrieved December 21, 2016.

Blizzard Entertainment. (2004). *World of Warcraft*. Blizzard Entertainment.

Bloom, B. (1968). Learning for mastery. In *Mastery Learning: Theory and Practice*. New York: Holt, Rinehart and Winston.

Bloom, B. S., Krathwohl, D. R., & Masia, B. B. (Eds.). (1956). *Taxonomy of Educational Objectives: The Classification of Educational Goals*. New York: Longman.

Brown, J. S. (2012, August 7). How World of Warcraft Could Save Your Business and the Economy | Think Tank. *Big Think*. Retrieved August 1, 2018, from https://bigthink.com/videos/how-world-of-warcraft-could-save-your-business-and-the-economy-2.

Bruce, T. (1987). *Early Childhood Education*. London: Hodder Education.

Bruner, J. S. (1960). *The Process of Education*. Cambridge, MA: Harvard University Press.

Bruner, J. S., & Sherwood, V. (1976). Peekaboo and the Learning of Rule Structures. In *Play: Its Role in Development and Evolution* (pp. 277–285). Harmondsworth: Penguin.

Carroll, J. B. (1968). Presidential Address of Division 15 on Learning from Being Told. *Educational Psychologist, 5*(2), 1–10. https://doi.org/10.1080/00461526809528955.

Carroll, J. B. (1989). The Carroll Model A 25-Year Retrospective and Prospective View. *Educational Researcher, 18*(1), 26–31. https://doi.org/10.3102/0013189X018001026.

Dewey, J. (1938). *Experience and Education*. New York: Macmillan Press.

Draper, S. (2005, March 15). Taxonomies of Learning Aims and Objectives: Bloom, neoBloom, and Criticisms. Retrieved April 10, 2013, from www.psy.gla.ac.uk/~steve/best/bloom.html.

Eidos Montréal. (2011). *Deus Ex: Human Revolution*. London: Square Enix.

Entwistle, N. J. (1987). A Model of the Teaching Learning Process. In J. T. E. Richardson, M. W. Eyesenck, & D. W. Piper (Eds.), *Student Learning Research in Education and Cognitive Psychology*. London: Open University Press.

FromSoftware. (2011). *Dark Souls*. San Jose, CA: Namco Bandai Games.

Gagné, R. M. (1977). *The Conditions of Learning* (3rd ed.). New York; London: Holt, Rinehart and Winston.

Gagné, R. M., & Briggs, L. J. (1974). *Principles of Instructional Design* (5th ed.). Belmont, CA; UK: Thomson/Wadsworth.

Gee, J. P. (2005a). Semiotic Social Spaces and Affinity Spaces. In D. Barton & K. Tusting (Eds.), *Beyond Communities of Practice: Language, Power and Social Context* (pp. 214–232). New York: Cambridge University Press.

Gee, J. P. (2005b). *Why Video Games Are Good for Your Soul: Pleasure and Learning*. Melbourne, VIC: Common Ground.

Gee, J. P. (2007). *What Video Games Have to Teach Us About Learning and Literacy* (2nd ed.). New York: Palgrave Macmillan.

Glasersfeld, E. v. (1995). *Radical Constructivism: A Way of Knowing and Learning*. London: The Palmer Press.

Granic, I., Lobel, A., & Engels, R. C. M. E. (2014). The Benefits of Playing Video Games. *American Psychologist, 69*(1), 66–78.

Greeno, J. G., Collins, A. M., & Resnick, L. B. (1996). Cognition and Learning. In D. C. Berliner & R. C. Calfee (Eds.), *Handbook of Educational Psychology* (pp. 15–46). London, UK: Prentice Hall International.

Guskey, T. R. (2007). Closing Achievement Gaps: Revisiting Benjamin S. Bloom's "Learning for Mastery.". *Journal of Advanced Academics, 19*(1), 8–31. https://doi.org/10.4219/jaa-2007-704.

Holland, J. G., & Skinner, B. F. (1961). *The Analysis of Behavior: A Program for Self-Instruction*. New York: McGraw-Hill College.

Hunicke, R., & Chapman, V. (2004). AI for Dynamic Difficulty Adjustment in Games (pp. 91–96). Presented at the Challenges in Game Artificial Intelligence AAAI Workshop, San Jose: Northwestern University. Retrieved from http://cs.northwestern.edu/~hunicke/pubs/Hamlet.pdf.

Huxley, A. (1932). *Brave New World*. Vintage Classics.

Illich, I. (1971). *Deschooling Society*. New York: Harper & Row. Retrieved November 3, 2013.

Infinity Ward. (2003). *Call of Duty*. Activision.

Johnson, S. (2005). *Everything Bad Is Good for You: How Popular Culture Is Making Us Smarter*. New York: Penguin.

Karpicke, J. D., & Blunt, J. R. (2011). Retrieval Practice Produces More Learning Than Elaborative Studying with Concept Mapping. *Science, 331*(6018), 772–775. https://doi.org/10.1126/science.1199327.

Kolb, D. A. (1983). *Experiential Learning: Experience as the Source of Learning and Development* (1st ed.). Upper Saddle River, NJ: Financial Times/Prentice Hall.

Laurillard, D. (2002a). *Rethinking University Teaching in the Digital Age*. Retrieved from http://net.educause.edu/ir/library/pdf/ffp0205s.pdf.

Laurillard, D. (2002b). *Rethinking University Teaching: A Conversational Framework for the Effective Use of Learning Technologies* (2nd ed.). London: Routledge.

Lave, J., & Wenger, E. (1991). *Situated Learning: Legitimate Peripheral Participation*. Learning in Doing: Social, Cognitive and Computational Perspectives. Cambridge: Cambridge University Press.

Lee, C. (2006, October 21). Video Games Aim to Hook Children on Better Health. *The Washington Post*. Retrieved January 10, 2012. http://www.washingtonpost.com/wp-dyn/content/article/2006/10/20/AR2006102001328.html.

Marton, F., & Säljö, R. (1976). On Qualitative Differences in Learning: I – Outcome and Process. *British Journal of Educational Psychology, 46*(1), 4–11. https://doi.org/10.1111/j.2044-8279.1976.tb02980.x.

Marton, F., & Säljö, R. (1997). Approaches to Learning. In F. Marton, D. Hounsell, & N. J. Entwistle (Eds.), *The Experience of Learning: Implications for Teaching and Studying in Higher Education* (pp. 39–58). Edinburgh: Scottish Academic Press.

Mayes, T., & de Freitas, S. (2006). *Stage 2: Review of e-learning Theories, Frameworks and Models*. JISC.

McGonigal, J. (2011). *Reality Is Broken: Why Games Make Us Better and How They Can Change the World*. Jonathan Cape.

Merians, A. S., Fluet, G. G., Qiu, Q., Saleh, S., Lafond, I., Davidow, A., & Adamovich, S. V. (2011). Robotically Facilitated Virtual Rehabilitation of Arm Transport Integrated With Finger Movement in Persons with Hemiparesis. *Journal of NeuroEngineering and Rehabilitation, 8*(1), 27. https://doi.org/10.1186/1743-0003-8-27.

Merrill, M. D. (2002). First Principles of Instruction. *Educational Technology Research and Development*, *50*(3), 43–59. https://doi.org/10.1007/BF02505024.

Miller, D. J., & Robertson, D. P. (2011). Educational Benefits of Using Game Consoles in a Primary Classroom: A Randomised Controlled Trial. *British Journal of Educational Technology*, *42*(5), 850–864. https://doi.org/10.1111/j.1467-8535.2010.01114.x.

Montessori, M. (1949). *The Absorbent Mind* (C. A. Claremont, Trans.) (7th ed.). Madras; London: Kalakshetra Publications; Distributed by Theosophical Publishing.

Moy, J. (1999). *The Impact of Generic Competencies on Workplace Performance: Review of Research*. Leabrook, SA: National Centre for Vocational Education Research. Retrieved May 10, 2013.

Moyles, J. (1989). *Just Playing?: Role and Status of Play in Early Childhood Education* (Illustrated ed.). Milton Keynes: Open University Press.

Neill, J. (2005). *John Dewey, the Modern Father of Experiential Education*. Retrieved May 11, 2013, from http://www.wilderdom.com/experiential/ExperientialDewey.html.

Nintendo Creative Department. (1985). *Super Mario Bros.* Nintendo.

Nintendo EAD. (1998). *The Legend of Zelda: Ocarina of Time*. Nintendo.

Papert, S. A. (1980). *Mindstorms: Children, Computers, and Powerful Ideas*. New York: Basic Books.

Papert, S., & Harel, I. (1991). Situating Constructionism. *Constructionism*, |*36*, 1–11.

Piaget, J. (1956). *The Child's Conception of Space*. London: Routledge & Kegan Paul.

Robertson, D., & Miller, D. (2009). Learning Gains from Using Games Consoles in Primary Classrooms: A Randomized Controlled Study. *Procedia – Social and Behavioral Sciences*, *1*(1), 1641–1644. https://doi.org/10.1016/j.sbspro.2009.01.289.

Savery, J., & Duffy, T. (1995). Problem Based Learning: An Instructional Model and Its Constructivist Framework. *Educational Technology*, *35*, 31–38.

Scholars' Open Letter to the APA Task Force on Violent Media Opposing APA Policy Statements on Violent Media. (2013, September 26). *Scribd*. Retrieved August 12, 2018, from https://www.scribd.com/doc/223284732/Scholar-s-Open-Letter-to-the-APA-Task-Force-On-Violent-Media-Opposing-APA-Policy-Statements-on-Violent-Media.

Shute, V. J., Ventura, M., & Ke, F. (2015). The Power of Play: The Effects of Portal 2 and Lumosity on Cognitive and Noncognitive Skills. *Computers & Education*, *80*, 58–67. https://doi.org/10.1016/j.compedu.2014.08.013.

Slavin, R. E. (1987). Mastery Learning Reconsidered. *Review of Educational Research, 57*(2), 175–213. https://doi.org/10.3102/00346543057002175.

Squire, K. (2003). Video Games in Education. *International Journal of Intelligent Simulations and Gaming, 2*(1), 49–62.

Squire, K. (2004). *Replaying History: Learning World History Through Playing Civilization III* Unpublished doctoral dissertation, Indiana University. Retrieved from http://website.education.wisc.edu/kdsquire/dissertation.html.

Squire, K. (2011). *Video Games and Learning: Teaching Participatory Culture in the Digital Age.* New York: Teachers' College Press.

Steinkuehler, C. A. (2004). Learning in Massively Multiplayer Online Games. In *Proceedings of the 6th International Conference on Learning Sciences* (pp. 521–528). Santa Monica, CA: International Society of the Learning Sciences. Retrieved August 19, 2018.

Steinkuehler, C., & Duncan, S. (2008). Scientific Habits of Mind in Virtual Worlds. *Journal of Science Education and Technology, 17*(6), 530–543. https://doi.org/10.1007/s10956-008-9120-8.

Team Meat. (2010). *Super Meat Boy.* Team Meat.

United States Army. (2002). *America's Army.* United States Army.

Vygotsky, L. S. (1930). *Mind in Society: the Development of Higher Psychological Processes* (A. R. Luria, M. Lopez-Morillas, M. Cole, & J. Wertsch, Trans.). Cambridge, MA; London: Harvard University Press.

Wankat, P. C., & Oreovicz, F. S. (1993). *Teaching Engineering.* New York: McGraw-Hill Inc., US.

Wenger, E. (2006). *Communities of Practice – A Brief Introduction.* Retrieved May 13, 2013, from http://www.ewenger.com/theory/communities_of_practice_intro.htm.

Wood, D., Bruner, J. S., & Ross, G. (1976). The Role of Tutoring in Problem Solving. *Journal of Child Psychology and Psychiatry, 17*(2), 89–100. https://doi.org/10.1111/j.1469-7610.1976.tb00381.x.

World Health Organization. (2019). International Classification of Diseases, 11th Revision (ICD-11). *WHO.* Retrieved June 2, 2019, from https://www.who.int/classifications/icd/revision/en/.

Wouters, P., & van Oostendorp, H. (2013). A Meta-analytic Review of the Role of Instructional Support in Game-Based Learning. *Computers & Education, 60*(1), 412–425. https://doi.org/10.1016/j.compedu.2012.07.018.

2

Graduate Attributes and Games

Also referred to as 'generic attributes', graduate attributes are a way of identifying and, to some degree, quantifying the skills and competencies that students are said to develop in higher education, over and above those that relate directly to their degree subject. Nicol (2010) offers the following definition of the term: "the skills, personal qualities, and understanding to be developed through the higher education experience so as to prepare graduates for life and work in the 21st century".

Graduate attributes are commonly aligned with the notion of the 'lifelong learner' (Candy et al. 1994) because they refer to skills and capabilities developed over time, from childhood onwards. In formal education, particularly at university level, generic attributes such as critical thinking, problem-solving, and the ability to self-organise are highlighted as skills that enhance graduates' employability. If studying for a degree can help develop these skills, so the argument goes, then graduates will be better placed to deploy them in the workplace. The Candy et al. (1994) report for the Australian government identified several characteristics of a lifelong learner, including an inquiring mind, helicopter vision, information literacy, a sense of personal agency, and a repertoire of learning skills. An enquiring mind suggests "a love of learning" and "a sense of curiosity",

© The Author(s) 2019
M. Barr, *Graduate Skills and Game-Based Learning*, Digital Education and Learning,
https://doi.org/10.1007/978-3-030-27786-4_2

for example, while helicopter vision entails "a sense of the interconnect-edness of fields" and associated "breadth of vision". Information literacy, according to Candy et al., requires "an ability to decode information in a variety of forms" and involves "critical evaluation of information". Meanwhile, personal agency is associated with "a positive concept of oneself as capable and autonomous" and learning skills include a "range of strategies for learning in whatever context one finds oneself".

Moy (1999), describing what she terms the "key competencies jour-ney", suggests that generic attributes are most readily developed through "active and interactive learning", placing emphasis on problem-solving and reflection so that "learners reflect on what has been learnt and the learning processes, as a critical aspect of competency development, self-awareness and the development of lifelong learning skills". Moy also sug-gests that, in order to support the development of such generic competencies, learning tasks should be relevant and meaningful to learn-ers. Of course, video games are inherently interactive and typically involve some form of problem-solving. Furthermore, those who play games most avidly will certainly attest to their relevance and meaning.

The question of whether university courses are explicitly designed to develop generic attributes is perhaps not satisfactorily answered in the literature, despite what universities and other institutions might claim. Arguably the leading researcher in the field, Barrie (2004), has noted that "university teachers charged with responsibility for developing students' generic graduate attributes do not share a common understanding of either the nature of these outcomes, or the teaching and learning pro-cesses that might facilitate the development of these outcomes". Therefore, despite institutional best intentions, it may be the case that the lack of a shared understanding of graduate attributes, and how to cultivate them, is one barrier to their development in higher education. Similarly, Green et al. (2009) note that graduate attributes can be difficult to develop due to the confusion that surrounds their definition and implementation, a problem exacerbated by institutional resistance and under-estimation of the resources required to embed related practices.

Ten years prior and using the term 'personal transferable skills' (PTS) rather than 'graduate attributes', Drummond et al. (1998) identified a variety of further problems associated with embedding such practices in higher education, despite some considerable investment in PTS initiatives. They noted that "effective skills development is difficult, if not impossible, to achieve in a system of teaching which is fundamentally based on lectures". They identified a lack of incentive for academics—for whom promotion and, indeed, continued employment are dependent on research outputs and successful funding applications—to engage with new teaching practices, particularly where the teaching does not relate directly to the work on which their research career is based. The image Drummond et al. project is of small pockets of good work rather than institution-wide efforts, concluding that "isolated, *ad hoc* initiatives do not amount to effective approaches to development". Given the challenges associated with integrating graduate attribute development in research-driven curricula, a task which Drummond et al. describe as being "difficult to operationalise effectively", another approach they identify is that of a stand-alone module or course:

> *Parallel (or stand-alone) development involves skills being developed in free-standing modules, which are not integrated into the curriculum. Some universities have accredited such schemes, e.g. student tutoring and student development programmes. Students generally do not appreciate the academic value of stand-alone modules. There are advantages to this approach though—not least in that the value of skills development is made explicit, and in a modular framework it allows students to involve themselves in a more varied learning experience.*

Stand-alone courses bring with them resourcing issues and, as Green et al. (2009) note, there is evidence of "polarised student responses" to such additions to the curriculum. In an ideal situation, perhaps, the development of graduate attributes should be embedded in university courses. However, there are undoubtedly challenges associated with doing so, particularly if the aim is to achieve parity across disciplines.

Despite the challenges associated with embedding graduate attribute development, de Corte (1996) argues that the best learning environments exhibit many features that relate directly to the development of generic attributes—features that higher education institutions can, and in many cases do, encourage. According to de Corte, such environments should provide a "good balance between discovery learning and personal exploration, on the one hand, and systematic instruction and guidance, on the other" while "allowing for the flexible adaptation of the instructional support to accommodate individual differences and stages of learning" and for "social interaction and collaboration".

A further issue to consider is the usefulness of the term "graduate attributes", especially when applied across multiple subjects or disciplines. The definition of such an idiom can be somewhat ambiguous, and prone to change over time. Haigh and Clifford (2011), for example, state that graduate attributes might be at the heart of what they perceive as a necessary shift to "focus on an agenda of personal responsibility, on individual and social interior attributes and to move away from [education's] present focus on exterior systems". In other words, they see a move towards attributes that relate to graduates' moral and social consciousness rather than skills that have traditionally appealed to employers.

So, what have video games got to do with graduate attributes and learning? Quite a lot, it may be argued. Take, for example, the characteristics of a life-long learner, as identified in the Candy report: are not explorers of game-based worlds driven by a 'sense of curiosity'? Many players relish the opportunity to uncover secrets and solve puzzles in intricate open worlds such as those offered by games such as *The Legend of Zelda: Breath of the Wild* (Nintendo EPD 2017) and *No Man's Sky* (Hello Games 2016) or series including *The Elder Scrolls* (Bethesda Softworks 1994–) or *The Witcher* (CD Projekt Red 2007–). Other parallels between these characteristics of life-long learning and the capabilities exercised by playing video games may be observed in titles that are built upon the need to decode and critically evaluate information. In games such as *Tacoma* (Fullbright 2017), *Observation* (No Code 2019), and *Her Story* (Sam Barlow 2015), for example, the player is fundamentally tasked with assembling a narrative from disparate and often inconsistent pieces of information.

The language used by de Corte to describe an optimal learning scenario, wherein opportunities for graduate attribute development are embedded, is directly relatable to the design of the best video games. Many commercial games rely on just this sort of balanced approach to learning by exploration and systematic guidance to lead players of differing experience and ability through the game. The aforementioned *Breath of the Wild*, for example, encourages the player to experiment with the complement of special powers bestowed upon the game's hero, Link, in order to learn how they might be used to solve environmental puzzles. Countless multiplayer games from *Team Fortress 2* (Valve Corporation 2007) through to the *Save the World* component of *Fortnite* (Epic Games 2017) are fuelled by the "social interaction and collaboration" espoused by de Corte. To a person familiar with games and their design, it seems clear that there is an argument to be made in favour of using video games as a means of helping to develop graduate attributes. Furthermore, if games are already capable of developing such attributes in players, they could be used to facilitate relatively low-cost, student-centred graduate attribute 'courses', sidestepping the operational difficulties identified by Drummond et al.

At this point, it is useful to return to James Paul Gee's game-based learning principles (Gee 2007) and examine how these compare with those developed in more conventional higher educational settings. Chickering and Gamson (1987) offer seven principles of good practice in undergraduate education, relevant to the higher education-focused work here:

1. Encourages student-faculty contact.
2. Encourages cooperation among students.
3. Encourages active learning.
4. Gives prompt feedback.
5. Emphasises time on task.
6. Communicates high expectations.
7. Respects diverse talents and ways of learning.

Stating that "while each practice can stand on its own, when all are present, their effects multiply", Chickering and Gamson suggest that these principles employ six powerful forces in education: activity, diversity, interaction, cooperation, expectations, and responsibility.

There are clear parallels between some of these principles and those espoused by Gee: cooperation, active learning, feedback, time on task, and diverse ways of learning are all key tenets of Gee's philosophy. Chickering and Gamson's principles, in turn, share similarities with other work on good quality higher education. A 1995 report led by Colorado

Governor Roy Romer, Chairman of the Education Commission of the States, identified several attributes of quality undergraduate education, based on a review of the existing research (Romer et al. 1995). For example, the report states that "quality begins with an organizational culture that values high expectations", while a "quality curriculum" requires "ongoing practice of learned skills" and "integrating education and experience". Further, "quality instruction" involves active learning, collaboration, and "adequate time on task".

While there are some obvious differences (e.g., where the importance of staff-student contact is concerned), the degree of commonality between Gee's game-based learning principles and those that are held in high esteem in higher education is striking.

Measuring Graduate Attributes

The previous chapter discussed means by which learning may be quantified or defined, but the specific challenge of measuring difficult-to-quantify graduate attributes (see Chong and Romkey 2012) must also be considered, if we wish to examine the potential for games—or any other form of intervention—to develop them.

General Measures

While many institutions list a series of discrete attributes that their graduates should possess, there is a sense in which the graduate may be more than the sum of these parts, leading to a notion of what Coetzee (2014) refers to as 'graduateness'. Coetzee proposes a 'Graduate Skills and Attributes Scale' as a holistic approach to quantifying the attributes of a given graduate, based on a review of the literature and, perhaps more importantly, employer surveys. Administered by questionnaire, 64 factors of 'graduateness' are addressed (e.g. "I find it easy to persuade, convince or influence others"), along eight dimensions (e.g. 'interactive skills') and grouped into three domains ('scholarship', 'global and moral citizenship', and 'life-long learning'). While such an approach is laudable in several respects—not least for its attempt to reflect employer priorities as well as the moral concerns highlighted by Haigh and Clifford (2011)— Coetzee's questions are rooted in the economic and management sciences and therefore reflect the specific concerns of that domain: how would such an approach work over multiple disciplines? Further, each of the eight dimensions—arguably important in their own right—are reduced to eight multiple-choice questions. In attempting to provide an overall measure of 'graduateness', Coetzee's approach lacks the granularity required here.

Popular in the US, the commercial Collegiate Learning Assessment or CLA+ is an open-ended test of analytic reasoning, critical thinking, problem-solving, and communication skills. Praised by the US Secretary of Education's Commission on the Future of HE[1] for promoting "a culture of evidence-based assessment in higher education" (US Department of Education 2006), the CLA was originally developed with the institution (not the individual student) as the object of measurement, although the latest CLA+ version now provides student-level metrics. The CLA+ aims to measure the 'value added' by attending one HE institution versus comparable students at another such institution and may also be used to measure the impact of pedagogic interventions. The actual tests comprise open-ended essay-style questions, rather than multiple-choice questions, wherein students are required to 'make or break' an argument, with more varied written tasks based on 'real-world' scenarios (see Klein et al. 2007 for a detailed example of such a scenario). These latter tasks are inspired by written tests developed by Klein (1983) for lawyers sitting the California state bar examination in the US, a lineage that suggests such tests are, at least, considered useful by the US legal profession. The CLA+ is administered entirely online, with essay-style questions assessed automatically by means of natural language processing software. It is of perceived value to universities because, as noted by Klein et al. (2007), the CLA+ claims to show an average improvement in test scores of greater than one standard deviation between first year students and graduates. As with Coetzee's attempt at providing a holistic approach to assessing graduates, the CLA+ acknowledges that each of the skills, competencies, or attributes that we hope to find and develop in graduates does not occur in isolation from another such attribute. As noted above, however, use of the otherwise promising CLA+ incurs a fee that precluded its use in the research described in this book.

The Australian Graduate Skills Assessment Test attempts to measure the generic skills of university students with respect to five cognitive dimensions: Critical Thinking, Problem-Solving, Interpersonal Understandings, Argument Writing, and Report Writing (Hambur et al. 2002). The test comprises a multiple-choice section and a section that requires a written response. The report by Hambur et al. on the validity of the measure is exceptionally detailed and concludes that ongoing assessment of the test's validity is required as it is developed in conjunction with stakeholders. Despite the authors' reservations, the test has been constructed in a thoughtful and transparent way, making it very appealing for use in work such as this. However, only one sample set of questions could be located, with answers freely available online, which might have implications for a pre- and post-test experiment design. Furthermore, the written portions of the test would need to be marked individually and this is not feasible if the measure was to be used on a large scale, even if a marking rubric were provided.

Measuring Individual Attributes

The Scottish university at which this work described in this book was carried out identifies ten graduate attributes: Investigative, Effective Communicators, Independent and Critical Thinkers, Adaptable, Resourceful and Responsible, Confident, Experienced Collaborators, Subject Specialists, Reflective Learners, and Ethically and Socially Aware.[2] This list of attributes may be viewed within the context of the Scottish Higher Education Enhancement Committee (SHEEC)'s 2008–11 Enhancement Theme, 'Graduates for the 21st Century'.[3] As noted by Nicol (2010), the development of graduate attributes in Scotland has drawn heavily on work carried out by Barrie (2004, 2006, 2007) in Sydney and Melbourne and, as a result, the attributes extolled by the host university are broadly comparable to those found at other international institutions. Further, experiments relating to this work necessarily involve students from the host university, so it is expedient and appropriate for that institution's attributes to form the basis of this work. Since the university already purports to develop this list of attributes in its students, it should be possible to determine if video games offer any advantages for attribute development over-and-above existing university provision.

These individual attributes, with the exception of Subject Specialists, are considered in more detail below. The omission of this attribute reflects its content-specific nature. Commercial games do not typically feature subject material that aligns closely with wide-ranging university curricula, although there are certainly aspects of individual games that draw on such content and may be useful as a subject-specific teaching aid, for example, the *SimCity* series (Maxis 1989–present) for Geography, or *Age of Mythology* (Ensemble Studios 2002) for Classics. Further examples of using commercial games to deliver subject material are discussed in Chap. 6, but the main purpose of this work is to determine if commercial games may be used to develop more generally useful skills and attributes in students.

Independent and Critical Thinkers

Robert Ennis defines critical thinking as "reasonable reflective thinking focused on deciding what to believe or do" (Ennis 1993). Ennis is responsible for the influential and widely used Ennis-Weir Critical Thinking Essay Test, developed in partnership with Eric Weir (Ennis and Weir 1985) and intended for use with high school and college students. The test asks participants to read and respond to a letter ('the Moorburg letter') written to a fictional newspaper editor in support of a proposal that concerns overnight street parking. The letter comprises eight numbered paragraphs that are intended to support the author's argument; however, each paragraph reveals some weakness in their reasoning and the participant is asked to evaluate the paragraphs in turn, as well as responding to the letter as a whole. Participants' ability to critically analyse the arguments contained in the letter are then graded by a person who is familiar with critical thinking (and has read the guidance supplied by Ennis and Weir). The test is intended to take around 40 minutes to complete (10 minutes for reading the letter and 30 minutes for composing a response). According to Ennis, grading of the test should take around six minutes per participant. The structured nature of the test—the participant is expected to formulate an individual response to each of the numbered paragraphs—and the discipline-agnostic content of the test make it a very promising candidate for assessing critical thinking ability as part of a larger experiment. In particular, the structure of the test means it may be readily adapted to online delivery, should the experiment be conducted remotely, or if there is a desire to retain and later analyse responses in digital form. The test is also freely available, allowing it to be used without restriction for research purposes. However, there are significant concerns about the practicality of grading a large number of such tests, if they were administered on a significant scale. Furthermore, a test based on the comprehension of a fixed text (the Moorburg letter) is not well suited to a pre/post-test experimental design: post-test, participants will have seen and responded to the letter already. Indeed, when the measures outlined here were piloted, there were audible groans (and some salty language) from participants faced with the Moorburg letter—and its tedious fictional author—for a second time, post-test. It is reasonable to assume that if participants did not relish a second opportunity to respond to the letter, it is unlikely that they gave doing so their full attention, which can only depress their scores.

The Cornell Critical Thinking Tests developed by Robert Ennis with Jason Millman of Cornell University comprise two levels: level X for pupils at grades five to twelve (in the US) and level Z for grades ten to twelve. However, the 50-minute level Z tests are also intended for use with "advanced or gifted high school students, college students, and other adults" (Ennis 1993). These tests require the administrator to purchase packs of testing booklets, in addition to an administration manual. For this work, a pack of test booklets was purchased for evaluation. Administration of the Cornell test is very straightforward, given its multiple-choice nature, but this mode of assessment may also be seen as a limitation: plausible, if not 'perfect', answers are not accommodated. While the test booklets may be reused by producing one's own answer sheets (respondents would note their answers on a separate sheet, leaving the test booklet unblemished), the test manual suggests that 'special answer sheets' may be purchased from the Critical Thinking Co., the owner of the test. It is thought that a suitable answer sheet may be developed and used without reference to the official sheets, as these amount to little more than 52 multiple-choice items with the option to mark the answer as A, B, or C. Having purchased the test booklets from the Critical Thinking Co., and read the associated manual, it is not believed that using one's own answer sheets is in breach of the licencing terms, but this remains a murky area, should other educators wish to follow suit.

The California Critical Thinking Skills Test (Facione 1991) is another multiple-choice test, composed of 34 items and taking 45–50 minutes to complete, while a companion instrument, the California Critical Thinking Disposition Inventory (Facione et al. 1994) may be completed in around 20 minutes, according to the authors. The former instrument is presented as a comprehension exercise, in much the same vein as the Ennis-Weir test, while the latter instrument is intended only to measure a respondent's willingness to think critically, not their ability to do so. Both instruments are based on the so-called Delphi Report's consensus definition of critical thinking (also authored by Facione, in 1990):

> We understand critical thinking to be purposeful, self-regulatory judgment which results in interpretation, analysis, evaluation, and inference, as well as explanation of the evidential, conceptual, methodological, criteriological, or contextual considerations upon which that judgment is based.

These instruments are not freely available, however, and appear to exist primarily in commercial form.[4] So, while the multiple-choice formulation of these instruments is initially appealing, their commercial availability and the fact that the test which actually measures critical thinking ability is presented in much the same manner as the freely available Ennis-Weir test, means that they are unlikely to be used in studies such as this. Other commercially available tests, such as the Watson-Glaser critical thinking appraisal (Watson 1980) were not considered here, for similar reasons. However, the use of these tests should be re-evaluated if any future work were to focus solely on critical thinking.

Investigative

While investigative skills are assessed explicitly as part of many school-level science courses and in certain other subject-specific domains such as History (Hillis 2005), there is currently no recognised, general-purpose instrument for measuring investigative ability. The host university states that investigative graduates are "able to locate, analyse and synthesise information from a variety of sources and media" and are thus "able to investigate problems and provide effective solutions".[5] It is perhaps unsurprising that the UK's security service, MI5, actively seeks employees with such skills and has, as a recruitment tool, developed an online test to "help you to assess your use of information and analytical skills".[6]

The online MI5 Investigative Challenge was "designed to broadly reflect some of the situations Intelligence Officers at MI5 are expected to deal with" and presents the potential applicant with a security-related scenario, described by means of a collection of text documents. Within a set period, the applicant is asked to make an assessment of the situation and answer four multiple-choice questions. These questions are intended to reveal how well the applicant has analysed and synthesised the available intelligence and translated this into security recommendations. With up to two points available for each answer (the best course of action is worth two points, other viable options one point), those who score highly are encouraged to apply for a position at MI5. While no validation of the instrument is available, that MI5 continues to use it may be seen as a warrant for its efficacy as an indicator of certain skills. However, questions of validity aside, the test is—like the Ennis-Weir critical thinking test—ill-suited to a pre/post-test experimental design as it involves analysis of a fixed 'text'.

Effective Communicators

Duran's Communicative Adaptability Scale (1983, 1992) is a self-reported measure of communication ability, framed in terms of communicative adaptability, which Duran defines as "the ability to perceive socio-interpersonal relationships and adapt one's interaction goals and behaviours accordingly". Such adaptability depends upon both "cognitive (ability to perceive) and behavioural (ability to adapt) skills". The scale, as reproduced in Duran (1992), comprises 30 statements (e.g. "I feel nervous in social situations") that relate to the six dimensions (Social Composure, Social Confirmation, Social Experience, Appropriate Disclosure, Articulation, and Wit) of the "social communication repertoire". Respondents are asked to indicate the degree to which each statement applies to them, on a scale from 1 ("never true of me") to 5 ("always true of me") and the responses summed for each dimension. Certain responses (e.g. "I sometimes use words incorrectly") are reversed before summing, for example, a 2 becomes a 4.

A salient feature of this scale, which makes it appealing for use in this context, is its focus on adaptability, as this is another commonly cited graduate attribute. Indeed, Duran (1992) states that "the most basic form of communication competence is fundamental competence", defined by Spitzberg and Cupach as "an individual's ability to adapt effectively to the surrounding environment over time" (1984, p. 35). Hullman (2007) demonstrated that the Communicative Adaptability Scale (CAS) instrument could also be used as a measure of adaptability. However, as McCroskey and McCroskey (1988) note, the insight provided by self-reported measurements is limited to that relating to the participants' self-perception and results are, therefore, confounded by the participants' self-confidence. In order to investigate actual communication competency, a tool that involves observation might be desirable, and such a tool may be used in conjunction with a self-reporting approach to correlate findings. However, self-report measures are used extensively in psychological research, and there is a prevailing wisdom that the best way to determine something about an individual is to ask them. Self-report measures are also favoured here due to the relatively fast and cheap nature of their deployment.

The SocioCommunicative Style Scale (Richmond and McCroskey 1990; McCroskey and Richmond 1995) is an initially promising instrument. It is designed to measure participants' perceptions of another individual's communication style in terms of assertiveness and responsiveness, and comprises a series of 20 personality characteristics to which respondents must assign a value of between 1 (strongly disagree that it applies) and 5 (strongly agree that it applies) in relation to a named individual. Assertiveness and responsiveness are deemed components that "make a substantial contribution to the prediction of communication and other social behavioural patterns" (Richmond and McCroskey 1990). Items that relate to these two components are presented in random order throughout the instrument. However, two problematic issues were identified when this instrument was considered for use here. First, from a practical point of view, each experiment participant would necessarily be required to demonstrate their communication abilities, perhaps by addressing a group of their peers who would, in turn, be tasked with using the instrument to gauge the speaker's communication style. While this approach is perfectly viable, it is also potentially very time-consuming to arrange for all participants to be able to speak on a topic, and rather demanding of the participants. Other practical concerns include controlling for increases in familiarity within the group of participants: given that the experiment described in the following chapter is designed to include pre- and post-intervention testing, McCroskey and McCroskey's data (and, indeed, common sense) would suggest that participants' self-perceived ability to communicate would increase as they had got to know one another over the course of the experiment. Overcoming this problem would require an additional cohort of participants—uninvolved in the game-based experiments—to act as assessors, using the instrument to assess people with whom they have not developed a relationship. These practical issues are not insurmountable: they may be reduced to concerns about the availability of suitable numbers of willing participants, and how much may be asked of them. However, a second, more fundamental issue is with the nature of the instrument: it is designed to measure two important components of communication but, as Richmond (2002) indicates, there is no 'correct' style: rather, better communicators are better able to adapt their communication style to reflect a given situation. The SocioCommunicative Style Scale, then, may be useful for detecting changes in communication style rather than measuring improvements in communication ability, assuming a practical and efficient means of administering the test may be devised.

Adaptable

The assessment of an individual's adaptability is hampered not only by the lack of an obvious, tangible measure but also by the ambiguity of the word itself. For the purposes of this work, the university's definition of the attribute's transferable dimension is instructive: "Demonstrate resilience, perseverance, and positivity in multi-tasking, dealing with change and meeting new challenges." The notion that being adaptable involves coping with the new and unfamiliar is echoed in the same attribute's personal dimension, described by the university as the ability to "respond flexibly and adapt their skills and knowledge to excel in unfamiliar situations".

With this understanding of what is meant by adaptability in the context of graduate attributes, a suitable measure of an individual's ability to adapt to new situations is required. While some tests actually rely upon game-like simulations to assess adaptability-related competencies, for example, the PC-based radar-tracking simulation used by Bell and Kozlowski (2008), it may be argued that laboratory tests of this nature are somewhat unrealistic. Furthermore, such testing bears little resemblance to the real-world concerns or responsibilities of those being tested.

Situational judgement tests (SJTs) are "measurement methods that present applicants with job-related situations and possible responses to these situations", which have been used to gauge individuals' ability to adapt to certain job conditions since at least World War II (Lievens et al. 2008). SJTs typically present respondents with descriptions of work situations and a number of alternative responses for each situation (Motowidlo et al. 1990). The most appropriate responses are pre-determined by, for example, the respondent's supervisor (in a work environment), allowing an individual employee's performance to be measured against their employer's expectations. A limitation of most SJTs, however, is that they are closely coupled with the domain in which they are developed and usually relate to a highly specific scenario, requiring those being tested to possess detailed subject knowledge. This limits the effectiveness of such tests in a broader, subject-neutral context.

Adam M. Grim's unpublished 2010 Master's thesis offers an account of a more generalised Adaptability SJT (ASJT). The test comprises a series of written work-based scenarios ('stems') for which the respondent must choose the course of action they would most likely take, from a list of five possibilities. In consultation with a panel of subject matter experts (SMEs), two versions of the instrument were developed, one drawing on critical incidents encountered in a military setting (tested with military personnel) and the other based on incidents that might occur in a more typical office environment (tested with call centre employees). Possible responses were rated by SMEs on a five-point Likert scale, where 1 corresponds to a highly non-adaptive response ("no behaviour change, not a functional response, and actions will probably make the situation worse") and 5 is a highly adaptable response ("behaviour change occurs and provides a response that will successfully resolve the problem"). Respondents' answers were then compared to the SME group's mean answer for each item.

Grim's approach is of interest for a number of reasons: this is a partially validated means of measuring adaptability that seeks to present respondents with recognisable situations, and it has been designed with reference to the established work of Pulakos et al. and Ployhart and Bliese (discussed below). The measure is only partially validated because the means by which the validity of the test was assessed—asking respondents' supervisors to assess their job performance and adaptability—was not, in itself, a validated method. While it was demonstrated that the ASJT was capable of predicting supervisor ratings of adaptability, it was determined that, for a student cohort with limited experience of 'typical' workplaces situations, the use of an SJT of this nature was potentially flawed. Grim also suggests that revisions of the ASJT are required before it may be used more widely.

Pulakos et al. (2000, 2002) developed a taxonomy of "adaptive job performance" and an instrument, the Job Adaptability Inventory (JAI), designed to validate this taxonomy. Pulakos et al. (2000) initially identified six dimensions of adaptive performance, based on an analysis of the existing literature: solving problems creatively; dealing with uncertain and unpredictable work situations; learning work tasks, technologies, and procedures; demonstrating interpersonal adaptability; demonstrating cultural adaptability; and demonstrating physically oriented adaptability. An initial study, examining a range of 'critical incidents' (work-based events that required employees to demonstrate adaptive performance), sought to find empirical evidence for the existence of these six dimensions and, as a result, two additional dimensions were identified: handling emergencies or crisis situations; and handling work stress. As one might expect, the study found that the requirement for adaptive behaviour varied with job type, and certain dimensions were of greater importance in certain types of job. Adaptive performance was found to be "multidimensional, encompassing a wide range of different behaviors" (Pulakos et al. 2000). The final version of the JAI instrument featured 68 items relating to the eight identified dimensions of critical incidents. Respondents were asked to rate the importance of, and time spent on, each of the dimensions and a criticality index calculated by doubling the importance rating, adding this to the time spent rating, and dividing by three (i.e. the importance rating was weighted twice as heavily as the time spent criterion).

This work is informative and represents one of the few empirical approaches to measuring adaptability within a work context. However, the JAI instrument seems better suited to analysing the nature of particular jobs or job families, and not individual adaptive performance. For example, on the 'Handling emergencies or crisis situations' dimension, the military police job family scored a criticality index of 3.74, versus a score of 0.30 for the research scientist family; 'Solving problems creatively' was scored 3.65 for research scientists but 1.63 for accountancy. These figures are credible, but not terribly useful for assessing or predicting adaptability. In a subsequent paper, however, Pulakos et al. (2002) present a range of "predictor and criterion measures to assess the eight dimensions of adaptive performance represented in the [2000] taxonomy". The authors refer to three adaptability measures related to experience, interest, and self-assessment. Some representative items for each measure are presented, which relate to the eight previously identified dimensions. For example, an experience item that relates to the 'Demonstrating cultural adaptability' dimension is given as "Making friends with people from different countries" with the respondent asked to rate the level of their experience of the item on the scale: 1 (never), 2 (once or twice), 3 (several times), or 4 (frequently or routinely).

The measures were successfully validated with military personnel by asking respondents' supervisors to independently assess their adaptive performance. While this approach suffers from the same limitations identified in Grim's study above, the work of Pulakos et al. was supported by funding from the US Army and thus enjoyed the resources to pilot test the rating measures used by supervisors. They were also able to fine-tune the selected critical incidents such that they accurately mirrored situations that may be encountered by the respondents in their military roles (e.g. "making quick decisions under life-threatening conditions"). However, as only representative items are published, these adaptability measures could not be in the study described here.

Building on the work of Pulakos et al. (2000, 2002), Ployhart and Bliese (2006) suggest a self-report measure of adaptability based on their own Individual ADAPTability (I-ADAPT) theory. They define individual adaptability as "a reasonably stable, individual difference construct that influences how a person interprets and responds to different situations" and present the I-ADAPT theory as a nomological network of knowledge, skill, ability, and other characteristics (KSAOs), performances, and situations. A potentially important distinction made by Ployhart and Bliese is between adaptability which is proactive and that which is reactive. The illustrative example provided by the authors is as follows:

> suppose an individual's behavior in a given situation is not producing the desired effect. Although the environment may not have changed, a more adaptive person will recognise this and change his/her behavior to change the situation in the intended manner. … Adaptability is proactive when an individual perceives a need to change even though the environment has not.

Based on the I-ADAPT theory, the I-ADAPT-M measure was developed with the practicalities of its use in mind, while addressing all eight of the dimensions identified by Pulakos et al. It is, therefore, relatively short (taking around ten minutes to complete) and is a self-report measure to "simplify administration and scoring, and to enhance applicability to multiple contexts". The measure has been tested and refined in collaboration with subject matter experts and validated by means of a confirmatory factor analysis. The 55-item survey asks respondents to indicate how well each of the items describes their preferences, styles, and habits at work, and each item is aligned with a particular dimension of adaptability. For example, the item "I work well with diverse others" relates to cultural aspects of adaptability. The instrument is freely available for research purposes and, given the apparent maturity of the measure, I-ADAPT-M is a plausible means of measuring adaptability as part of this work, or in other higher education contexts.

Resourceful and Responsible

While no obvious quantitative measures exist for the responsibility aspect of this attribute, work to operationalise and measure resourcefulness has been conducted. Kanungo and Menon (2005), for example, describe a 29-item instrument intended to measure managerial resourcefulness that the authors suggest may be used to identify potential leaders. The instrument is derived from an empirical study of 485 managers that identified affective, intellectual, and action-oriented competencies believed to underpin managerial resourcefulness. Items include "I think it is necessary to use formal authority positions to get others to do what I want" and "I share what I know". While the instrument is shown to exhibit high degrees of validity, the focus on managerial roles is arguably too narrow for use as a general measure of resourcefulness in students.

Another measure that is commonly associated with resourcefulness (see McWhirter et al. 2008) is Rosenbaum's Self-Control Schedule (Rosenbaum 1980). The 36 items that comprise this instrument relate to several dimensions of self-control, including the handling of negative emotions, breaking bad habits, completing undesirable tasks, and delaying gratification. The instrument has been shown to possess good reliability and consistency and has been used widely since its publication. The issue with this measure is that it was not designed to quantify resourcefulness, specifically. Of course, there is significant overlap between the concepts of self-control and personal resourcefulness, but self-control is arguably a *component* of resourcefulness while the Rosenbaum measure also places greater emphasis on self-efficacy than is typically associated with being resourceful.

Zauszniewski et al. (2006) present a 28-item Resourcefulness Scale that measures resourcefulness along two dimensions: personal ("the ability to independently perform daily tasks") and social ("to seek help from others when unable to function independently"). 16 of the 28 items relate to personal resourcefulness (e.g. "When faced with a difficult problem, I try to approach its solution in a systematic way"), with the remaining 12 designed to measure social resourcefulness (e.g. "When I am feeling sad, it helps to talk to other people"). Items are presented on a 6-point scale ranging from 0 ("not at all like me") to 5 ("very much like me") and respondents asked to indicate how descriptive each of the items is of them. Significantly, the Resourcefulness Scale draws heavily on Rosenbaum's Self-Control Schedule in its conception and realisation, featuring many of the same items while downplaying the emphasis on self-efficacy, which LeFort (2000) found did not correlate strongly with accepted conceptualisations of resourcefulness.

The scale was developed and validated in a two-phase study with chronically ill elderly patients. The authors found that the scale had acceptable internal consistency (a = 0.85) and state that it may be used with younger and middle-aged adults as well as the elderly. Thus, given its specific focus on resourcefulness, the scale is thought to be suitable for use in this work and higher education more generally, where this attribute is concerned.

Confident

The university defines confidence in terms of the personal dimension: "possess excellent interpersonal and social skills fostered within an internationalised community" and the transferable dimension: "demonstrate enthusiasm, leadership and the ability to positively influence others". When approaching confidence as a distinct, measurable attribute, however, this definition is not helpful, as it does not indicate what is unique about confidence. Interpersonal skills, leadership, and international awareness are all covered, to some extent, elsewhere and, while the form of confidence described here is creditable, the level of confidence that might be described as useful is somewhat subjective. It is conceivable, too, that an excess of confidence may be undesirable in an employee. Defining a simple measure of confidence, then, is problematic, as the ideal degree and nature of confidence exuded by an individual is not fixed.

If confidence was to be measured, and considered analogous to self-efficacy, then the ten-point General Self-Efficacy Scale (Schwarzer and Jerusalem 1995) might be a suitable candidate instrument. While notions of self-efficacy are arguably associated with what one might generally term confidence, it is not a perfect fit for the university definition of the attribute. Removed further still from how the university definition may be interpreted, self-esteem is another trait that may be measured, for example, using the ten-point Rosenberg Self-Esteem Scale (Rosenberg 1979) and considered somewhat equivalent to confidence. A potential limitation of both these self-rating measures is their attitudinal nature: confidence is arguably a phenomenon that is better measured through the observation of behaviour. However, simple self-report measures are more practical to administer when resources are limited, and volunteers are unlikely to be compensated for their time: constructing scenarios under which additional volunteers may be recruited to observe and rate other participants' confidence is prohibitively resource intensive in most higher education contexts.

While neither of these measures represents an ideal fit for the some-what prosaic university definition, their brevity—just ten items apiece—makes them interesting candidates for inclusion in the battery of tests used to measure attribute attainment, as they do not place significant additional demands on study participants.

Experienced Collaborators

The university defines experienced collaborators in terms of the personal dimension: "are experienced in working in groups and teams of varying sizes and in a variety of roles"; and the transferable dimension: "conduct themselves professionally and contribute positively when working in a team". Beyond the confines of the university, however, collaboration is not so easily defined. As Wood and Gray (1991) note, the literature presents "a welter of definitions, each having something to offer and none being entirely satisfactory by itself". Further, much of the work on collaboration is concerned with conceptualising and measuring the process at an organisational level (see, e.g., Thomson et al. 2009). This makes good sense, as it is only within (and between) organisations or groups of individuals, that collaboration may occur. From a higher education point of view, however, the focus is not on organisational policies and procedures but on individual attitudes and experience. Here, a possibly flawed assumption in the university definition is revealed: graduates are expected to have gained experience of working collaboratively (the personal dimension above) and, it is implied, that this experience results in conduct that is positive and professional (the transferable dimension). It does not necessarily follow, however, that mere experience of being forced to work as part of a group will develop a professional attitude in such situations. While some work exists on measuring attitudes to collaboration, the instruments used are highly specific to the setting in which they are administered (e.g. health care—see Hojat and Gonnella 2011) and therefore not more generally applicable. Collaboration is closely related to communication, of course, and so measures of communication—coupled with some qualitative data collection, may be the only practical means of 'measuring' this attribute.

Reflective Learners

The university defines reflective learners in terms of the personal dimension: "set aspirational goals for continuing personal, professional and career development"; and the transferable dimension: "identify and articulate their skills, knowledge and understanding confidently and in a variety of contexts". This latter dimension seems very closely related to effective communication, discussed above. Thus, it might be said that aspects of this attribute are captured in measures of communication, but this is a somewhat unsatisfactory position. It might be possible to construct a test that attempts to measure reflective learning, but such a test would lack validity without extensive work to develop it. So, the potential for games to encourage reflective learning is probably best explored by qualitative means and, as such, this is discussed in Chaps. 4 and 5.

Ethically and Socially Aware

The university defines ethical and social awareness in terms of the personal dimension: "welcome exposure to the richness of multi-cultural and international experiences, opportunities, and ways of thinking"; and the transferable dimension: "have a practical and contemporary knowledge of relevant professional, ethical, and legal frameworks". The personal dimension might be interpreted as being equivalent to political correctness, but this is of limited use in terms of devising a robust measurement because what constitutes 'politically correct' ways of thinking may vary from person to person, between cultures, and over time. The university-approved personal dimension also places emphasis on *welcoming exposure* to varying experiences and cultures, rather than simply accepting these as valuable. The transferable dimension, which refers to knowledge of legal frameworks, is also unhelpful in this context as such knowledge is necessarily subject-specific: an architect needs to understand the legal obligations and liabilities associated with their profession but not those of a surgeon, for example.

While ethical and social awareness is not formally tested for in most universities, the Associateship of King's College (AKC) is a taught programme and associated award that "aims to promote intelligent, open-minded reflection on religious, philosophical and ethical issues".[7] The AKC originated as the award given to all graduates of King's College, London, and is now an optional part of any King's student's curriculum. The modern AKC "seeks to foster an understanding of different ideas, beliefs, and cultures that can be taken into wider society", which is somewhat relevant to the definition of ethical and social awareness discussed above. However, while the AKC is assessed (by means of a two-hour examination), it does not represent an ideal candidate for measuring the Ethically and Socially Aware attribute due to its reliance on taught material. The examination at King's is based directly on lectures delivered over the course of two semesters. Thus, while this is clearly a suitable and successful means of assessing students taking the AKC, it would not function as a general-purpose test of the degree to which students "welcome exposure to the richness of multicultural and international experiences, opportunities and ways of thinking". Indeed, the guidance provided to students at King's states that "as each AKC unit is unique, looking at past papers for revision purposes may not be very helpful", suggesting that the material taught each year is what is being assessed, rather some attitudinal aspect of the students.

Again, in the absence of a readily deployed quantitative measure, students' attainment of this difficult to measure attribute may be explored qualitatively.

Summary

This chapter has highlighted the relevance of video games to higher education. The suggestion made here is that, in this context, the utility of games lies in their potential to develop desirable skills and attributes, rather than their capacity for course content delivery. To put this idea to the test, it follows that we must be able to measure the impact of a game-based intervention intended to develop graduate attributes. Indeed, if we are to make *any* claims about the development of graduate attributes at university, some means of quantifying gains in attribute attainment are required.

Measuring graduate attribute attainment is not straightforward, however. In this chapter, potential quantitative measures have been discussed for a range of typical graduate attributes, but it is clear that many such attributes are not readily quantified. In determining which measures should be used in the work described here, a number of guiding principles were applied, informed by a small pilot project wherein potential measures were trialled with students (see Barr 2016). First, in order to minimise the demands on participants, concise and easy-to-administer instruments were favoured over more complex, time-consuming measures. Multiple-choice surveys, for example, are more practical to administer than more involved observational approaches. Efficient administration and analysis are also important considerations for any educator seeking to measure graduate attribute attainment, as the ease of a measure's administration has resourcing implications. This relates to the second principle applied to the selection of attribute measures: that the instruments should be free to use. As well as acknowledging that few higher education institutions enjoy a budget dedicated to graduate attribute development, ensuring that the instruments used here are free to use also helps ensure the reproducibility of the work. Third, measures were selected on the basis of their published validity. For example, the MI5 Investigative Challenge was not intended for research use and thus comes with no indication of its validity. On the other hand, measures such as the Resourcefulness Scale are published alongside an account of the means by which they have been validated. Finally, it must be accepted that not everything can be measured in a quantitative fashion. Some attributes, such as those concerned with ethical and social awareness or reflective learning, are probably best explored by qualitative means: often the best way of finding something out about a person is simply to ask them.

Notes

1. Known as the Spellings' Commission after the US Secretary of Education (2005–2009), Margaret Spellings.
2. http://www.gla.ac.uk/students/attributes/.
3. https://www.enhancementthemes.ac.uk/completed-enhancement-themes/graduates-for-the-21st-century.
4. https://www.insightassessment.com/Products/Products-Summary/Critical-Thinking-Skills-Tests/California-Critical-Thinking-Skills-Test-CCTST.
5. https://www.gla.ac.uk/students/attributes/yourattributes/investigative/.
6. https://www.mi5.gov.uk/careers/opportunities/investigations.
7. http://www.kcl.ac.uk/aboutkings/principal/dean/akc/AKC-Handbook/starting/values.aspx.

References

Barr, M. (2016). Using Video Games to Develop Graduate Attributes: A Pilot Study. In The University of the West of Scotland (Ed.), *Proceedings of the 10th European Conference on Games Based Learning* (pp. 41–49). Paisley, Scotland, UK: Academic Conferences and Publishing Limited.

Barrie, S. C. (2004). A Research-Based Approach to Generic Graduate Attributes Policy. *Higher Education Research & Development, 23*(3), 261–275. https://doi.org/10.1080/0729436042000235391.

Barrie, S. C. (2006). Understanding What We Mean by the Generic Attributes of Graduates. *Higher Education, 51*(2), 215–241. https://doi.org/10.1007/s10734-004-6384-7.

Barrie, S. C. (2007). A Conceptual Framework for the Teaching and Learning of Generic Graduate Attributes. *Studies in Higher Education, 32*(4), 439–458. https://doi.org/10.1080/03075070701476100.

Bell, B. S., & Kozlowski, S. W. J. (2008). Active Learning: Effects of Core Training Design Elements on Self-Regulatory Processes, Learning, and Adaptability. *Journal of Applied Psychology, 93*(2), 296–316. https://doi.org/10.1037/0021-9010.93.2.296.

Bethesda Softworks. (1994). *The Elder Scrolls.* Bethesda Softworks.

Candy, P., Crebert, G., & O'Leary, J. (1994). *Developing Lifelong Learners Through Undergraduate Education.* Canberra, Australian Capital Territory: Australian Government Publishing Service.

CD Projekt Red. (2007). *The Witcher.* Atari.

Chickering, A. W., & Gamson, Z. F. (1987). Seven Principles for Good Practice in Undergraduate Education. *AAHE Bulletin.* Retrieved November 4, 2013.

Chong, A., & Romkey, L. (2012). Adapting Existing Assessment Tools for Use in Assessing Engineering Graduate Attributes. In *Proceedings of the 2012 Canadian Engineering Education Association (CEEA12) Conference,* Winnipeg, MB.

Coetzee, M. (2014). Measuring Student Graduateness: Reliability and Construct Validity of the Graduate Skills and Attributes Scale. *Higher Education Research & Development.* https://doi.org/10.1080/07294360.2014.890572.

de Corte, E. (1996). New Perspectives on Learning and Teaching in Higher Education. In S. A. Burgen (Ed.), *Goals and Purposes of Higher Education in the 21st Century* (pp. 112–132). London: Jessica Kingsley Publishers.

Drummond, I., Nixon, I., & Wiltshire, J. (1998). Personal Transferable Skills in Higher Education: The Problems of Implementing Good Practice. *Quality Assurance in Education, 6*(1), 19–27. https://doi.org/10.1108/09684889810200359.

Duran, R. L. (1983). Communicative Adaptability: A Measure of Social Communicative Competence. *Communication Quarterly, 31*(4), 320–326. https://doi.org/10.1080/01463378309369521.

Duran, R. L. (1992). Communicative Adaptability: A Review of Conceptualization and Measurement. *Communication Quarterly, 40*(3), 253–268. https://doi.org/10.1080/01463379209369840.

Ennis, R. H. (1993). Critical Thinking Assessment. *Theory Into Practice, 32*(3), 179–186. https://doi.org/10.1080/00405849309543594.

Ennis, R. H., & Weir, E. (1985). *The Ennis-Weir Critical Thinking Essay Test.* Pacific Grove, CA: Midwest Publications.

Ensemble Studios. (2002). *Age of Mythology.* Microsoft Game Studios.

Epic Games. (2017). *Fortnite.* Epic Games.

Facione, P. A. (1990). *Critical Thinking: A Statement of Expert Consensus for Purposes of Educational Assessment and Instruction. Research Findings and Recommendations.* Fullerton, CA: Peter A. Facione.

Facione, P. (1991). *Using the California Critical Thinking Skills Test in Research, Evaluation, and Assessment.* Millbrae, CA: California Academic Press.

Facione, N. C., Facione, P. A., & Sanchez, C. A. (1994). Critical Thinking Disposition as a Measure of Competent Clinical Judgment: The Development of the California Critical Thinking Disposition Inventory. *The Journal of Nursing Education, 33*(8), 345–350.

Fullbright. (2017). *Tacoma.* Fullbright.

Gee, J. P. (2007). *What Video Games Have to Teach Us About Learning and Literacy* (2nd ed.). Basingstoke: Palgrave Macmillan.

Green, W., Hammer, S., & Star, C. (2009). Facing Up to the Challenge: Why Is It So Hard to Develop Graduate Attributes? *Higher Education Research & Development, 28*(1), 17–29. https://doi.org/10.1080/07294360802444339.

Grim, A. M. (2010). *Use of Situational Judgment Test to Measure Individual Adaptability in Applied Settings.* Unpublished thesis. George Mason University, Fairfax, VA.

Haigh, M., & Clifford, V. A. (2011). Integral Vision: A Multi-Perspective Approach to the Recognition of Graduate Attributes. *Higher Education Research & Development, 30*(5), 573–584. https://doi.org/10.1080/0729436 0.2011.598448.

Hambur, S., Rowe, K., & Luc, L. T. (2002). *Graduate Skills Assessment: Stage One Validity Study.* Canberra: Australian Council for Educational Research.

Hello Games. (2016). *No Man's Sky.* Hello Games.

Hillis, P. (2005). Assessing Investigative Skills in History: A Case Study from Scotland. *History Teacher, 38*(3), 341–360.

Hojat, M., & Gonnella, J. S. (2011). An Instrument for Measuring Pharmacist and Physician Attitudes Towards Collaboration: Preliminary Psychometric Data. *Journal of Interprofessional Care, 25*(1), 66–72. https://doi.org/10.310 9/13561820.2010.483368.

Hullman, G. A. (2007). Communicative Adaptability Scale: Evaluating Its Use as an 'Other-Report' Measure. *Communication Reports, 20*(2), 51–74. https:// doi.org/10.1080/08934210701643693.

Kanungo, R. N., & Menon, S. T. (2005). Managerial Resourcefulness: Measuring a Critical Component of Leadership Effectiveness. *The Journal of Entrepreneurship, 14*(1), 39–55. https://doi.org/10.1177/097135570401400103.

Klein, S. P. (1983). *Relationship of Bar Examinations to Performance Tests of Lawyering Skills.* Santa Monica, CA: The Rand Corporation.

Klein, S., Benjamin, R., Shavelson, R., & Bolus, R. (2007). The Collegiate Learning Assessment: Facts and Fantasies. *Evaluation review, 31*(5), 415–439. https://doi.org/10.1177/0193841X07303318.

LeFort, S. M. (2000). A Test of Braden's Self-Help Model in Adults with Chronic Pain. *Journal of Nursing Scholarship, 32*(2), 153–160. https://doi.org/10.1111/j.1547-5069.2000.00153.x.

Lievens, F., Peeters, H., & Schollaert, E. (2008). Situational Judgment Tests: A Review of Recent Research. *Personnel Review, 37*(4), 426–441. https://doi.org/10.1108/00483480810877598.

Maxis. (1989). *SimCity.* Maxis.

McCroskey, J. C., & McCroskey, L. L. (1988). Self-Report as an Approach to Measuring Communication Competence. *Communication Research Reports, 5*(2), 108–113. https://doi.org/10.1080/08824098809359810.

McCroskey, J. C., & Richmond, V. P. (1995). *Fundamentals of Human Communication: An Interpersonal Perspective.* Prospect Heights, IL: Waveland Press Inc.

McWhirter, B. T., Burrow-Sanchez, J. J., & Townsend, K. C. (2008). Measuring Learned Resourcefulness in College Students: Factor Structure of the Self-Control Schedule (SCS). *College Student Journal, 42*(4), 1099–1109.

Motowidlo, S. J., Dunnette, M. D., & Carter, G. W. (1990). An Alternative Selection Procedure: The Low-Fidelity Simulation. *Journal of Applied Psychology, 75*(6), 640–647. https://doi.org/10.1037/0021-9010.75.6.640.

Moy, J. (1999). *The Impact of Generic Competencies on Workplace Performance: Review of Research.* Leabrook, SA: National Centre for Vocational Education Research. Retrieved May 10, 2013.

Nicol, D. J. (2010). *The Foundation for Graduate Attributes: Developing Self-Regulation Through Self and Peer-Assessment.* The Quality Assurance Agency for Higher Education.

Nintendo EPD. (2017). *The Legend of Zelda: Breath of the Wild.* Nintendo.

No Code. (2019). *Observation.* Devolver Digital.

Ployhart, Robert E., & Paul D. Bliese. (2006). Individual Adaptability (I-ADAPT) Theory: Conceptualizing the Antecedents, Consequences, and

Measurement of Individual Differences in Adaptability. In *Understanding Adaptability: A Prerequisite for Effective Performance within Complex Environments* (Vols. 1–0, Vol. 6, pp. 3–39). Bingley: Emerald Group Publishing Limited.

Pulakos, E. D., Arad, S., Donovan, M. A., & Plamondon, K. E. (2000). Adaptability in the Workplace: Development of a Taxonomy of Adaptive Performance. *Journal of Applied Psychology, 85*(4), 612–624. https://doi.org/10.1037/0021-9010.85.4.612.

Pulakos, E. D., Schmitt, N., Dorsey, D. W., Arad, S., Borman, W. C., & Hedge, J. W. (2002). Predicting Adaptive Performance: Further Tests of a Model of Adaptability. *Human Performance, 15*(4), 299–323. https://doi.org/10.1207/S15327043HUP1504_01.

Richmond, V. P. (2002). Socio-communicative Style and Orientation in Instruction: Giving Good Communication and Receiving Good Communication. In J. L. Chesebro & J. C. McCroskey (Eds.), *Communication for Teachers* (pp. 104–115). Boston: Allyn & Bacon.

Richmond, V. P., & McCroskey, J. C. (1990). Reliability and Separation of Factors on the Assertiveness-Responsiveness Measure. *Psychological Reports, 67*, 449–450.

Romer, R., Ewell, P., Jones, D., & Lenth, C. (1995). *Making Quality Count in Undergraduate Education. A Report for the ECS Chairman's 'Quality Counts' Agenda in Higher Education* (p. 34). Denver, Colorado: Education Commission of the States.

Rosenbaum, M. (1980). A Schedule for Assessing Self-Control Behaviors: Preliminary Findings. *Behavior Therapy, 11*(1), 109–121. https://doi.org/10.1016/S0005-7894(80)80040-2.

Rosenberg, M. (1979). *Conceiving the Self.* New York: Basic Books.

Sam Barlow. (2015). *Her Story.* Sam Barlow.

Schwarzer, R., & Jerusalem, M. (1995). Generalized Self-Efficacy Scale. In M. Johnston, S. C. Wright, & J. Weinman (Eds.), *Measures in Health Psychology: A User's Portfolio. Causal and Control Beliefs* (pp. 35–37). Windsor: NFER-NELSON.

Spitzberg, B. H., & Cupach, W. R. (1984). *Interpersonal Communication Competence.* Beverly Hills: SAGE Publications.

Thomson, A. M., Perry, J. L., & Miller, T. K. (2009). Conceptualizing and Measuring Collaboration. *Journal of Public Administration Research and Theory, 19*(1), 23–56. https://doi.org/10.1093/jopart/mum036.

US Department of Education. (2006). *A National Dialogue: The Secretary of Education's Commission on the Future of Higher Education.* Washington, DC. Retrieved April 21, 2019.

Valve Corporation. (2007). *Team Fortress 2.* Valve Corporation.

Watson, G. (1980). *Watson-Glaser Critical Thinking Appraisal.* New York: Psychological Corporation.

Wood, D. J., & Gray, B. (1991). Toward a Comprehensive Theory of Collaboration. *The Journal of Applied Behavioral Science, 27*(2), 139–162. https://doi.org/10.1177/0021886391272001.

Zauszniewski, J. A., Lai, C.-Y., & Tithiphontumrong, S. (2006). Development and Testing of the Resourcefulness Scale for Older Adults. *Journal of Nursing Measurement, 14*(1), 57–68. https://doi.org/10.1891/jnum.14.1.57.

3

Playing Games at University

Previous chapters have discussed graduate attributes and presented the idea that video games might be used to develop them: the question now is whether this idea has merit. In this chapter, a randomised controlled study is described, wherein a cohort of undergraduate students played specified games under controlled conditions over a period of one semester. Participants' graduate attribute attainment was tested at the beginning and the end of the study, with a pre-test battery of measures administered immediately following an initial survey of game play habits. This testing was followed by an eight-week programme of game play comprising drop-in sessions with specified games in a lab environment. The semester concluded with a round of post-test graduate attribute measurement and interviews with participants.

Since graduate attribute test scores were compared on a participant-by-participant basis, this pre- and post-test design controlled for differences between individual participants; however, it did not control for confounding outside influences. Perhaps the most obvious of these outside influences (over and above the process of personal development one might expect of an individual over time) is the effect that attending university is supposed to have on all students: graduates are expected to have

© The Author(s) 2019
M. Barr, *Graduate Skills and Game-Based Learning*, Digital Education and Learning,
https://doi.org/10.1007/978-3-030-27786-4_3

developed the range of attributes detailed in Chap. 2 as an ancillary (or perhaps primary) outcome of their degree. For this reason, a randomly assigned control group was tested on the same schedule, comprising students who match the intervention group in terms of demographic background, degree subject, and year of study as closely as possible.

Thus, student participants were randomly assigned to one of two groups:

* An intervention group that would be asked to complete a battery of online tests at the beginning and the end of the semester and play selected video games under lab conditions.
* A control group that would be asked only to complete the tests at the beginning and the end of the semester.

Student participants were recruited to the study by means of an email invitation with a link to an online form. The email was targeted at year one and year two students at the host institution and explained that the study may involve playing video games and completing surveys. The email indicated that participants who completed all assigned tasks would be entered into a prize draw for an Amazon voucher at the end of the semester. Potential participants were told that they may be randomly allocated to one of two groups but were not given any advance indication of what the tests might be intended to measure.

The online form asked participants for some basic demographic information, including age, gender, and subjects studied. In addition, participants were asked to estimate the frequency with which they played video games, if they played them at all.

Selected Measures

Based on the principles outlined in the previous chapter, and the experience of running a pilot project to trial the use of potential graduate attribute measures (Barr 2016), three attribute-specific instruments were identified for use in this study: the Communicative Adaptability Scale (Duran 1983, 1992), the I-ADAPT measure, or I-ADAPT-M (Ployhart and Bliese 2006), and the Resourcefulness Scale (Zauszniewski et al. 2006). In addition, the General Self-Efficacy Scale (Schwarzer and Jerusalem 1995) and the Rosenberg Self-Esteem Scale (Rosenberg 1979) were administered as proxies for confidence.

Selected Games

Games were selected with input from colleagues in the games industry and academia, who were presented with a list of graduate attributes and asked to suggest commercial titles that might exercise each. This list of games was then filtered through practical concerns including cost, compatibility with available hardware, and quality. A poor-quality game is of little utility here: well-received titles are more likely to be representative of those that players would choose to play on their own time, and a particularly poor game is likely to impact negatively on the participants' willingness to engage in the study. While game quality is somewhat subjective, aggregated review scores published on sites such as Metacritic[1] are used by industry and consumers alike to determine a game's excellence (Graft 2011). Metacritic scores—which convert the scores awarded by critics to games, films, and music into a convenient, if opaquely calculated, percentage value—are not without their critics (Dring 2010) but they undoubtedly provide an easily quantifiable means of determining the relative merits of a game. For the purposes of this study, no game with a Metacritic score of less than 80 was considered, with scores ranging from 82 to 95. A brief description of each of the selected games is provided below.

Borderlands 2

Borderlands 2 (Gearbox Software 2012) is a cooperative role-playing first-person shooter game, which allows up to four players to "team up with other players for online co-op goodness". Importantly, the game also allows for LAN (Local Area Network) multiplayer, meaning the cooperative elements function without an internet connection where institutional firewalls prohibit access to games servers. The game also permits players to drop in and drop out as required. This allowed participants who arrived after others had already embarked on a mission to join the team without being forced to wait for the beginning of the next mission or requiring the others to start again from the beginning. One player, however, must host the game, to which the other players then connect.

Borderlands 2 players work together to obtain loot and weaponry while battling a range of foes against a colourful cartoonish backdrop and attendant story (Fig. 3.1). A variety of play styles are supported through the choice of character classes presented to the player, ranging from a tank-like 'Gunzerker' to a stealthier assassin. The emphasis is very much on cooperation and, as such, there are no overtly competitive elements, although players receive points for completing missions that they may use to 'level up' their character.

Minecraft

Minecraft (Mojang 2011) is a procedurally generated sandbox game with construction, exploration, and survival elements. In single-player mode, players are free to explore the world and collect ('mine') resources such as stone, wood, and metal to create ('craft') a virtually limitless range of buildings, tools, and weapons. Multiplayer mode is similarly non-prescriptive in terms of what it permits (or requires) players to do: the

Fig. 3.1 Players combine forces to take on a pair of 'Bullymongs' in *Borderlands 2* (Source: http://gearboxsoftware.com)

main difference is that the world is shared, so players may choose to work together, often on very large collaborative projects (see "All of Denmark virtually recreated" 2014). Here, a *Minecraft* server was created to facilitate player cooperation in a persistent world that permitted all participants to share the same space and did not require an individual player to host the game.

The game server was left running indefinitely, with participants logging in from their individual workstations as and when they arrived in the lab. The persistent game world meant that structures constructed by players, along the lines of that seen in Fig. 3.2, could be used and extended (or, indeed, destroyed) by anyone, and returning players were not required to start from scratch each time. The persistent, shared nature of the world also provided greater scope for more ambitious collaborative efforts, given the larger pool of collaborators and increased cumulative duration of play.

Portal 2

Valve's *Portal 2* (Valve Corporation 2011) is described by the developer as "a hilariously mind-bending adventure that challenges you to use wits over weaponry in a funhouse of diabolical science". The game features a particularly robust and inventive cooperative mode, which requires two players to work together to traverse a series of challenging virtual spaces. Both players may create a pair of joined portals, through which either

Fig. 3.2 Players cooperate on some construction work in *Minecraft* (Source: http://minecraft.gamepedia.com)

player may pass, thus opening up possibilities for reaching new areas and creating opportunities for physics-based interactions with the environment. For example, in order to advance through one cooperative level, the first player must create a pair of portals for the second player to continually fall through in order to gain momentum until they exit the portal with sufficient velocity to reach a raised platform. Cooperating players are afforded their individual views of the action via a split screen, such that a player may observe what their partner is doing while controlling their own on-screen avatar. In order to aid collaboration, players are also granted the ability to 'point' to important aspects of the game world, for example, to indicate where they believe their partner should go next.

Lara Croft and the Guardian of Light

The cooperative, isometrically presented *Lara Croft and the Guardian of Light* (Crystal Dynamics 2010) also places emphasis on cooperation to solve puzzles and progress. The game is something of a departure from previous titles featuring the eponymous heroine, which are traditionally branded as *Tomb Raider* games and typically feature a third-person perspective and single-player gameplay. For the *Lara Croft* titles, a fixed isometric view of the world is presented, and the game is intended to be played with a friend. One player assumes the role of the gun-toting Lara while the other plays as Totec, a Mayan warrior who comes equipped with a spear that is useful for creating impromptu ladders and bridges.

Cooperative players share the same screen (although online co-op is an option in most versions of the game) and for this study both players were provided with a game console-style controller. This arrangement was intended to provide a more convenient means of cooperative play than crowding two players around a shared keyboard. The game's design clearly encourages verbal communication between players, often taking the form of one player solving the puzzle at hand and explaining to the other player what is required of them. Of course, if the solution to the puzzle is plain to both players it is still beneficial, and usually essential, for the players to communicate their intentions. Figure 3.3 provides a simple example of the cooperative nature of the gameplay, where Lara has used her rope to

Fig. 3.3 Players must work together to traverse the obstacles presented in *Lara Croft and the Guardian of Light* (Source: http://laracroftandtheguardianoflight. com)

create a precarious-looking bridge for Totec to cross the spike-filled pit below. Once Totec has crossed, he will be required to create a bridge for Lara to follow him by throwing his spear into the wooden planks that adorn the wall behind the pit. Only Lara possesses a rope and only Totec can throw spears—spears too weak to support the weight of the hulking warrior himself—meaning that this and numerous other obstacles may only be traversed by means of carefully planned teamwork. While the demise of a player's on-screen avatar results in little more than a brief inconvenience, there is an element of competition introduced by a points system that rewards players for their individual success in collecting artefacts and dispatching enemies. This dynamic does not lessen the fundamentally cooperative nature of the game, but it does add some small significance to the quick-fire negotiations that mediate the allocation of spoils such as health.

Warcraft III

Released in 2002, *Warcraft III: Reign of Chaos* (Blizzard Entertainment 2002) was the oldest game used in the study. The rationale for its inclusion was based on its strategic multiplayer mode, which may be played over a local network without an internet connection. While *Warcraft III* was not mentioned specifically by the panel of experts involved in

selecting the games, a number of its derivatives were, namely: the ubiqui-
tous *World of Warcraft* (*WoW*) (Blizzard Entertainment 2004) and *Dota 2*
(Valve Corporation 2013). These are quite different games, belonging to
different genres: *Warcraft III* is a Real-Time Strategy (RTS) game whereas
WoW is a Massively Multiplayer Online Role-Playing Game (MMORPG)
based on the lore of the RTS series which preceded it; *Dota 2* is a
Multiplayer Online Battle Arena (MOBA) game and sequel to a mod
('modification') of *Warcraft III*. However, certain shared elements—the
online cooperation of *WoW* and the strategic combat of *Dota 2*—made
Warcraft III an interesting candidate for inclusion in the study.

Warcraft III is played on a pseudo three-dimensional map with up to
four races (Orcs, Humans, Night Elves, and Undead) vying for domina-
tion (Fig. 3.4). Each player controls one of these races and must collect
resources—gold and lumber—to develop and construct buildings, units,
and weaponry with the ultimate aim of obliterating their opponents from
the map. The game's multiplayer mode supports team play, meaning that
participants in the study could work together (even as different races) to
defeat a computer-controlled adversary. Unlike *Lara Croft*, many different multiplayer configurations are supported, from the previously
described two-versus-one scenario through to any combination of human
and computer teams.

Fig. 3.4 A Night Elf (turquoise) encampment comes under Human (blue) attack
in *Warcraft III* (Source: http://us.blizzard.com/en-us/games/war3) (Color figure
online)

Participants were instructed to play cooperatively (i.e. on the same team) in pairs or groups. If sufficient participants were available, competitive play was permitted (e.g. a team of two participants against another two) but cooperation was encouraged.

Team Fortress 2

Valve's *Team Fortress 2* (Valve Corporation 2007) is the multiplayer-only sequel to a popular mod of the 1996 first-person shooter, *Quake* (id Software 1996). While it does feature in-game purchases—players may opt to buy particular upgrades and other content—the core game is free-to-play, making it an attractive option where budgets are limited. The free-to-play tag is often synonymous with lower quality titles; however, the game was also critically well received, with a Metacritic score of 92. Crucially, multiplayer games may be hosted on a local server, again avoiding the need for an internet connection to facilitate matchmaking.

Gameplay in *Team Fortress 2* is, as one might expect, team based. Players may join the game at any time by dropping into the current match and choosing to side with either the RED ('Reliable Excavation & Demolition') team or the BLU ('Builders League United') team. Similar to *Borderlands 2*, players may select from a range of character classes that allow for experimentation with different play styles, ranging from the slow but formidable Heavy to the elusive Spy (Fig. 3.5).

Fig. 3.5 BLU versus RED combat during a Capture the Flag game in *Team Fortress 2* (Source: http://wiki.teamfortress.com)

The structure of the game sees competing teams thrown into conflict on a time-limited or objective-based map. When a team meets the victory conditions—or time runs out—the next map is loaded, and a new objective pursued. Each map operates in a pre-determined game mode, such as Capture the Flag, Payload, or King of the Hill, with the objective of each mode explained by means of a short video shown at the beginning of play. In Capture the Flag mode, for example, both teams are tasked with stealing a briefcase of intelligence from the depths of the opposing team's base and transporting it back to their own, with the briefcase standing in for the titular flag. Players must therefore decide how much emphasis to place on defence of their own intelligence versus making an offensive move to capture the enemy's briefcase.

Regardless of game mode, the team-based gameplay means that communication is critically important. At a basic level, communication may comprise little more than desperate pleas for assistance when an enemy agent gains the upper hand. However, a successful team will communicate in a more sophisticated manner to convey strategies and status updates, often under the direction of a de facto leader.

Papers, Please and *Gone Home*

Described by its developer as a "dystopian document thriller", *Papers, Please* (3909 LLC 2013) is a British Academy of Film and Television Arts (BAFTA) winning game in which the player is cast as an immigration officer, deciding whom to let in and whom to turn away from the border of the fictional former communist state of Arstotzka. The player performs this role by critically (and increasingly quickly) assessing the documentation presented by each potential immigrant in light of the ever-changing rules and regulations imposed by the state (Fig. 3.6). As well as exercising critical judgement and dealing with change, the player is presented with an opportunity to reflect on the ethical and social consequences of their in-game actions. A player may reflect on how their actions impact the lives of the fictional immigrants and citizens of Arstotzka (terrorist attacks are a distinct possibility, should the wrong person be permitted access to the country) and also on the personal price to be paid by the family of the player's

Fig. 3.6 Players must analyse evidence presented in *Papers, Please* and respond accordingly (Source: http://papersplea.se)

character. Failure to meet state-imposed quotas for processing immigrants results in reduced pay and, ultimately, a choice to be made between paying fuel bills or buying life-saving medicine for a family member.

Fullbright's *Gone Home* (The Fullbright Company 2013) might be described as a first-person interactive story or adventure (the designers term it a "story exploration video game") wherein the player, assuming the role of a young woman returning to her family home after a yearlong absence, explores an apparently abandoned house. In doing so, the player may uncover a number of storylines, the most significant of which relates to the protagonist's younger sister. There are no explicit goals and interaction is relatively limited—such games are occasionally, and somewhat derogatorily, referred to as "walking simulators"—with plot developments uncovered by reading discarded letters and examining ephemera such as concert ticket stubs and television viewing guides.

These two single-player games differed in nature from the majority of the titles used in the study, which emphasised cooperation and communication in a multiplayer environment. However, both games may be viewed as requiring the player to exercise critical thinking and to demonstrate resourcefulness and adaptability. While these latter attributes were measured here by quantitative means, it was thought useful to discuss the possibility of these games being used to develop less tangible attributes—such as ethical and social awareness—with participants in the interviews that followed.

Lab Configuration

The gameplay labs operated on a drop-in basis, open for students to come and play the specified games between the hours of 9 am–5 pm three days a week (Fig. 3.7). Participants were thus permitted to play the games as and when fitted with their existing schedules, provided they logged the requisite number of minutes of play time on each. Time played was logged by participants on exiting the lab, and play sessions ranged in duration from little more than a few minutes to sometimes more than two hours. The flexible drop-in structure partially addresses a common criticism of laboratory-based video game studies, where an arbitrarily defined time limit on play does not mirror the circumstances under which players normally play games (Egenfeldt-Nielsen et al. 2008, p. 233). While participants were asked to log 120 minutes of play on most games, time management was their responsibility, meaning they could choose to play for "just five minutes more" or leave when they had

Fig. 3.7 Lab environment used in the experimental study

a class to attend. Participants did occasionally opt to play for longer than the prescribed period, either because they were simply immersed in an enjoyable experience, or because it is more natural to stop playing at a suitable juncture in the game, for example, at the completion of a level or mission. In this sense, the lab was arranged to provide better ecological validity than would have been afforded by imposing a rigid temporal structure on proceedings. No player welcomes being told to stop when they are in the middle of a game they are enjoying, and many players—particularly those less accustomed to lengthy sessions of video game play—might find being asked to endure two hours of an unfamiliar game prohibitively tiring.

In total, seven tasks were set for participants in the experimental group, comprising the eight games described above. Most tasks involved the participants playing a prescribed game for two hours, with the exception of the final task that comprised an hour each of two comparatively short single-player titles that differed from the more open-ended multiplayer games of tasks one to six.

The lab environment consisted of 12 very modestly specified Windows workstations with flat screen monitors, games controllers, and optional headphones. The lab's pre-existing network infrastructure was not initially connected to the internet, but all of the machines were connected to a network hub, allowing for cooperative and competitive LAN play were supported by the games. The network ports required to connect to the Steam platform were eventually opened by the university's network administration team, allowing for more straightforward purchase, download, and patching of the games software. These ports are typically blocked by higher education IT services for perhaps obvious reasons: games are not generally encouraged at university, and every open port increases the potential area of attack available to malicious parties outside of the institution.

Potentially more problematic was the use of Valve's Steam service to facilitate matchmaking, mediating the connections between players that are required for multiplayer gaming. By default, Steam is used to facilitate the multiplayer component of *Portal 2* and *Team Fortress 2*—both titles produced by Valve. An unforeseen additional complication with Steam matchmaking related to the limitations placed on newly created

Steam accounts. In order to purchase and install multiple copies of each game, a Steam account with an associated email address was created for each machine in the lab and games bought—as gift purchases, via an existing Steam account—for each. However, in order to "protect our users from spamming, phishing, and other abuse, Steam prevents some accounts from accessing certain community and social features". To this end, Steam limits the ability of accounts that have spent less than five US dollars to engage in multiplayer activity, such as sending friend invites. As all of the purchasing was done through a single account, this restriction remained in place for all of the accounts used in the lab. Furthermore, the creation of multiple shared Steam accounts may be in breach of the service's terms and conditions, and it is hoped that Valve's legal team don't read this book.

However, solutions were found for both games. A local dedicated server was created for *Team Fortress 2*, to which participants' games connected instead of looking to Steam for potential opponents. This was very straightforward to accomplish as LAN play of this nature is supported by default in the game. The solution for *Portal 2* was slightly less straightforward, as LAN co-op is not an option available to players when they launch the game and, while the functionality does exist in the game's code, it may only be accessed by entering command line instructions via a normally concealed console. A more user-friendly workaround was found that, through the modification of one of the game's configuration files, allowed the option to connect to games on specified lab computers to be added to the game's menu. Participants were then instructed to choose the relevant menu option, depending on whether they were to host or connect to a game. In the latter case, they were instructed to choose the option that would connect them to the machine hosting the game, as identified by its IP address, which was clearly displayed on each machine.

More mundane were the issues relating to the available hardware. As noted above, the machines used in the lab were not especially well specified, and certainly not intended for gaming. They did, however, prove perfectly usable for most games, especially when graphical options were adjusted to reflect the limited capabilities of the machines' graphics cards. The exception to this was perhaps *Lara Croft and the Guardian of Light*, which, even on the lowest performance settings, was somewhat sluggish and occasionally unresponsive. Such issues did not prove critical to participant engagement, however.

Results

In total, 100 level one and two undergraduate students were recruited to the main experimental study. These participants were randomly assigned to either the control group or intervention group. 36 of the 50 potential participants assigned to the control group completed the first battery of online tests while 36 of the intervention group completed the same before playing any of the selected games. All subsequent analysis treats the completion of these tests as part of the entry criteria for the study. This approach differs from the 'intention to treat' of many medical studies (Hollis and Campbell 1999) wherein all participants are included in the analysis regardless of whether they completed the study or received any treatment. However, as no relevant data pertaining to the absent participants was available prior to beginning the study (as might be the case in a medical trial, e.g., where pre-existing medical records for those who did not complete any treatment might be used to establish a baseline), this approach was thought most appropriate here.

Data collected via the online battery of tests are considered below on an attribute-by-attribute basis, noting any findings that may support, disprove, or otherwise speak to the hypothesis that playing certain commercial video games is associated with gains in each attribute. The control and intervention groups were assessed for similarity at baseline (taken to mean the point at which the first battery of tests was completed, following randomisation) by comparing demographic factors and baseline test scores by attribute (Table 3.1). Correlations for all measures at baseline (week one) are for all participants: week one is when most data are available, and there is no issue with combining data because all participants are pre-intervention. All comparisons were by Fisher's exact test for categorical variables (e.g., year of study), and by t-test measures (Welch's t-test) assuming unequal variance between groups for continuous variables such as those numerical values derived from attribute tests.

Table 3.1 indicates that there were no significant differences between the randomly assigned control and intervention groups, with p-values ranging from 0.271 to 0.973. The mean age of the intervention group (M = 21.09) was slightly higher than that of the control group (M = 19.8), with a larger standard deviation (SD = 5.95 versus SD = 3.41), but otherwise the groups were remarkably similar. Differences in key characteristics such as gender, year of study, and time typically spent playing video games per week were all well within acceptable bounds; for example, the percentage of participants who did not play video games at

Table 3.1 Summary of week one test scores and demographic information by control/intervention group

		Control	Intervention	p
N		36	36	
Measures				
Group (%)	Control	36 (100.0)	0 (0.0)	
	Intervention	0 (0.0)	36 (100.0)	
I-ADAPT-M (mean (SD))		**202.69 (19.70)**	**200.36 (37.65)**	**0.743**
Communicative Adaptability Scale (mean (SD))		**100.14 (8.92)**	**99.06 (17.88)**	**0.746**
Resourcefulness Scale (mean (SD))		**82.75 (19.75)**	**81.44 (23.33)**	**0.798**
Rosenberg Self-Esteem Scale (mean (SD))		22.56 (3.30)	23.25 (3.28)	0.374
General Self-Efficacy Scale (mean (SD))		31.00 (3.57)	31.69 (6.23)	0.563
Demographic information				
Note that one participant in both groups did not complete the demographic survey, so N = 35 for these data.				
Year (%)	Level 1	22 (62.9)	24 (68.6)	0.801
	Level 2	13 (37.1)	11 (31.4)	
Age (mean (SD))		19.80 (3.41)	21.09 (5.95)	0.271
Gender (%)	Female	18 (51.4)	20 (57.1)	0.346
	Male	14 (40.0)	15 (42.9)	
	Other	3 (8.6)	0 (0.0)	
Hours spent playing video games per week (%)	0	10 (28.6)	9 (25.7)	0.973
	1–4	12 (34.3)	14 (40.0)	
	4–8	6 (17.1)	6 (17.1)	
	>8	7 (20.0)	6 (17.1)	
Retention (%)	Completed	20 (55.6)	16 (44.4)	0.48
	Lost to follow-up	16 (44.4)	20 (55.6)	

Includes only those participants who completed surveys at baseline (week one). Highlighted bold rows are those that refer to key attribute-measuring scores all was 25.7% for the intervention group and 28.6% for the control. Exposure to games outside of the study was an important variable that randomisation was intended to control—this was, perhaps, the factor most likely to skew the results of the intervention.

Total scores for each attribute were calculated, in accordance with the published scoring mechanisms, for each participant at each time point they completed testing. To assess students' attribute attainment over the period in question, a summary measure of 'score change' was calculated for each attribute by subtracting week one score from week eight score for each participant with available data. Thus, each participant has a score change for each attribute, which is negative if their score worsened, and positive if their score improved. The distribution of score changes was assessed in both groups (control and intervention) for each attribute as follows:

- Score changes were assessed for normality by graphical means, using histograms (see Fig. 3.8; distributions for each of the key attribute-testing measures are also visualised using violin plots under the relevant sections below);
- Each participant's week one score was plotted against their week eight score in a scatter plot, such that participants with positive score changes lay above the diagonal, and negative score changes below diagonal (providing a visualisation of how score change differed across the range of week one scores);
- Differences in score change between the groups were formally assessed by calculating a Cohen's d for difference in the means for the groups and tested using t-test assuming unequal variance.

The parametric statistical tests used here rely on the assumption that data are distributed normally. The study's relatively small sample sizes were thought to prohibit assessing normality based on the changes in overall score change (as used in the analysis of the measures above). Therefore, normality was assessed by plotting histograms for each measure, showing the changes recorded for individual questions, as opposed to the overall score for each participant. This approach provided a great deal more data to plot and thus a more reliable assessment of

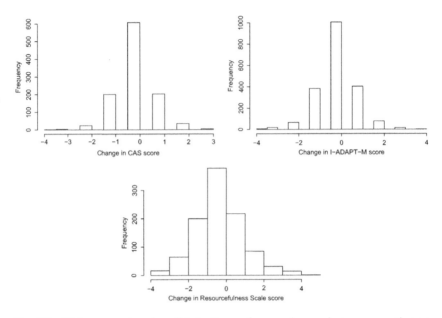

Fig. 3.8 Histograms showing distributions of score change between week one and week eight for each measure (CAS, I-ADAPT-M, and Resourcefulness Scale), for all participants

normality. As shown in Fig. 3.8 below, a classically normal distribution may be observed for all the attribute-measuring instruments. In order to check that distributions for both groups (control and intervention) were similar, the same data were plotted again on a per group basis, again revealing a classically normal distribution in all cases (not shown here).

While randomisation helps control for differences between the intervention and control groups—differences such as age, gender, and game-playing habits—an additional concern here is retention bias. This refers to the problems that can occur when there is something different about the participants who choose to stick with the study, compared to those who drop out (or are 'lost to follow-up'). If, for example, a disproportionate number of the most avid gamers dropped out of the study, then this could skew the results. What if those who already played video games for many hours a week were largely unaffected by the game-based intervention? If they all dropped out of the intervention group, leaving only those

Table 3.2 Summary of week one test scores and demographic information by completed/lost to follow-up

		Completed	Lost to follow-up	p
N		36	36	
Group (%)	Control	20 (55.6)	16 (44.4)	0.48
	Intervention	16 (44.4)	20 (55.6)	
I-ADAPT-M (mean (SD))		**200.22 (19.06)**	**202.83 (37.97)**	**0.713**
Communicative Adaptability Scale (mean (SD))		**97.72 (8.41)**	**101.47 (17.94)**	**0.26**
Resourcefulness Scale (mean (SD))		**80.94 (18.09)**	**83.25 (24.60)**	**0.652**
Rosenberg Self-Esteem Scale (mean (SD))		22.67 (3.02)	23.14 (3.55)	0.546
General Self-Efficacy Scale (mean (SD))		31.03 (3.65)	31.67 (6.18)	0.595
Demographic information				
Note that one participant in both groups did not complete the demographic survey, so *N* = 35 for these data				
Year (%)	Level 1	19 (54.3)	27 (77.1)	0.078
	Level 2	16 (45.7)	8 (22.9)	
Age (mean (SD))		21.06 (4.28)	19.83 (5.36)	0.293
Gender (%)	Female	20 (57.1)	18 (51.4)	0.714
	Male	13 (37.1)	16 (45.7)	
	Other	2 (5.7)	1 (2.9)	
Hours spent playing video games per week (%)	0	7 (20.0)	12 (34.3)	0.32
	1–4	14 (40.0)	12 (34.3)	
	4–8	5 (14.3)	7 (20.0)	
	>8	9 (25.7)	4 (11.4)	

Highlighted bold rows are those that refer to key attribute-measuring scores

who rarely played video games, the effects of gameplay on attribute attainment might appear inflated. So, baseline features were also compared between those with and without week eight (end of study) scores, that is, those participants who completed the study and those that were lost to follow-up (Table 3.2).

While there are no significant or troubling differences between those participants who completed the study and those who dropped out, a number of interesting features are revealed in this analysis. For example, it may be noted that a slightly higher proportion of participants in the intervention group were lost to follow-up. This is almost certainly explained by the demands placed on the game-playing participants, which included finding around two hours per week to attend the lab. On reflection, it is easy to imagine that falling behind on the game-playing tasks may result in a participant disengaging with the study, particularly as other university-related demands increased. One of the more pronounced differences between those participants who completed and those who dropped out was in year of study, where 27 of 46 (58.7%) level one students failed to complete compared with 8 of 24 (33.3%) level two students. This difference is not thought to have had any impact on the findings of the study and might be explained by considering that first year students may be less able to estimate their availability later in the semester. It is likely that first-time students underestimated the demands placed on them as the semester progresses and finding time for this study may not have been a priority in the face of university exams, coursework, and extracurricular responsibilities. Average baseline (week one) scores for each of the key attribute-testing measures were comparable between the two groups.

For each attribute measure, 95% confidence intervals and p-values for statistical significance in the difference between mean control and intervention group scores were calculated. These data are summarised in Table 3.3. By convention, p-values of ≤ 0.05 are considered significant, while 95% confidence intervals that do not cross zero suggest that the mean change in score may be expected to be either positive *or* negative in 95% of cases, should the experiment be repeated. Here, a negative difference in means indicates improved scores for the game-playing intervention group so, for example, in the case of the Communicative Adaptability Scale (CAS) scores, it may be expected that the mean difference between control and intervention groups would fall between −12.79 and −2.69. In other words, should the exercise be repeated under the same conditions, the game-playing intervention group would likely score between 2.69 and 12.79 points higher than the control. That the confidence interval (CI) does not cross zero means that it does not contain the null hypothesis value: a difference of zero between the two groups would mean there was no difference between the two, thus supporting the null hypothesis. The absolute difference in the mean for CAS scores was 7.74, meaning that, on average, the intervention group scores were 7.74 points higher on the Communicative Adaptability Scale. However, p-values and confidence intervals are concerned only with the probability of a difference

Table 3.3 Summary of score changes from week one to week eight

Measure	Control		Intervention		Difference in means			
	Mean	SD	Mean	SD	Absolute	95% CI	Adjusted	p
CAS	-2.80	5.65	4.94	8.41	7.74	-12.79 to -2.69	1.10	0.004
I-ADAPT-M	-8.25	15.99	11.31	18.07	19.56	-31.32 to -7.80	1.15	0.002
Resourcefulness	0.25	9.71	9.69	11.42	9.44	-16.77 to -2.11	0.90	0.013
Self-efficacy	-1.55	6.29	0.75	3.53	2.30	-5.69 to 1.09	0.44	0.176
Self-esteem	-0.05	5.76	1.13	6.38	1.18	-5.36 to 3.01	0.19	0.571

Highlighted bold rows are those that refer to primary attribute-measuring scores. Adjusted differences in mean are Cohen's d occurring between the two groups; it is also necessary to determine if the size of the difference—the effect size—is large or small. The scales associated with each measure used here are essentially arbitrary (is a difference of 7.74 points on the Communicative Adaptability Scale a large difference?) and certainly not comparable to one another (the absolute difference in means for CAS is less than half that for I-ADAPT-M, so is it less important?) In order to gauge effect size, then, Cohen's d (the 'Adjusted' column below) was calculated for each difference in mean. Cohen's d expresses the size of the difference in terms of standard deviations, otherwise known as the average deviation from the mean. Cohen (1988, pp. 25–27), while noting that the terms 'small', 'medium', and 'large' are relative, suggested that d-values of between 0.2 and 0.5 represent small effect size, values between 0.5 and 0.8 represent medium effect, and values of greater than 0.8 represent large effect sizes.

On the 'secondary measures' used as proxies for confidence, the intervention group generally fares better, in small and statistically insignificant ways. In terms of both self-efficacy (Cohen's d = 0. 44, p = 0. 176) and self-esteem (Cohen's d = 0. 19, p = 0. 571), the intervention group saw a slight improvement in mean scores over the course of the semester, while the control group saw a small fall in mean scores. However, given the absence of statistical significance or large effect sizes, and the fact that these measures do not relate directly to graduate attributes, they are not analysed in any further detail here.

For each of the three primary measures, the box plots below (Figs. 3.9, 3.10, and 3.11) show pre/post differences in mean score for both control and intervention groups; these plots are thought to be particularly useful as they show the distribution of all data, with interquartile range (IQR) and outliers clearly indicated. Violin (kernel density) plots (Figs. 3.12, 3.13, and 3.14) provide an alternative means of visualising mean score distribution. Pre/post scatterplots show week one and week eight scores for each individual participant. The scatterplots for the scores on each measure (Figs. 3.15, 3.16, and 3.17) suggest that, generally, week one score predicts week eight score, for most participants: the upward slope observed on these plots indicates the trend is for higher week eight scores where week one scores are higher. Further, week eight scores are generally higher for participants in the intervention group than those in the

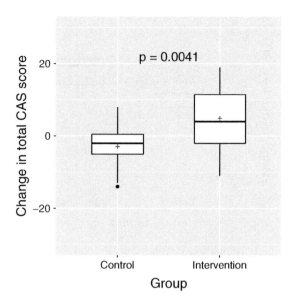

Fig. 3.9 Box plot comparing distribution of total Communicative Adaptability Scale (CAS) score change from week one to week eight between control and intervention groups. The horizontal line is the median score change for the group, the crosses represent mean change, the box represents interquartile range, whiskers show the two standard deviation range used to define outliers, and outliers are plotted as dots

control group, as indicated by the plotting of the line of best fit for the intervention group above that for the control group. It may also be observed that the higher week eight scores for intervention group participants appear to occur across the range of week one scores. This is suggested by the approximately parallel arrangement of the lines of best fit for both groups: had the effect of the intervention been greater for those participants with high baseline scores, for example, the lines of best fit would diverge towards the origin but converge at the higher end of the x-axis. While lines of best fit act merely as a guide, a brief visual inspection of the CAS, I-ADAPT-M, and Resourcefulness Scale plots clearly supports these general observations, with, for example, a preponderance of intervention participants plotted above each scatterplot's diagonal and control participants below. Tables 3.4, 3.5, and 3.6 summarise changes in score for each measure for both groups, providing a

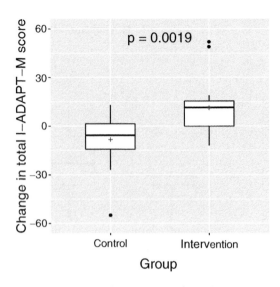

Fig. 3.10 Box plots comparing distributions of total I-ADAPT-M score change from week one and week eight between control and intervention groups. Horizontal line is median score change for group, cross is mean score change, box is IQR, whiskers are range, and outliers are plotted as dots

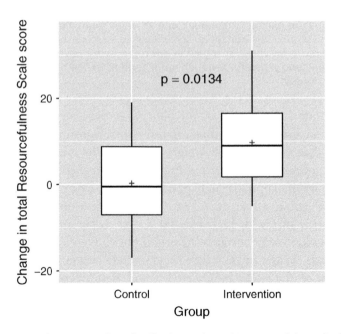

Fig. 3.11 Box plots comparing distributions of total Resourcefulness Scale score change from week one and week eight between control and intervention groups. Horizontal line is median score change for group, cross is mean score change, box is IQR, whiskers are range, and outliers are plotted as dots

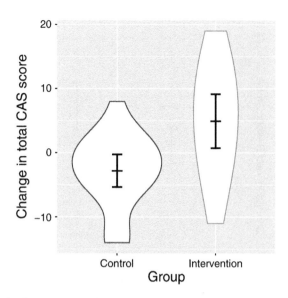

Fig. 3.12 Violin (kernel density) plot showing distribution of total Communicative Adaptability Scale (CAS) score change from week one to week eight by control and intervention groups. Error bars are two standard errors of the mean

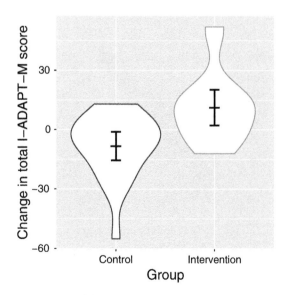

Fig. 3.13 Violin (kernel density) plot showing distribution of total I-ADAPT-M score change from week one to week eight by control and intervention groups. Error bars are two standard errors of the mean

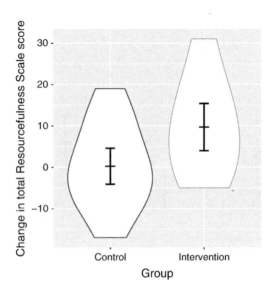

Fig. 3.14 Violin (kernel density) plot showing distribution of total Resourcefulness Scale score change from week one to week eight by control and intervention groups. Error bars are two standard errors of the mean

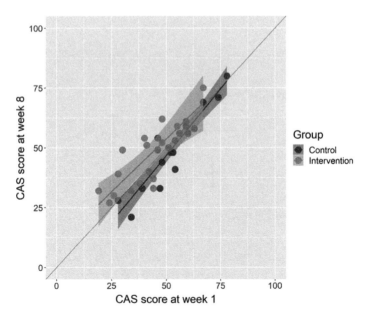

Fig. 3.15 Scatterplot of Communicative Adaptability Scale scores for week one and week eight for both control and intervention groups. Line of equality for week one and week eight scores is shown (diagonal), and a line of best fit (least squares method) is plotted for each group

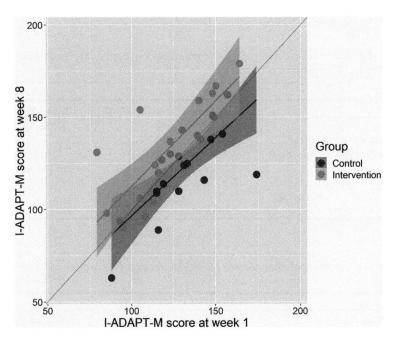

Fig. 3.16 Scatterplot of I-ADAPT-M scores for week one and week eight for both control and intervention groups

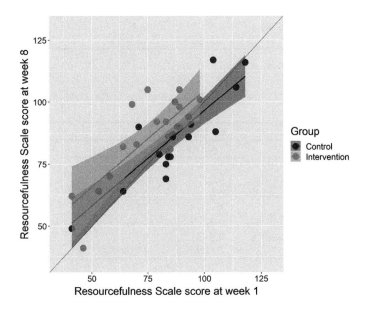

Fig. 3.17 Scatterplot of Resourcefulness Scale scores for week one and week eight for both control and intervention groups

Table 3.4 Summary of changes in Communicative Adaptability Scale scores for control and intervention groups

Change	Group		
	Control	Intervention	Row total
Negative (N)	15	5	20 (56%)
Negative (N/row total)	0.75	0.25	
Negative (N/column total)	0.75	0.31	
Positive (N)	5	11	16 (44%)
Positive (N/row total)	0.31	0.69	
Positive (N/column total)	0.25	0.69	
Column total	20 (56%)	16 (44%)	36 (100%)

Table 3.5 Summary of changes in I-ADAPT-M scores for control and intervention groups

Change	Group		
	Control	Intervention	Row total
Negative (N)	12	4	16 (44%)
Negative (N/row total)	0.75	0.25	
Negative (N/column total)	0.60	0.25	
Positive (N)	8	12	20 (56%)
Positive (N/row total)	0.40	0.60	
Positive (N/column total)	0.40	0.75	
Column total	20 (56%)	16 (44%)	36 (100%)

Table 3.6 Summary of changes in Resourcefulness Scale scores for control and intervention groups

Change	Group		
	Control	Intervention	Row total
Negative (N)	12	3	15 (42%)
Negative (N/row total)	0.8	0.2	
Negative (N/column total)	0.6	0.19	
Positive (N)	8	13	21 (58%)
Positive (N/row total)	0.38	0.62	
Positive (N/column total)	0.4	0.81	
Column total	20 (56%)	16 (44%)	36 (100%)

sense of the general (positive or negative) trend for the two groups. For example, Table 3.4 indicates that a majority (11 out of 16, 69%) of intervention participants saw a positive change in their CAS scores from week one to week eight.

Effective Communicators

The percentage of participants in the intervention group (69%, 11 of 16) with improved CAS scores was significantly greater than the percentage of participants in the control group (25%, 5 of 20) with improved CAS scores (p = 0.016, Fisher's exact test). Mean score change on the Communicative Adaptability Scale was −2.8 (SD = 5.65) in the control group and 4.94 (SD = 8.41) in the intervention group (absolute difference in means = 7.74, 95% CI 2.69 to 12.79, Cohen's d 1.1).

Adaptable

Mean score change on the adaptability scale was −8.25 (SD = 15.99) in the control group and 11.31 (SD = 18.07) in the intervention group (absolute difference in means = 19.56, 95% CI 7.8 to 31.32, Cohen's d 1.15).

Resourceful and Responsible

No instrument for measuring responsibility was identified: only the resourcefulness aspect of this attribute is measured here. Mean score change on the Resourcefulness Scale was 0.25 (SD = 9.71) in the control group and 9.69 (SD = 11.42) in the intervention group (absolute difference in means = 9.44, 95% CI 2.11 to 16.77, Cohen's d 0.9).

Discussion

For each of the graduate attribute measures, the data indicate a significant increase in mean scores for participants in the intervention group over those in the control group when week one scores are compared against week eight scores. The very low p-values for the remaining measures suggest that Type I errors (incorrect rejection of a true null hypothesis, or a false positive) are unlikely. The quantitative data, then, appear to support the hypothesis that playing selected video games can improve scores on certain self-report measures of communication, resourcefulness, and adaptability.

An issue that must be addressed, however, is that of the loss of function observed in control group participants, particularly where CAS and I-ADAPT-M scores were concerned. On the CAS measure of communication, 75% of control group participants showed an apparent drop in communication skill, while 60% saw a drop in adaptability, as measured by the I-ADAPT-M instrument. It may also be noted that the standard deviation for score change in both the control and the intervention groups is greater in magnitude than the mean change in all the attribute scores (see Table 3.3). In addition, the mean score change for the intervention group, while positive, is less than one standard deviation greater than zero for all attribute measures, which is indicative of the loss of function observed in some participants in the game-playing group. Furthermore, the distribution of changes in score illustrated by the box plots above shows that for the CAS and I-ADAPT measures, the interquartile range for the control group's score change falls almost entirely below zero in both cases, reflecting the preponderance of control group scores that deteriorated over the course of the semester. Such negative score changes can only serve to exaggerate the positive gains made by the intervention group, and the apparent loss of function may be interpreted in a number of ways.

First, it may be argued that the observed deterioration in the control group's attribute scores calls into question the reliability of the measures used. Some deterioration in students' skills over time is not unprecedented, however. In their account of a skills development initiative carried out at Napier University, for example, Laybourn et al. (2013, p. 53) note that their control group (in this case, a group of students from another university, for whom no explicit skills development training was provided) saw a deterioration in four of the nine skills tested. The skills examined in that study did include communication skills, amongst others, although it is not clear in which of these skills the deterioration in control group scores was observed. There is also evidence to suggest that the very act of sitting exams—and most of the participants here would have been taking exams or preparing to do so—can have a detrimental effect on students' intrinsic motivation (Remedios et al. 2005). While motivation is not directly linked to any of the attributes measured here, it is interesting to note that such a mechanism, whereby the experience of taking examinations can result in negative psychological effects, has been shown to exist.

It is conceivable, then, that the stress associated with the end of semester—and the attendant assessment deadlines and examinations—is reflected in the control group's reduced scores. At the point of taking the final battery of tests, the students involved are perhaps at something of a low ebb, mentally. It might be surmised that participants in the intervention group were either less susceptible to these stresses, or that the gains in function afforded by the game-playing experience offset the losses that are otherwise associated with the end of term. While the negative effects of stress on the control group's scores may only be supposed, interviews conducted with intervention group participants at the end of the study revealed a belief among the students involved that playing video games on campus or between classes helped alleviate stress. This aspect of the study is discussed, and interview data presented, in the following chapter.

As the box plots above also show, outliers were observed in both groups, but the observed effect of the intervention was broadly similar across the range of baseline scores, as shown in the scatterplots above. As a sensitivity analysis, data were re-analysed with outliers (as defined by greater than two standard deviations from the mean) excluded; this made no substantive difference to the results of t-tests.

It may also be argued that the mean positive and negative shifts in self-report scores for the intervention and control groups, respectively, might be due to changes in self-confidence. As noted in the discussion of measures above, confidence is certainly a component of communication, in particular, but may also be seen as a factor that influences adaptability and resourcefulness, in that a more confident person may be more willing to experiment with new methods, for example. This may be a problematic argument, however. If confidence—or some aspect of confidence—really is an important part of what makes us more effective at communicating, then it is quite appropriate that the communication measures employed here should detect an increase in this aspect. Confidence was not measured as part of the study per se, but self-esteem, which might be defined as confidence in one's own abilities, was measured, using the Rosenberg Self-Esteem Scale.

As Fig. 3.18 shows, however, there is no significant difference in self-esteem between the control and intervention groups, with differences in scores at week one and week eight clustered around zero for both groups. Although, as the data in Table 3.3 indicate, the intervention group did see small, non-significant positive gains in mean self-esteem scores.

Self-efficacy—which might be thought of as one's belief that one can succeed, and therefore related to confidence—was also measured, using the General Self-Efficacy Scale. These data showed remarkably little difference between the two groups, as Fig. 3.19 illustrates, although, again, the intervention group saw small and non-significant positive gains in mean scores for self-efficacy.

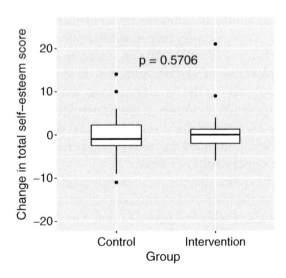

Fig. 3.18 Box plot comparing distribution of total Rosenberg Self-Esteem Scale score change from week one and week eight between control and intervention groups. Horizontal line is mean score change for group, box is IQR, whiskers are range, and outliers are plotted as dots

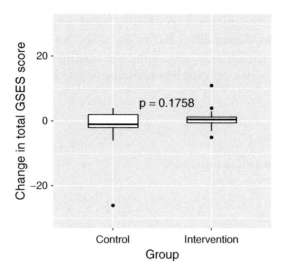

Fig. 3.19 Box plot comparing distribution of total General Self-Efficacy Scale score change from week one and week eight between control and intervention groups. Horizontal line is mean score change for group, box is IQR, whiskers are range, and outliers are plotted as dots

Summary

These quantitative data show significant differences in mean score change for three measures directly related to certain graduate attributes. It appears that playing selected video games under specific circumstances can improve graduate skills including communication, resourcefulness, and adaptability. While the supplementary data is largely insignificant, the intervention group fares better than the control and these data offer some small clues as to some of the underlying factors, such as confidence. However, quantitative data are only part of the picture. Student attitudes to game-based learning are also sought here, because learners' 'buy-in' is equally important to future initiatives based on the quantitative gains in attribute attainment described in this chapter. Furthermore, as noted in Chap. 2, quantitative measures do not exist for several of the university's graduate attributes, meaning that qualitative data is the most obvious means of gauging how these more elusive phenomena might be affected by the intervention. A mixture of quantitative and qualitative methods has been used in many instances of educational research (see Devlin et al. 2013; Hess and Gunter 2013; Barendregt 2011) and the following chapter continues in this vein, describing the qualitative data collected by means of interviews with student participants involved in the trial.

Note

1. http://www.metacritic.com/.

References

3909 LLC. (2013). *Papers, Please*. 3909 LLC.
All of Denmark Virtually Recreated. (2014, April 25). Retrieved June 17, 2019, from https://www.bbc.com/news/technology-27155859.
Barendregt, W. (2011). The Influence of the Level of Free-Choice Learning Activities on the Use of an Educational Computer Game. *Computers & Education, 56*(1), 80–90. https://doi.org/10.1016/j.compedu.2010.08.018.
Barr, M. (2016). Using Video Games to Develop Graduate Attributes: A Pilot Study. In The University of the West of Scotland (Ed.), *Proceedings of the 10th European Conference on Games Based Learning* (pp. 41–49). Paisley, Scotland, UK: Academic Conferences and Publishing Limited.
Blizzard Entertainment. (2002). *Warcraft III: Reign of Chaos*. Blizzard Entertainment.
Blizzard Entertainment. (2004). *World of Warcraft*. Blizzard Entertainment.
Cohen, J. (1988). *Statistical Power Analysis for the Behavioral Sciences* (2nd ed.). New York; London: Psychology Press.
Crystal Dynamics. (2010). *Lara Croft and the Guardian of Light*. Square Enix.
Devlin, A. M., Lally, V., Canavan, B., & Magill, J. (2013). The Role of the "Inter-Life" Virtual World as a Creative Technology to Support Student Transition into Higher Education. *Creative Education, 04*(7), 191. https://doi.org/10.4236/ce.2013.47A2025.
Dring, C. (2010, July 20). EA's Moore: Metacritic Mania a 'Slippery Slope'? *Develop Online*. Retrieved 24 March 2016, from http://www.develop-online.net/news/ea-s-moore-metacritic-mania-a-slippery-slope/0107404.
Duran, R. L. (1983). Communicative Adaptability: A Measure of Social Communicative Competence. *Communication Quarterly, 31*(4), 320–326. https://doi.org/10.1080/01463378309369521.

Duran, R. L. (1992). Communicative Adaptability: A Review of Conceptualization and Measurement. *Communication Quarterly, 40*(3), 253–268. https://doi.org/10.1080/01463379209369840.

Egenfeldt-Nielsen, S., Smith, J. H., & Tosca, S. P. (2008). *Understanding Video Games: The Essential Introduction* (New ed.). New York: Routledge.

Gearbox Software. (2012). *Borderlands 2.* 2K Games.

Graft, K. (2011, March 9). Take-Two's Zelnick Stresses Importance of Metacritic Scores. Accessed March 24, 2016, from http://www.gamasutra.com/view/news/33092/TakeTwos_Zelnick_Stresses_Importance_Of_Metacritic_Scores.php.

Hess, T., & Gunter, G. (2013). Serious Game-Based and Nongame-Based Online Courses: Learning Experiences and Outcomes. *British Journal of Educational Technology, 44*(3), 372–385. https://doi.org/10.1111/bjet.12024.

Hollis, S., & Campbell, F. (1999). What Is Meant by Intention to Treat Analysis? Survey of Published Randomised Controlled Trials. *British Medical Journal, 319*(7211), 670–674. https://doi.org/10.1136/bmj.319.7211.670.

id Software. (1996). *Quake.* GT Interactive.

Laybourn, P., Falchikov, N., Goldfinch, J., & Westwood, J. (2013). Evolution of Skills Development Initiatives. In S. Fallows & C. Steven (Eds.), *Integrating Key Skills in Higher Education: Employability, Transferable Skills and Learning for Life.* London: Routledge.

Mojang. (2011). *Minecraft.* Mojang.

Ployhart, Robert E., & Paul D. Bliese. (2006). Individual Adaptability (I-ADAPT) Theory: Conceptualizing the Antecedents, Consequences, and Measurement of Individual Differences in Adaptability. In Understanding Adaptability: A Prerequisite for Effective Performance Within Complex Environments (Vols. 1–0, Vol. 6, pp. 3–39). Bingley: Emerald Group Publishing Limited.

Remedios, R., Ritchie, K., & Lieberman, D. A. (2005). I Used to Like It But Now I Don't: The Effect of the Transfer Test in Northern Ireland on Pupils' Intrinsic Motivation. *British Journal of Educational Psychology, 75*(3), 435–452. https://doi.org/10.1348/000709904X24771.

Rosenberg, M. (1979). *Conceiving the Self.* New York: Basic Books.

Schwarzer, R., & Jerusalem, M. (1995). Generalized Self-Efficacy Scale. In M. Johnston, S. C. Wright, & J. Weinman (Eds.), *Measures in Health Psychology: A User's Portfolio. Causal and Control Beliefs* (pp. 35–37). Windsor: NFER-NELSON.

The Fullbright Company. (2013). *Gone Home.* The Fullbright Company.

Valve Corporation. (2007). *Team Fortress 2.* Valve Corporation.

Valve Corporation. (2011). *Portal 2*. Valve Corporation.

Valve Corporation. (2013). *Dota 2*. Valve Corporation.

Zauszniewski, J. A., Lai, C.-Y., & Tithiphontumrong, S. (2006). Development and Testing of the Resourcefulness Scale for Older Adults. *Journal of Nursing Measurement, 14*(1), 57–68. https://doi.org/10.1891/jnum.14.1.57.

4

The Student Perspective

The previous chapter presented quantitative data that suggests participants in a game-playing intervention made significant gains in graduate attribute attainment. In this chapter, a qualitative approach is taken to explore whether the students involved in the study perceived any benefits to playing the games. This provides an opportunity to obtain a deeper understanding of how the three attributes discussed in the previous chapter (communication skill, adaptability, and resourcefulness) were developed but also to gain insight into how other attributes, not measured by quantitative means, might have been exercised.

Each of the participants in the game-playing intervention group who saw the study through to its conclusion was interviewed, an exercise which comprised 20 interviews in total. The interviews began with an open question: do you think the games we played might have helped develop any skills or competencies? The remainder of the interview script was structured around the host university's stated graduate attributes,[1] with each considered in turn. The interview data are presented in this chapter, with more detailed reflections on their implications in the chapter that follows. For more information on how the interviews were conducted and the data analysed, see Barr (2018).

© The Author(s) 2019
M. Barr, *Graduate Skills and Game-Based Learning*, Digital Education and Learning,
https://doi.org/10.1007/978-3-030-27786-4_4

Effective Communicators

Responses to the question of whether the games played could have helped develop the Effective Communicators attribute were positive. Participants agreed that communication played a significant part in the games played, with many going on to state that this experience helped develop their communication skill:

Definitely, yeah, because they all have a multiplayer aspect to them, and you're having to work with other people and talk to each other. (Participant L, female, age 18)

Yeah, definitely. Especially, like, negotiating with people, trying to figure out where you were going to go, and stuff like that. (Participant M, female, age 17)

One of the more cautious comments came from a mature student:

I don't know if I communicated very clearly or confidently. I communicated effectively because we got through it but, yeah, I don't know if I was very clear. (Participant A, male, age 32)

Participant C (male, age 19) agreed that effective communication was necessary when playing the games provided but was unable to say for certain that the experience helped improve his skills:

Definitely, it did require communication. I don't know if it helped improve it necessarily but, for sure, you notice how you communicate with others. But I think definitely there was a lot of communication needed. Not necessarily developed, but then we played only two hours per week.

Participant C was one of the more dedicated game players taking part in the study, however, estimating that he played more than eight hours per week outside of the lab. Considering these playing habits, it is perhaps unsurprising that this participant was unsure if the relatively insignificant time he spent playing games in the lab could have influenced his own communication abilities.

Another participant was very positive about the relationship between the games played and certain aspects of effective communication:

I think communicating confidently, definitely, because you don't want to lose the game. So, you have to be able to tell people, even if you've just met them, "excuse me, sir, don't be such a fool, defend this base", and such. And negotiating, for sure, is another one because, again, the game itself becomes the priority, so you do have to communicate quite well. (Participant T, male, age 19)

However, while the games might have required confident communication and deft negotiation, Participant T, echoing Participant A's reservations, was less certain that his in-game communication possessed clarity:

You know, you'd like to be a calm and collected individual who can clearly articulate in a calm manner what you'd like to happen but instead you go, you know, you just scream at each other. (Participant T)

The idea that communicating with fellow players in a pressurised gaming scenario might result in a successful outcome despite a lack of clarity was suggested by another participant:

it kind of depended on the game because some of them where, you know, if there's people coming at you, it's kind of hard to communicate clearly and confidently. It ends up being "ahh, someone's over there to your left, kind of, sort of … oh, is that where you are? Oh God, oh God…." So that's maybe not as clear and confident as one would normally like in a standard job situation but at least communication was there. (Participant G, female, age 22)

Some participants offered ideas about which aspects of the experience were most valuable in terms of improving communication skill. For example, Participant H (female, age 23) pointed to how the disparity in her fellow participants' game-playing ability enriched the experience:

I definitely think that the game sessions we played in the lab helped with communication because we did co-op. Because we get to do it with people that have different levels of experience. We get to do it with people that are experts at the game, or people who are completely new to it, people who have played it sometimes, so they have a general grasp, and you get to compare yourself to them but also learn from them or help others. So, I definitely think that the game sessions here do a whole lot to develop communication skills.

While she did not necessarily enjoy playing with less experienced players, another participant alluded to the need to adapt the nature of their communication in order to progress, which might be thought of as useful experience:

Yeah, you kind of have to communicate if you're doing a team game but it just depends on who I'm playing with. Like, I think it was Borderlands *I was playing, at first, we were playing with a few girls who were pretty decent at it, you know, it was the first time they'd played it but they knew what to do. Whereas someone else came in and they obviously hadn't played anything before and I was just like, "ah, ffff ..."* [sound of frustration] *Like, just, "that's how you walk forward".* (Participant G)

For another participant, the fact that many of the games involved "communication with others in the room, many of whom complete strangers who you are now relying on for the success of your goal" (Participant F, male, age 19) was part of what made the experience interesting. He pointed to the procedurally generated world of *Minecraft* (Mojang 2011) in particular:

Minecraft *especially surprised me with the amount of communication involved. I was willingly taking advice from a person I'd never met, allowing him to guide me and give me tips for success, whilst at other times I was placed in his position, giving others advice on how to play. When random strangers are dropped together in an unknown and sometimes dangerous world, they bond together and have to have clear communication in order to get their points across and survive together. It was great!* (Participant F)

Only one participant entirely rejected the notion that the game-related communication was useful:

Not really, the communication was more about sharing feedback with each other ("Dammit! I thought I killed you!") than trying to communicate effectively in order to solve problems. (Participant Q, male, age 18)

Observations about the influence of gender on communication were also made, primarily in relation to collaboration, and this is discussed under Experienced Collaborators below.

Experienced Collaborators

The collaborative nature of the game play sessions was frequently cited in response to the initial open question, with six of the twenty interviewees suggesting that useful experience of collaborating—more commonly referred to here as teamwork—was gained. Responses to the open question ranged from the non-committal ("Em, maybe teamwork?"—Participant D, female, age 18) to the somewhat more definite ("Maybe teamwork. I think teamwork is one."—Participant N, male, age 18). The overtly cooperative nature of certain games was also highlighted in responses to the initial question, and typically associated with the idea of teamwork. For example:

Probably teamwork. Especially the likes of [Team Fortress 2]. *Learning how to work with new people as well.* (Participant L)

Also in response to the open question, one participant noted that the experience was beneficial because she was not normally fond of teamwork:

Working in a group when you have to rely on people and make sure that everyone does their part, that's quite useful. And, I'm not really a team player, so that helps me gain patience and stuff. (Participant E, female, age 20)

When asked specifically if the games had helped provide experience of collaborating, the response from participants was overwhelmingly positive: "Yeah. Yeah, definitely." (Participant D); "Yeah, for sure, yeah." (Participant R, female, age 18). Participant F was quite confident that this experience was relevant beyond the games:

In many of the games you are simply forced to work with others and change positions as well. There is often no single leader, the roles switch as different people's strengths come into play or depending on your prior knowledge of the game. Almost every game on the study required teamwork, you are doing just as you would if you were working together to solve a problem in the workplace— just it's in a virtual environment. To say one demonstrates and advances skills of working in a team whilst another doesn't hardly makes any sense.

There was agreement from Participant L that the collaborative experience ("especially when you're working with different people all the time") had benefits beyond the lab:

Yeah, I think definitely a lot of the skills learnt you could apply outside of video games, things like the confidence and teamwork. Yeah, I think you could apply [them] to uni, work, just everyday life.

Participant K (male, age 18), however, was not convinced that the collaboration—which he did agree had occurred—was relevant outside the games:

Yes, yeah.
    Interviewer: *Useful experience?*
    Em … useful within games.

Participant C is a practised player who believed the collaborative experience was, for him, enhanced by the need to play with less knowledgeable players ("I gained experience of working in a group of people that were not my same skill level"). He also noted the potential for collaboration in the single-player games, played in the same room as others:

We can speak to each other and we're enquiring, 'what happens on your side, how can I get there?' And, 'oh you should try that' so it's a common investigation of the same issue but from a different perspective and getting a different understanding of what's going on.

Another participant agreed that being asked to collaborate with players of differing abilities was also a useful, more challenging experience:

Yes, definitely [...] *Outside* [the lab] *I didn't* [play multiplayer] *as much, or I may do it with just one person that I play with very often, so I know that we're pretty much at the same level of expertise. It's actually harder to collaborate with others if they have a different level of experience.* (Participant H)

Other participants noted that the games provided opportunities for players to take on different roles. Participant A, for example, recalled how he fell into a supporting—albeit important—role:

I did find myself taking, or kind of seeking, a secondary role in co-op games, and just being happy. On Team Fortress *I ended up being the person who pushed the bomb along.*

While leadership is considered under the Confident attribute below, one participant was enthusiastic about the possibility of taking on a leading role, but also assuming a secondary role, as required. He compares his experience in *Minecraft* with that in *Warcraft III* (Blizzard Entertainment 2002):

For Minecraft *I was kind of helping a couple of other people with the ropes and you kind of know to take a slightly more leader-y 'OK, I know what I'm doing'* [role]. *And then, equally, there were games where I knew absolutely nothing, like* Warcraft, *and so I'd take a back seat and people would say 'do this' and I would do that, go fight that person.* (Participant T)

Participant T was also able to generalise what he had learned from his experience of playing multiplayer games, such that it might prove useful beyond the games:

So, yeah, I suppose it helps in regards to knowing when to take a little bit of control and when to sit back and let the people who know what they're doing, do it.

A less positive response came from a mature student (Participant A) with extensive work experience:

Possibly … I mean … it's kind of an environment that I'm comfortable in, being part of the team, because I'm a mature student so I've been a chef for about ten years. I mean, if you're not part of the team, you're out the door. I play in bands and things as well. I play drums and I like collaborating with people in that way. So, I think … I probably wouldn't have noticed, because I'm so used to being [collaborative].

Finally, some participants alluded to gender differences in the collaborative approach taken to playing *Borderlands 2* (Gearbox Software 2012). One participant had this to say:

There was a lot of collaborative effort, because I think especially with the three girls that were playing, well, me and two other girls that were playing, it was like 'I'm going to come over and heal you!', 'I'll come over and do all this stuff'. Whereas with, I don't know if this is like a sexism thing, whereas with the two guys, they were like 'I'm just going to go and kill things' and I was like, 'where are you? I can't even help you when you're over there'. So, that was quite interesting. Just as a side note, I think the girls were better at like tacit, implied, 'I'm going to come over and help you if you're in trouble' whereas with the guys you had to clearly state 'could you, like, not do that?' (Participant J, female, age 29)

Adaptable

The response to this attribute was also broadly positive, with several participants highlighting that the variety of games played in the study required some adaptability on the part of the player, for example:

I think it's when we're playing a different game every week and most of them, I hadn't played before either […] You do have to adapt slightly depending on what you're playing. (Participant L)

Participant K also felt that the variety of games played was the important factor: "To an extent, I imagine the games did, but probably getting a variety of games helped more than the individual games themselves." Another participant described the feeling of being "dropped into it" with each successive game:

Most of the games, especially Borderlands, *we were just kind of dropped into it, like, 'I don't know what this does' and you kind of figure it out relatively quickly. So, I think that kind of shows adaptability in a way that, you know, you have to learn how to navigate the game.* (Participant J)

Another participant agreed that the variety of games was important but noted diversity within the games, too:

Yeah, I do think that the game sessions helped because we not only played a variety of different games like shooters or adventures but in the same game you can have lots of different tasks that require different skills. (Participant H)

Participant E agreed that different missions or levels within the same game each required a different response: "Yeah, I think if you do different missions every time you need to find a new approach to solve the mission [...] so I think that that helps as well." She cited *Portal 2* (Valve Corporation 2011) as an example of a game that required this form of serial adaptability. Participant O suggested that the dynamic scenarios presented by *Team Fortress 2* were also relevant: "when things would go really bad, you just had to get through it, adapt to the changing situations". Continuing this theme of dealing with ever-changing scenarios, Participant F highlighted the unique worlds of *Minecraft*, "again for the unfamiliarity of the vast world with new explorations and findings causing change in goals and priorities".

A point made by Participant S (female, age 18)—that participants were required to adapt to a "foreign" environment, including the lab and the other participants—was echoed by a number of other interviewees. For example, one participant noted the need to adapt to unfamiliar cultural norms:

Well, I think playing with another person does [require adaptability] *because of how they are used to do things is not the same. Probably because they are from here, or England, or from other countries and I'm from Spain, it's very different from every culture.* (Participant P, male, age 27)

Another participant highlighted the need to adapt to the differing levels of gaming experience in the room, a recurring theme that also featured in the discussion around communication and collaboration:

> *To be honest, it was probably more other people responding to my lack of experience with games but, yeah, I think just like working with other people with different abilities probably helps.* (Participant D)

Another, more experienced player (Participant R) also noted that a disparity in gameplay ability required her to adopt a certain role—that of a teacher—while playing, supporting Participant D's idea that more able players had to adapt to working with novices. Some participants, however, were uncertain about the transferable value of the experience, indicating that while they were required to adapt their game-based skills from title-to-title, this was not relevant beyond gaming. Participant G, for example, had this to say:

> *I mean, obviously again it depends what sort of job or thing I'd be doing, outside of gaming, but I suppose it could help with some things, like systems. And I think there were a couple of games that were quite strategic, so, I guess it makes you think.*

Other participants referred to adaptability only in terms of video game play ("I think so, the more games I played the less time it took me to learn new gameplay mechanics"—Participant Q), although this kind of response does not preclude the notion that the experience was more generally useful. One participant made a connection between skills acquired in the real world and applying them within a game, a reversal of the idea being explored here:

> Papers, Please *was a good example of using previously acquired information and time management skills to complete a virtual and unknown task. Every single game in some way required you to take things you have learnt elsewhere and enforce them in new situations, therefore allowing the brain to understand new ways of applying those skills.* (Participant F)

Experienced players expressed some scepticism, suggesting that their knowledge of a wide variety of games resulted in few 'unfamiliar situations' to which they had to adapt ("Em, well the thing is I've played most of the games before, so it was all kind of familiar to me"—Participant N). Participant B was similarly unsure that the games required adaptability on her part, as she took each new challenge in her stride: "I mean, I don't know. In each game I had to learn, I had to play it from the beginning, then. I don't know, it was easy." Meanwhile, Participant A was the only interviewee who was certain that the games did not require adaptability on his part, responding to the question of whether they did so as follows: "Hmm … [long pause] No, no."

Resourceful and Responsible

Resourcefulness, as understood by the participants, was frequently described as being related to how they responded to the often-unfamiliar games.

a lot of them I had absolutely no clue what I was doing, so I would have to make things up as I went along. And just sort of work with the little knowledge of games I had and just try and patch something together with that. It worked most of the time. (Participant L)

Specifically, the constraints imposed by the limited time spent on each game in the study, and relative lack of instruction, were cited as factors which required resourcefulness (while echoing some of the sentiments expressed in relation to adaptability above):

Probably. Just because … you don't [get] much in the instructions, so if you haven't done it before, you kind of have to figure it out for yourself. (Participant D)

because we only had two hours, you really wanted to make something of the game in the two hours, so you kind of hit the ground running. And that meant you had to be resourceful [...] in that you have to do what you can do to be good and try and get other people to also be good, so you can make something of it. (Participant T)

Participant T also related resourcefulness with teamwork and effective collaboration:

I mean, with Borderlands 2, *we sat down, and we were like, 'we've got two hours, let's try to make it to Sanctuary* [ostensibly the first geographic goal in the game] *in this two hours'. And so, we were totally in the zone, right, OK, let's properly work with each other, let's do this. What are you good at? What am I good at? OK, you go to the front and shoot this guy and I'll stay at the back and shoot this guy. Let's see what we can do.*

So, while some of the discussion of this attribute was at the edges of what might constitute resourcefulness, ideas relating to meeting fellow players' expectations and demonstrating determination in the face of the unfamiliar—aspects of the university definition of resourcefulness—are clearly articulated. Another participant made the connection between carrying out independent work—also a component of the university definition—and the single-player nature of the final two games played: *Gone Home* (The Fullbright Company 2013) and *Papers, Please* (3909 LLC 2013).

When it says, "independent work", like, can I manage to do everything I have to do by myself? Well, in the last two games—because those were the only two where we played by ourselves—yes, it does [require resourcefulness]. (Participant P)

While the associated quantitative instrument measured only resourcefulness, interviews provided an opportunity for participants to comment on the 'responsible' aspect of the attribute. Participant A, for example, highlighted the in-game responsibilities associated with assuming a particular role:

a sense of responsibility, yeah.
Interviewer: *OK, in what way? Just knowing your ... knowing your place.*
Going back to Team Fortress, *even though I was just pushing the bomb.*
Interviewer: *That was your responsibility?*
Yeah, I kind of knew, it was kind of clear. ... I mean, there has to be, in games like that, there has to be a clear divide, I think. Someone has to do one thing and the other person takes care of another aspect.

The idea that players were responsible for contributing to the progress of their in-game team also resonated with Participant H: "especially if you are playing in co-op, if you slack off, that's not really gonna help the team". Participant C framed their team responsibilities in terms of what he perceived as his inadequacies as a game player. Drawing on some of the language of the university definition, he suggests that his main influence was to 'ruin the experience' for others, remarking that "maybe that's part of it, managing your own performance to meet expectations. Not necessarily improving it, but more managing it."

A couple of participants suggested that they felt they should manage in-game resources in a responsible manner, an idea which falls somewhere between a literal interpretation of what it means to be resourceful and a perfectly reasonable conception of responsibility. Participant S, for example, suggested that "in *Minecraft*, you have to think about which things you are going to use and which you are going to save [for others]". *Minecraft* was also cited by another participant, who similarly linked responsibility with sharing resources with other players:

Like going around and having to find resources and having to kind of like collaborate with people to make sure you've got enough stuff to make weapons and armour and things like that. (Participant M)

And, while her response was framed in terms of resourcefulness, the pooling of resources Participant J described was similarly responsible (and collaborative) in nature:

Oh, well I think Minecraft *is good for resourcefulness, especially, at least when I was playing, I kind of was looking around like 'what can I make, what do we need?' I say 'we' as in the collective group of whoever is going to be playing after me as well—what might they need?—and we came up with that idea of having a chest of stuff.*

Extending the collaborative theme, the same participant elsewhere noted that one's teammates might be considered a resource to be managed, citing *Lara Croft and the Guardian of Light* (Crystal Dynamics 2010) as an example:

in Lara Croft *you kind of have to, you know, almost use each other's skills to navigate certain puzzles and issues so I think that kind of demonstrates resourcefulness.* (Participant J)

While most participants had something positive to say about one or other aspect of this attribute, there were those who could not make any connection between the games played and being resourceful or responsible ("Mmm … I don't know"). Others, however, were more confident in their dismissal of the idea: "Yeah, I'm not sure that this one would be helpful, like from the games" (Participant E); "Yeah, I think there is room for it, but I don't think I experienced it" (Participant R).

Finally, a wry comment from one participant, which certainly appears to speak to the definition of 'resourcefulness':

Well at some point I played co-op Lara Croft *with two controllers on my own which I had never done before, and developed strategies to do well anyway. I think that demonstrates a good amount of self-sufficiency and motivation …?* (Participant Q)

Investigative

In line with the host university's definition, mentions of problem-solving were treated as components of the Investigative attribute. Indeed, investigating and solving problems (or puzzles) was the most commonly cited facet of this attribute, while Valve's *Portal 2* dominated the discussion when participants sought to provide examples of their problem-solving ("Yeah, definitely. Especially in *Portal*."—Participant S; "*Portal*. Just *Portal*."—Participant M). As has been observed already, there is clear overlap between the attributes, as illustrated by Participant I's response to the 'investigative' question, which makes a connection to teamwork: "Yeah, yeah. I think especially in the one when you had to work in a team, the teamworks to solve the problem."

One participant was particularly enthusiastic about this attribute, and cited no fewer than three of the games played in the study:

This is an interesting one, because I would say every game developed this skill but did it through different aspects of investigation. For example, location, between the vast and seemingly endless world of Minecraft *to the restricted yet intricate house in* Gone Home *or like finding out information about all the necessary states in* Papers, Please. *[…] These experiences which we likely wouldn't get to have in real life, allow us to apply the investigation skills we've learnt so far and attribute it to new experiences which could allow them to develop.* (Participant F)

The single-player games mentioned by Participant F, *Gone Home* and *Papers, Please,* were cited by several other participants:

Yeah, I think that games are really useful for this.
    Interviewer: *And the games that we played, there was some of that in there?*

In Papers, Please, *you had to like, go through everything, and investigate everything.* (Participant E)

everything else was basically problem solving. So, yeah, a lot of that going on, especially with the likes of Papers, Please *and* Gone Home, *that was very investigative. You were kind of left to your own devices with a lot of the games to just come up the solutions yourself, so there was a lot of that involved.* (Participant T)

In general, the response to this attribute was almost universally positive: the participants here are in little doubt about the fact the games played—particularly those with a puzzle element—required them to be investigative. However, the interview data also suggest a small note of caution:

Yeah, I think especially in the likes of Portal, *there's a lot of problem solving in that. Although I did get* [another participant] *to do most of the problem solving in that one. I just sort of went into the mazes and did what he told me.* (Participant L)

If one player was to dominate in a game such as *Portal 2*, it is difficult to say that the other player is really exercising their investigative skills, or many of the other skills and competencies being considered here.

Certainly, there is a subtle distinction to be made between recognising that a fellow team member's ability exceeds one's own in a certain area, and exploiting this, versus taking a back seat entirely, and failing to engage with any of the game's intellectual challenges.

Independent and Critical Thinkers

This attribute also touches upon problem-solving, albeit from the point of view of using critical thinking to arrive at the solutions. As such, there is overlap with the previously discussed Investigative attribute, the university definition of which also makes direct reference to problem-solving. *Portal 2*, *Gone Home*, and *Papers, Please* were again amongst the most frequently cited games, which perhaps reflects the overlap between these two attributes. For example:

> *Yeah, sure* [laughs]. *I mean, you almost always use critical thinking ... or maybe should. For example, in the last games, like* Gone Home [*and* Papers, Please], *but also in* Portal, *it was demanding. In all games you have to think, usually critically, about what you are doing.* (Participant S)

Therefore, there was some agreement on the particular games that exercised this attribute. However, an interesting source of disagreement was the team-based shooter *Team Fortress 2* (Valve Corporation 2007). One participant, who stated that *Portal 2* "kind of demanded" critical thinking of the player, was somewhat less positive about *Team Fortress*:

> *I mean, stuff like* Team Fortress, *I didn't really think at all!* [...] *I just got lost in my own base which was really bad. And then I started putting some more thought into where I was and alternative routes, and things like that. But yeah, I just thought of* Team Fortress *as a shooter, which means 'walk into a room and blindly blast everything and hope for the best'.* (Participant A)

Another participant agreed that *Team Fortress* was not one of the games that demanded critical thinking, citing the apparent lack of strategy involved:

I think it probably comes down to again the sort of Portal, Warcraft, *the strategy games over the sort of* Team Fortress *types where you actually have a puzzle that you need to solve, and you're given information and you have to figure out what to do with it.* (Participant R)

However, more than one participant cited *Team Fortress* as an example of a game that did require critical thinking, even if this was not immediately apparent:

it's all about judgement, it's all about, 'OK, what does this do, what does this do? What's the best way of organising everything in order to win this game?' And I think a lot of the games are like that as well, even Team Fortress, *you have to know 'OK, the enemy are three guys with guns, am I going to do that as well, am I going to fight fire with fire here, or am I going to be the sneaky guy and come up behind and attack?'* (Participant T)

And, for another participant, when asked if the games required critical thinking, *Team Fortress* was the exceptional game that required such thinking:

Not much, but if it did, I think it would be through Team Fortress. *When the same approach gets you killed every time, you are forced to find another way to attack, another angle that gets you less exposed, on your own.* (Participant Q)

Participant R was not alone in equating this attribute with strategic thinking, and several participants also made a connection with puzzle games, echoing comments made in relation to the Investigative attribute. For example:

Yeah, especially, following on from the puzzle game thing, you're supposed to think critically through, 'how would you solve this problem, what would be the answer to this problem?' Also, stuff like Warcraft *as well, you have to think strategically, so you have to think what would work in this scenario.* (Participant N)

Papers Please *was for sure the most obvious example of a game requiring critical thinking, as the entire game is one massive puzzle to solve and closely examine.*

Portal 2 *follows closely behind, especially when you get to the advanced stages, with the puzzles involving a major sense of 'thinking outside the box' in order to complete the puzzle.* (Participant F)

A theme that runs through many of the participants' responses to this attribute is that of judgement, picking up on the "critical judgement in evaluating sources of information" that the university definition mentions. As Participant T asserted above, playing video games is "all about judgement". Participant K agreed, stating that there was "a lot of judgement required" as the story of their character developed.

Aside from Participant A's derisory comments about *Team Fortress*, there was little resistance to the idea that the games played might have exercised critical—if not imaginative—thinking. There was, however, another mention of the potentially problematic imbalance in mental effort devoted to the games within a pair of players: "Yeah, *Portal 2* was probably critical thinking because you had to figure it out. I think [another participant] probably did most of the work on that one" (Participant D).

Confident

Based on the university definition, several themes were coded as being related to the Confident attribute, including leadership and social skill. When these aspects of the definition are considered, participants had a substantial amount to say about games and confidence, most of it positive ("Yes, definitely in my case, I was beginning to gain more confidence over time"—Participant S). One participant, responding by email, was effusive about the confidence-enhancing properties of video games, especially where playing with other people was involved:

Definitely in the times in which there were others in the video game lab and we had to work together, confidence was really tested as these could be people I'd never met before. (Participant F)

The same participant went on to relate his previous game-playing experience to his real-world confidence, citing Multiplayer Online Battle Arena (MOBA), *League of Legends* (Riot Games 2009) as an example:

I know for a fact that a lot of the confidence I have today has been built by talking and working together in chat rooms when teaming in online games such as League of Legends *et cetera. Mainly because you don't just have to be a nice person, but you need to prove to the group that you are competent, sharp, and good at what you do.* (Participant F)

For Participant H, confidence was gained from the sense of achievement that video games can produce in the player:

I feel like, after I play, I feel more confident.
Interviewer: *Really?*
Yes, I don't know, maybe it's because they give you achievements to complete. So definitely that.

Relating confidence to the aspect of the university's Experienced Collaborators attribute which states that graduates should "contribute positively when working in a team", Participant H explains:

Mainly, the confidence comes from being able to see that I was able to complete a task on my own but also to know that I wasn't a burden to the people I was in co-op with. I actually had the drive to do my best, so I was really satisfied after I completed a game and I see that I haven't done a bad job. It makes me feel a lot better. I'm a lot more convinced about what I can do.

Interpersonal and social skills improving over the course of the lab sessions was a feature of several other participants' responses, including Participant L "definitely as I went along, I got a lot more confident, a lot more comfortable just going in and playing a game with a few people". Other participants elaborated:

Yeah … obviously it kind of ties in because [I'm] *a first year student coming to uni, and with the video game study—I've become much more confident, just talking to people, and not being afraid to just start conversations and just ask people stuff.* (Participant M)

I guess it was good practice for, like, being in a social area, talking to people, like 'oh, can you help me with this?' In the multiplayer games, if I needed help, I'd just be like 'I don't know what I'm doing' and somebody would help me. (Participant O)

Another participant, who stated "when I play video games I tend to just play with my friends", connected developing the confidence to speak to others with the ability to lead, noting that the labs required him to play with those outside his existing circle of friends:

So, when you open it up to people you don't know very well at all, it sort of gives you that nudge [...] to go for it, to be the first person to speak, to be the first person to take leadership of the team and devise a strategy, devise a plan. [...] It gives that sort of ... it gave me the confidence to be the first person to speak anyway. (Participant K)

Leadership was mentioned specifically by several participants. One participant recounted how she assumed the role of leader after the previous *de facto* leader left during a *Borderlands 2* session:

suddenly I was the only person playing who had actually been in that part before and suddenly I had to take up the mantle, as it were, and be like 'well, I think it's over there because we've done that and X, Y, Z, and that's where the map is pointing. So, you kind of have to step up and say, 'well, this is the knowledge I have and be willing to share so that we as a team can not die'. (Participant J)

This need for somebody to be confident enough to assume the role of leader was identified by other participants, too:

The confidence to be the first person to say something and be the person to say 'oh, you do this'. Like, the leadership, throwing yourself into it, especially when everyone else was not speaking, to be the first person to go 'OK, so, maybe we should have a plan, have a strategy?' I sort of found that a lot easier as the weeks went on, to be the first person to say, 'look guys, this is what we need to do, this is where we need to be headed'. (Participant R)

Another participant describes how the unexpected opportunity to lead was a boost to her confidence:

When you figure out the bits, like when you can actually do something, and you can, like, tell other people what to do, that's quite good because you feel like you can lead a bit. (Participant D)

There were few instances of participants rejecting the idea of a link between confidence and gameplay altogether, but there was some scepticism about the usefulness of any such link. While Participant Q offered only a flat "No" when asked if such a link existed, Participant B was noncommittal ("Yeah, maybe"). Participant I, meanwhile, was unconvinced of the transferable benefits: "Well, I'm more confident talking about games! [laughs] I don't really think that it impacted on my confidence as a person." Participant E noted that they felt their confidence improved as they played the game, but suggested that this was true of any activity that may be practiced:

> I don't think it's the game itself that helps you gain confidence but the more you play it, the more confident you feel [...], it's just like you improving when you play it more and more and more, so that's just like it comes from you ... so it's just practice.

Ethically and Socially Aware

The final, single-player games included in the study—*Gone Home* and *Papers, Please*—were intended to touch on this attribute. The ethical dilemmas presented by *Papers, Please* were referred to by many participants ("you actually had to think on an ethical basis"—Participant H), although the degree to which these dilemmas were taken seriously differed. For example:

> This one became most relevant in Papers, Please, *when you were forced to make quick decisions between doing your job correctly and getting paid or facing the possibility of ruining someone else's life. You were made to consider, within seconds, whether you would doom a husband and wife to the terrors of war or have enough money for your family to eat. Heavy stuff for a rather brief game.* (Participant F)

> Yeah, definitely. I can think of a lot of times when there's been people in Papers, Please *where you've had to make a sort of ethical judgement or like a moral judgment on something. You kind of grow numb to it after a while. That's really bad!* [laughs]. (Participant R)

According to Participant A, *Gone Home* opened up possibilities about "what a game can be", featuring a female lead character and themes of sexuality. Another participant agreed:

> *Oh, in* Gone Home*! It was the only game about lesbians! I loved it! That was good. Because all the rest of the games we played* [...] *it was just mainly, like you play a stereotypical game person.* (Participant O)

For Participant N, *Gone Home* provided an opportunity for him to explore some unfamiliar territory:

> *Em, yeah, I suppose, because, well* ... Gone Home *was obviously about a lesbian story, so. Yeah, kind of like different kind of culture, well, not different kind of culture but you know what I mean.*
> Interviewer: *Like a different perspective?*
> *Yeah, I mean, I'm not a lesbian, so.*

Many participants commented on the potential for personal interactions in the game lab to expose participants to new cultures and new ways of thinking. For example:

> *Yeah, I think the games helped with that because there was so many different people, different types of people that you were playing with. People from different countries and things as well.* (Participant L)

Several of the participants were aware that they were playing with students from other countries with whom they might not otherwise interact, as Participant P indicated when discussing adaptability. One participant noted that communicating with players from different backgrounds (those who do not "who live down the road in Glasgow or in Edinburgh or wherever") required some experimentation, given the active, collaborative nature of the games:

> *So, if you're sitting next to a Spaniard or an Italian, you don't know if you're going to get the same response from somebody who is from a very different cultural background by being very blunt with them and saying, you know, 'you're*

*doing terribly at this game, please stop'. […] You have to try it out, you have to
see what people are going to be like and you tend to find that we are all the
same.* (Participant T)

Speaking from the perspective of one such overseas student, for whom
English is not their first language, one participant noted the benefits of
engaging in the sort of natural conversation that a shared gaming experience can elicit:

*foreign people will be better to learn the language because in games people are
always talking and you will listen to what they say. Not only the good English,
but also the slang, how they use it in games, for example the 'LOL' and that
kind of thing that people use a lot on video games and that kind of things.*
(Participant P, male, age 27)

Participant P's comment about how players from different countries
operate differently is reflected in a number of other comments that treat
gaming as an aspect of our culture, an aspect that varies from country to
country and person to person:

*I ended up interacting with a lot of people through the video games study that
I wouldn't normally talk to […] meeting up with people who are from the
Canary Islands, and Italy, and kind talking about that and seeing the different
types of games that they play and seeing how their skills translate into that, see-
ing their different experiences and how that plays out in a video game context.*
(Participant M)

However, another participant stated that his co-players' various backgrounds were irrelevant:

*Well, it doesn't really matter who else is playing, because essentially, they're still
… they're just another player, so it doesn't really matter who they are.*
(Participant K)

Beyond the games played in the lab, some participants speculated that
playing video games in general might expose players to new cultures and
new ways of thinking. One participant had this to say:

I think the whole idea of placing a person into an environment unknown to them—virtual included—makes them look around and consider what's happening. […] I think most games would make someone more ethically and socially aware if they were playing it properly, specifically if it was the case that a new world has been created in the game which is made to mirror the issues within real life. (Participant F)

Participant O, while effusive about *Gone Home*, also notes that many of the games played feature stereotypical (male, straight) protagonists. When suggesting that games such as *Gone Home* could challenge what a game can be, Participant A also noted that female protagonists are rare in mainstream games:

I mean, there's still so few female lead characters in video games. I remember Metroid (Nintendo R&D1 and Intelligent Systems 1986) *and …* Perfect Dark (Rare 2000). *They're about the only two I can remember. And* Lara Croft*!* (Participant A)

The issue of representation in games, and the implications for using games to develop related attributes, are discussed in the following chapter.

Reflective Learners

Of all the attributes considered, Reflective Learners was found by participants to be the least obviously relevant beyond the games played. Whereas many of the responses above clearly imply a transferable dimension to the skills and experience gained from playing, the responses here largely refer to how participants reflect on what they have learned about the games played, and how this reflection influences subsequent play ("You need to learn from your mistakes in the game"—Participant B). There is evidence of reflection, then, but the participants' ability to articulate their skills and understanding in other contexts is less well evidenced.

While a single participant (Participant O) responded with a flat 'no' (accompanied by laughter) in response to the question of whether games could make players more reflective learners, the occurrence of reflective learning—pertaining to the games—was referenced in numerous other responses:

Yes. Every single game method ever can be attributed to the 'learning from your mistakes' ethos. It's practically how gaming works—it's part of what keeps people hooked. (Participant F)

learning from mistakes actually in the games themselves, plenty of that, that's the only way you can play these games is by getting them wrong the first time [...] it's very trial and error. (Participant T)

The idea of a 'second chance' was mentioned by several participants, highlighting that games provide an environment in which it is acceptable to fail and try again, following some period of reflection. As Participant I describes:

Yeah. Like, in relation to the games, if you made a mistake you tried to correct it the second time. And in the game, you had more lives.
Interviewer: *It didn't matter if you died...*
Yes. So, I think in this matter I can be more confident, going back to confidence, because you don't have anything to be afraid of. Because if you die.
Interviewer: *You can just start again?*
Yes.

Referring to games such as *Team Fortress 2*, where a player may choose to play as a different class of character when they die and 'respawn' in the game, Participant Q identifies an opportunity to reflect and adapt before taking a different approach with a different character class.

In every game we played, if you are losing, it is sometimes because you are not doing well enough, but more often because you are not doing it in the best way possible. You are forced to find better ways to confront problems and adapt. (Participant Q)

Some participants made observations relating to the timescale on which reflection occurred. While the *Team Fortress 2* example above indicates that reflection on the game could occur in mere moments, others suggested that a longer period of reflection, away from the game, was beneficial:

the trial and error, being able to look back reflectively on what you've done or if you play for one hour and go away and come back another day for like another hour you can base your next hour on how you did the last hour and kind of figure out what to do. (Participant M)

While most participants confined their discussion of reflection to game play alone, a few did attempt to connect this reflection with the world beyond. One participant had this to say:

I know it sounds kind of stupid, but … [laughs] Because you actually have to think about what you're doing while you're playing the game, but you sort of think back to it after you've played. Not just to prepare for other games but it's just because a lot of those skills help you in all kinds of aspects, I think, of like logic, sense of direction, reflexes, all these things, like confidence, being able to communicate and cooperate with others. So, I definitely think that, even just two hours a week, helped a lot. (Participant H)

Confidence and teamwork were cited by other participants in relation to reflection, too:

It's something that sort of sits with you, like, the experiences that you've had, the teamwork and the sort of problem solving that you've done, you become more confident in your ability to be able to do that kind of thing in other situations. So, it's not a case of actually, literally applying what you've done but it does give you that, the self-confidence to sort of be flexible. (Participant R)

Finally, however, one participant was keenly aware that the trial and error approach that many games encourage was not necessarily applicable to university life:

usually I'll look at a game and I'll play it and even if I make a mess of it, you can always go back again and re-do it. You can't do that with your semesters [laughs]. (Participant G)

Summary

In this chapter, the attitudes and experiences of students involved in a game-based learning intervention have been explored. Most of the student participants were positive about video games' capacity to develop a range of graduate attributes, with potential increases in confidence, communication skill, and critical thinking ability featuring prominently in discussion. Participants were also positive about the potential for games to provide experience of collaborating with others, and to enhance their ethical and social awareness through such collaboration. There were some notes of scepticism, however, particularly around the transferability of skills beyond games. The implications of these interview data, and some of the ways in which they connect with previous research, are discussed in the next chapter.

Note

1. http://www.gla.ac.uk/students/attributes/.

References

3909 LLC. (2013). *Papers, Please*. 3909 LLC.
Barr, M. (2018). Student Attitudes to Games-Based Skills Development: Learning from Video Games in Higher Education. *Computers in Human Behavior, 80*, 283–294. https://doi.org/10.1016/j.chb.2017.11.030.
Blizzard Entertainment. (2002). *Warcraft III: Reign of Chaos*. Blizzard Entertainment.
Crystal Dynamics. (2010). *Lara Croft and the Guardian of Light*. Square Enix.
Gearbox Software. (2012). *Borderlands 2*. 2K Games.
Mojang. (2011). *Minecraft*. Mojang.
Nintendo R&D1 and Intelligent Systems. (1986). *Metroid*. Nintendo.
Rare. (2000). *Perfect Dark*. Rare.
Riot Games. (2009). *League of Legends*. Riot Games.
The Fullbright Company. (2013). *Gone Home*. The Fullbright Company.
Valve Corporation. (2007). *Team Fortress 2*. Valve Corporation.
Valve Corporation. (2011). *Portal 2*. Valve Corporation.

5

Reflections on Game-Based Learning

The previous chapter presented interview data obtained from participants in a game-based intervention designed to develop graduate attributes in students. In this chapter, the implications of the interview data, collected at the conclusion of the original study, are considered. Each attribute is considered in turn and the chapter concludes with a brief overview of the skills and experience that students suggest they developed in addition to the stated graduate attributes.

Effective Communicators

Overall, study participants felt that the experience of playing the selected games—most of which featured some form of multiplayer component—was likely to have had a positive effect on their ability to communicate. This outcome is supported by the quantitative data described in Chap. 3, and so the interview data help shed some light on aspects of the experience the participants felt were most relevant to improving communication skill. Chief among these factors, based on participant interviews, is the simple fact that multiplayer video games require players to communicate in order to succeed. This is hardly a revelation, but what is interesting to note here

© The Author(s) 2019   **127**
M. Barr, *Graduate Skills and Game-Based Learning*, Digital Education and Learning,
https://doi.org/10.1007/978-3-030-27786-4_5

is that the players' intuition about such games' utility for developing communication ability is apparently well founded. Another relevant factor identified by participants is the time-sensitive, high-pressure nature of the scenarios presented by video games that require players to communicate efficiently in order to progress. Again, this seems entirely plausible on paper, and very much the kind of experience an employer might seek in a potential employee: the issue is that the experience is gained by playing video games, a means that may not be recognised by employers as legitimate. A final factor revealed in the participants' responses is that of being required to communicate with players of differing ability and experience. This necessitates more experienced players to adapt their approach to communicating with their teammates. Furthermore, in this case, the experienced players' teammates are students with whom they often have no existing rapport or comparable experience on which to draw, as might be the case when playing with their own friends. Less experienced players, too, must learn to listen to their more knowledgeable peers if the team is to achieve its in-game goals, and be ready to ask questions in a clear and efficient manner, as well as make sense of the answers received.

Van Lier (2004), in his discussion of the "ecology of language learning", frames Bruner's concept of pedagogical scaffolding (discussed in Chap. 1) as occurring on three timescales: macro, meso, and micro. The last of these timescales refers to the "interactional unfolding of learning activities" rather than the premeditated, structured approach to scaffolding that a teacher or tutor may take. It is defined as comprising the "contingent interactional processes of appropriation, stimulation, give-and-take in conversation, collaborative dialogue and so on" to which several of the interviewees here alluded. Van Lier also suggests that the learning of language "crucially relies on how the learner, as an active participant in meaningful activity, learns to perceive activity" and is a process that takes place within a semiotic context. There are clear links here to Gee's broader theories of learning in games, wherein the game is the semiotic context (or domain) and the learners/players are active participants in constructing meaning, here understood to be a shared language or means of communicating. Players learn through activity that is not limited to the spoken word but encompasses the deixes or contextual knowledge that players of the same game share, as well as gestures and utterances that, in a different context, might be meaningless. Van Lier also presents three interlocutor configurations, based on their inter-relationships. *Primary intersubjectivity* relates to face-to-face exchanges and is characterised by communication between infant and caregiver. *Secondary intersubjectivity* refers to shared observation of an object, a triadic interaction between two interlocutors and an object; it is characterised by an older infant and their caregiver referring to the object in question, initially by means of pointing. *Tertiary intersubjectivity* is characterised by the ability to refer to phenomena that are temporally or spatially distal and begins to occur in children from around age three. This final mode of communication is essential to most forms of multiplayer video games, as the interview data illustrate: tertiary intersubjectivity is required for relaying players' relative positions in *Team Fortress 2* (Valve Corporation 2007), sharing the location of certain resources in *Warcraft III* (Blizzard Entertainment 2002), or describing an off-screen clue in *Gone Home* (The Fullbright Company 2013). In fact, the complexity of these communications—exacerbated by the different perspectives on the game world offered by individual players' screens—suggests a *quaternary intersubjectivity* configuration. Here, the interlocutors are discussing objects of which there are multiple copies, and which are virtually distal—that is, they exist only in a virtual world—in addition to being temporally and spatially distal. This subtle increase in complexity, which is manifest in a first-time player's bewilderment, may be part of what makes video games suitable for developing communication skill. Furthermore, in a world where business is increasingly conducted online, the ability to exercise this quaternary intersubjectivity may be all the more valuable.

In Chap. 4, Participant T appeared sceptical that merely screaming his co-player's name is effective but given the context in which he is doing so—and the shared nature of their experience—this, in fact, may be a sufficiently clear and efficient means of communicating with his partner. This is not the form of communication this participant or, indeed, most of us have been taught to value, but it is true that brevity is key to successful communication in many real-world domains (e.g., the military, or air traffic control). There are echoes here of Grice's (1969) distinction between what is uttered and what is intended to be understood by the utterer. This idea of communicative intention has been taken up by relevance theorists (see Stojanović-Prelević 2011) and described in terms of explicature and implicature. Here, explicature consists of causal and temporal conclusions about what is said, for example, the shouting of a fellow player's name, a description of an enemy or obstacle that makes sense only within the context of the game, at that moment. Implicature consists of implied premises and conclusions about what is meant, for example, the identity of the person best placed to help, and the nature of the problem at hand. So, while the participant's chosen mode of communication is far from sophisticated, there may a useful lesson to be learned here if players were to reflect on the efficacy of their in-game communication, and to consider if the message they intended is being delivered.

Of course, many activities may provide a context in which communication may be developed. Video games, however, offer a means of creating shared and dynamic contexts that are not readily matched—in terms of fluidity, complexity, and authenticity—by conventional classroom experiences.

Experienced Collaborators

Given that students have been found to value teamwork and collaborative learning experience (Crebert et al. 2004), the overwhelmingly positive response to the idea that games could provide useful experience of collaboration is encouraging. Furthermore, teamwork is amongst the skills most commonly sought by employers, with Tempone (2012) finding that, alongside communication and self-management, teamwork was one of the three most critical generic attributes for graduates to possess. Matsouka and Mihail (2016), following interviews with 29 companies which were actively recruiting at the time, found that 'teamwork' was sought after by 89.7% of employers, just ahead of communication (89.6%) and adaptability (86.2%). More telling, still, is the fact that only 34.5% of companies felt that graduates possessed the necessary experience of working as part of a team. If playing video games at university can provide meaningful experience of collaboration, as the students interviewed in Chap. 4 clearly believe, then perhaps a game-based approach to developing team working skills would help address the apparent shortcomings in this area of student development. Beyond the more overtly cooperative titles, such as *Portal 2* (Valve Corporation 2011) and *Lara Croft and the Guardian of Light* (Crystal Dynamics 2010), participants were observed to engage in *ad hoc* cooperative endeavours, including the construction of a mountaintop lair and the creation of a chest intended to store communal supplies in *Minecraft* (Mojang 2011). However, with no game-enforced requirement to cooperate in *Minecraft*, not all participants engaged in meaningful collaboration. Some would explore the world by themselves, albeit occasionally conversing with players in the same world, while others would play in pairs that reflected existing relationships, interacting very little with other participants.

It was suggested in the interview data that female students might have proved more adept at collaborating with one another as they played the games. This idea is interesting because violent shooter games—which might include *Borderlands 2* (Gearbox Software 2012)—are often considered masculine spaces (Assunção 2016). If female players' collaborative and communicative abilities were, in fact, superior to those of their male counterparts, this might suggest they possessed some advantage in a game that apparently relies upon collaboration and communication. Indeed, there is evidence in the literature to suggest that women are better at collaborating or, at least, more disposed towards collaboration than men. For example, in a study that used co-authorship of scientific papers as a proxy for research collaboration, Abramo et al. (2013) demonstrated that female researchers show greater propensity towards collaboration than male researchers at "general level, intramural level and domestic extramural level", while noting that "a gap remains in the propensity to collaborate at the international level". The authors speculate that this gap may be indicative of the reduced opportunity for mobility that women can encounter in the workplace, rather than a disinclination towards international collaboration, however. Gender differences in attitudes to collaboration and competition have also been observed in the workplace. Kuhn and Villeval (2014), for example, cite a range of previous work showing that women shy away from competitive work environments while presenting data that suggests women are more likely to opt to collaborate with colleagues than men, driven by a more positive view of colleagues' abilities.

Differences between how men and women communicate—and the capacity for such differences to result in miscommunication—are described by Maltz and Borker (1982). The differences they identify include how women and men perceive questions, with the former viewing them as "part of conversational maintenance" and the latter as "requests for information". They also note that men are more likely to assume the verbal sharing of a problem is an explicit request for a solution, which may be dispensed regardless of the (male) interlocutor's understanding of the topic at hand (a phenomenon otherwise known as mansplaining), and that men and women perceive the role of verbal aggressiveness differently (p. 213). Coates (2015, p. 161) draws attention to Maltz and Borker's characterisation of girls' talk as 'collaboration-oriented' and boys' as 'competition-oriented', suggesting that while men are more inclined to talk loudly, swear, and ignore other men's utterances, women, when talking to other women, use so-called powerless language to express mutual support and solidarity (pp. 139–140). It is not difficult to imagine how the latter female approach might offer some advantages when playing cooperative video games. However, as Canary and Hause (1993) note, a reliance on stereotypes and the polarisation of the sexes can muddy the waters where research into gender differences in communication is concerned, and these issues undoubtedly persist where research pertains to collaboration. Reeder (1996) also notes that research into gender differences in communication is often hampered by studies that conflate gender with biological sex, and those that treat gender as a predictor variable or reduce gender to a binary construct. This implicitly ignores the reverse relationship between communication and gender, wherein aspects of what define a person's gender are created by the way in which they communicate.

The implications of this idea are not entirely clear. It might be suggested that male players could stand to gain from being asked to play with female players, from whom they may learn to collaborate more effectively. If female players are generally better at collaborating, then, it might also follow that they have less to gain from taking part in such game-based activities, although experience of working with less able male players may prove, in itself, useful. However, these gender differences are largely speculative: there is little qualitative evidence here to suggest any significant disparity between male and female players. Perhaps the differences are so slight as to render them unobservable in situations such as these or, as one participant in this study indicated, perhaps concerns about appearing sexist discourage comment on any observed differences. However, if this work were to be carried out on a larger scale, potential gender differences should be examined in more detail. With a more detailed knowledge of the differences and interactions between genders, future interventions could be modified to address any potential issues and capitalise upon any potential advantages, for example, in the gender balance of game-playing groups.

Collaboration and communication are skills that clearly require active participation to develop, as the above discussion of Van Lier's and Gee's ideas indicates. As suggested in Chap. 1, there is a potential link between the active nature of game-based learning and deep learning, and the higher levels of Bloom's taxonomy of learning. This, in turn, is why games may offer an opportunity to develop these skills, and, indeed, many of the other attributes considered here. It may be further argued that for learned skills to be transferable, the learning must be deep in nature—the simple memorisation of facts is largely irrelevant when it comes to learning about how to communicate and collaborate: the ability to abstract meaning and a deeper understanding of reality are required, to use Marton and Säljö's (1997) terminology. Therefore, it is interesting to note Participant J's scepticism about the applicability of their game-based experience of collaboration beyond games. This is in contrast to Participant Q's assertion that playing games 'globally enhanced' such skills, and a general agreement among participants that aspects of their game-playing experiences were relevant in 'real life'. It also contrasts with the findings of Toups et al. (2011), who showed that even a 'zero fidelity' simulation game—one that does not attempt to accurately portray a real-world scenario, but rather, an abstraction thereof—was effective in improving team coordination amongst first-response emergency workers. The fact that the experience was gained within a game that bears no resemblance to an external reality was, in this case, irrelevant to the transferability of the skills. Thus, the unrealistic nature of games such as *Borderlands* or *Team Fortress* may not, in fact, hinder the transfer of communication and collaboration skills.

Adaptable

Smith et al. (1997) note that the modern workplace requires less of what may be termed 'routine' expertise (required to solve familiar problems), and more adaptive expertise. And, in the two decades since, adaptive expertise has only become more vital in the workplace where the idea of a 'job for life' has crumbled in the face of globalisation and automation. Adaptive experts can recognise when to try alternative approaches to novel problems, just as several participants here described how they would experiment with different tactics in the face of some new in-game problem. For the participants here, the need to exercise adaptability arose from both the variety of games played and the range of problems encountered within each game. Some participants did question the transferability of learning to adapt to ever-changing in-game circumstances. However, it may be argued that it's the act of adapting to unfamiliar situations that is of importance here, not the ability to adapt an understanding of a particular game mechanic to a non-game context. The transferable dimension of the university's attribute definition states that graduates should "demonstrate resilience, perseverance, and positivity in multi-tasking, dealing with change and meeting new challenges". In fact, there is evidence in the responses of several participants to suggest that many, if not all, of these criteria have been touched upon in their experience of playing these games at university. Resilience in the face of the unfamiliar is what is transferable here, not the ability to understand a specific game or gaming convention.

It is worth noting, perhaps, that certain of the examples cited by participants in relation to the Adaptable attribute have clear connections with other attributes. For example, the need to adapt to playing with people of differing gaming ability—raised by several participants—is also mentioned in relation to the Experienced Collaborators attributed above. Adapting to playing with—or working with—a diverse range of unfamiliar individuals is arguably an increasingly important form of adaptability, due to the effects of globalisation on the job market (Lord and Smith 1999). Certainly, many of the students involved here were conscious of the need to adapt their approach to the games in order to succeed as a team, just as they might in the workplace.

Pulakos et al. (2000) developed an eight-dimension taxonomy of adaptive job performance by analysing over 1000 'critical incidents' in workplace environments. Many of these eight dimensions—which are cited by Ployhart and Bliese (2006) in their development of the I-ADAPT measure used in this study—are evident in the interview data. For example, several participants referred to the need to cooperate with a variety of unfamiliar people, which is encapsulated in the "demonstrating interpersonal adaptability" component. The discussion of participants adapting to the cultural norms of their fellow players clearly relates to the 'demonstrating cultural adaptability' component. The unpredictability of *Minecraft's* procedurally generated worlds, and the unfamiliar scenarios presented by games that participants had never played before, have clear parallels to the "dealing with uncertain and unpredictable work situations" component of adaptability identified by Pulakos et al. White et al. (2005) suggest that "behavior change is at the core of the definition" of adaptability. Based on this definition, and the various components of adaptability described above, the qualitative evidence strongly supports the notion that video games—particularly when played under the circumstances described here—can exercise a player's adaptability.

Finally, it may be noted that several other attributes were mentioned by participants when discussing the games' influence on their adaptability, including confidence and communication. After considering just a few typical graduate attributes, it is clear that there is overlap between these attributes, or, at least, there are relationships between them.

Resourceful and Responsible

Recalling the conceptualisation of resourcefulness on which Zauszniewski et al. (2006) based their Resourcefulness Scale, this attribute comprises two dimensions: personal resourcefulness (maintaining independence in the face of challenging circumstances) and social resourcefulness (knowing when to seek help from others). Broadly speaking, the former of these dimensions is more evident in player interview responses: when participants refer to being able to advance despite a lack of instruction or a limited amount of time, they are demonstrating independence in the face of challenging circumstances. Evidence of participants seeking help from other players—of social resourcefulness—was lacking. However, it should be noted that interview questions were based on the university definitions of the relevant graduate attribute, not the definition of resourcefulness offered by Zauszniewski et al. Social resourcefulness naturally underpins much of Zauszniewski et al.'s Resourcefulness Scale, and, given that the intervention group demonstrated a significant increase on resourcefulness as measured by this scale, it is logical to assume that many of the interviewees were socially resourceful. Indeed, there is qualitative evidence to support this supposition, although it is not presented in relation to gameplay: it is revealed in participants' answers to a question about how they might cope with being asked by an employer to carry out an unfamiliar or ill-defined task (which, in turn, was based on items present in the quantitative Resourcefulness Scale). For example, Participant M (female, age 17) replied "I'd probably try it first and if I still couldn't quite figure out what was going on, I'd ask someone and ask them if they could help me out". Similarly, Participant N (male, age 18) responded, "Well, I'd kind of ask them for help when doing it first, just to help me understand it properly".

So, while participants are certainly capable of exercising social resourcefulness, it is not reported in relation to gameplay. This is not unexpected, given that the university definition for this attribute—to which respondents were asked to refer during interviews—does not make reference to seeking help when required. Indeed, the phrase "self-sufficient individuals capable of substantial independent work" seems to preclude this aspect of resourcefulness. The university definition combines resourcefulness with responsibility, and, in the discussion of the latter, there is evidence of help being *given*, if not sought—for example in participants' collaborative *Minecraft* efforts. Elsewhere, experienced players describe the help they bestowed upon less experienced participants, out of an unspoken sense of responsibility. So, unless all of this help was unsolicited, it seems likely that some participants did actually seek help when required, thus demonstrating social resourcefulness.

As with all of the attributes under consideration here, there is a distinction to be made between experiencing something and internalising that experience such that it influences or informs subsequent behaviour. So, while the quantitative measure for resourcefulness provides some tangible evidence that this attribute was improved in a majority of the intervention group participants, it is more difficult to say that simply because the participants could provide examples of responsibility from their experience of the study, this experience made them any more responsible. The wording of the university attribute definitions does, in places, acknowledge this distinction: it is suggested that graduates be 'experienced collaborators' rather than 'skilled collaborators', for example. However, as the discussion of this attribute demonstrates, there are still questions about what exactly the university experience—or interventions such as this—can impart to a student.

Investigative

Participant C (male, age 19) described the "common investigation of the same issue but from a different perspective" that occurred in the lab as a group of participants played a single-player title simultaneously, again alluding to collaboration. Heller et al. (1992) describe an experiment in which problem-solving is taught to college Physics students through cooperative group learning. Their finding that better solutions were produced by students working collaboratively to solve problems, compared to those working independently, is reflected in the collaborative approach to problem-solving participants opted to take here. Heller et al. also noted that collaborative problem-solving exercises improved problem-solving skill across the range of abilities in the class, which may suggest that the collaborative approach taken to solving game-based problems here is beneficial to all concerned. Heller et al. also observed the significant influence of peer interaction and support within their groups, recalling the kind of peer tutoring observed in mixed ability pairs in this study:

In well-functioning cooperative groups, students can share conceptual and procedural knowledge and argument roles, and request clarification, justification, and elaboration from one another. [...] The results of this study suggest that this type of collaboration did occur. (Heller et al. 1992)

Indeed, pairs—or dyads—may be the optimal configuration for collaborative game-based learning. Students who played the water quality game in Barab et al.'s (2009) study in pairs out-performed not only those students who learned from a textbook but also those who played the game alone. Schwabe et al. (2005) also found that teams of two were optimal, at least in terms of fun and immersion, while teams of four or more, or single players, were less motivated to learn from a game. Related to the Experienced Collaborators attribute above, Schwabe et al. also found that dyads were the optimal configuration for team building. However, the effects on learning were less clear.

The frequency with which *Portal 2* was associated with investigating and solving problems is also of note, particularly if the study were to be repeated or rolled out in any more formal capacity—Valve's 'physics-based puzzler' is clearly a candidate for inclusion, based on these data. However, other titles, such as *Lara Croft*, were also cited as requiring investigative and problem-solving skills.

The idea that players may accumulate individual 'investigation skills' of subsequent utility seems to echo Anderson's (1993) conceptualisation of human problem-solving as the acquisition of 'production rules'. Anderson also highlights the importance of the 'strength' of the example from which a production rule is learned: the participants here are suggesting that the examples afforded by the games are strong enough to support the development of such rules, and thus enhance players' problem-solving ability.

While, in many cases, pairs may be the optimal configuration for learning and enjoyment, it is useful to recall that several participants here admitted that they opted to 'take a back seat' when investigating in-game problems with a partner. So, it may not be assumed that individuals within a game-playing dyad are applying their problem-solving skills in equal measure. However, with these caveats in mind, it may be concluded from the qualitative data that participants saw opportunities to exercise their problem-solving abilities using the games played. Furthermore, the problems presented by video games may be complex and varied, reflecting the nature of problems encountered in real life, and in many workplaces.

Independent and Critical Thinkers

Robert H. Ennis, one of the authors of the Ennis-Weir Critical Thinking Essay Test (see Chap. 2), defines critical thinking as "reasonable reflective thinking focused on deciding what to believe or do" (Ennis 2015) and there is a clear emphasis on deciding what to do in the interview responses. Participant C, for example, frames his experience of *Minecraft* in terms of the question "what do I need to do?", while Participant T noted that playing video games was "all about judgement", which is, perhaps, another way of interpreting Ennis' definition. However, while this is a neat and very credible definition of critical thinking, Ennis and others have identified numerous facets to the concept, each of which may be considered individually. For example, Norris and Ennis (1989, p. 12) identify a list of critical thinking dispositions that includes trying to be well informed and seeking a statement of the thesis or question at hand. Exploring each of the dispositions and abilities that comprise critical thinking was beyond the scope of these interviews, which were focused on the university definitions of the graduate attributes in question. However, there is sufficient evidence here to warrant further work that explores video games' relationship with the more detailed conceptions of critical thinking that exist in the literature. Furthermore, other work has suggested that problem-based learning (PBL) is effective in improving critical thinking skills (see, e.g., Williams 2001, for an overview of the literature on the use of PBL to develop students' critical thinking). As Connolly et al. (2004) have noted, game-based learning draws on concepts related to PBL, so it is quite plausible that games can exercise players' critical thinking. Further exploration of the relationship between video games and critical thinking, however, will require an alternative means of measuring any gains associated with playing, as the pilot mentioned in Chap. 2 illustrated the problems associated with using the Ennis-Weir test in a pre-/post-test experiment.

As the sixth attribute to be considered by interviewees, the critical thinking responses highlighted more than any previous discussion the extent to which these attributes inter-relate: "I don't know, yeah, all the games had a bit of each thing" (Participant B); "Well, in every game you have always in the beginning [the question of] what to do, right?" (Participant C). And, regardless of the attribute to which problem-solving is thought to most closely relate, for Participant J this aspect of the critical thinking attribute definition is common to all: "Some of these things, they just all sound like problem-solving to me! Just different aspects of problem-solving, I guess."

It may be argued, however, that the critical thinking attribute appeared to overlap with so many others not simply because it was discussed later in the interview, but because critical thinking underpins many of these other attributes. Nicol (2010) has asserted that "critical evaluative experience" may foster the development of a range of different attributes, for example. The limited qualitative data presented here may be seen as supporting this assertion, bearing in mind that critical thinking was discussed following consideration of several other attributes.

Confident

The Confident attribute is one of several graduate attributes that may well be influenced by playing video games but, based on the quantitative and qualitative data collected here, it is not possible to isolate this influence from the combined effects of playing the selected games under lab conditions. That is to say, the effects—measured or perceived—may be attributed to the overall experience of the participants playing the games together in the lab over a period of weeks. As one participant noted, under normal conditions, he would play games with his friends, which would not require him to engage in potentially confidence-building conversations with strangers. Furthermore, the quantitative General Self-Efficacy Scale measure, included in the main experiment as a proxy for confidence, revealed only a small, statistically insignificant difference between the control and intervention groups. That said, it has been argued that confidence is not a distinct, measurable attribute. Stajkovic (2006), for example, suggests that confidence is a higher-order construct that is manifested by hope, self-efficacy, optimism, and resilience. If this is the case, the quantitative measure used to gauge any gains in self-efficacy is telling only part of the story. A more sophisticated understanding of confidence may be bound up in aspects of other attributes; for example, where resilience is considered to be a component of resourcefulness.

The interview data, however, clearly show that participants see a link between playing the games in the lab and developing confidence. At the root of this belief is the idea that "you don't have anything to be afraid of" if you make a mistake in a game, as one participant puts it. This view is entirely in line with Gee's "Psychosocial Moratorium" Principle, which states that "learners can take risks in a space where real-world consequences are lowered" (2007, p. 64). Gee's principle borrows its name from the work of Erikson (1959), which concerns the development of an individual's identity, and so it follows that the principle may be connected with the player's development as a (more confident) person. However, another of Gee's principles, the Practice Principle (2007, p. 68) also appears relevant when examining the interview data: participants here describe how, for example, playing the games improved their confidence by providing them with an opportunity to practice being in social situations. The idea that games' utility to support skills development lies in the potential they offer for practice is also discussed by game developers in Chap. 7.

The popular notion—espoused by John Seely Brown (2006, 2012)—that multiplayer video games can develop leadership skills was not quantitatively measured, but the interview data suggest that participants were aware of the need for leadership, making frequent reference to their lab experience in relation to both confidence and that required to lead. One participant, for example, describes how playing the games gave him the confidence to "take leadership of the team". Indeed, there is some precedent for the idea that playing video games may help develop leadership skills. Xanthopoulou and Papagiannidis (2012), for example, describe a one-month longitudinal study wherein the results "supported the direct spillover of transformational leadership, as well as the boosting effect of high game performance in this spillover effect". Given that several participants here questioned the transferability of leadership skills, such 'spillover effects' are important to note. Nuangjumnong (2016), using self-report measures to quantify leadership skills exhibited by MOBA (Multiplayer Online Battle Arena) players, also found that the practice of in-game leadership corresponded with the development of real-world leadership skills. Concluding that playing such video games can help improve leadership ability, that study offers further evidence that the effects on players' ability to lead are, indeed, transferable.

Ethically and Socially Aware

The attainment of this attribute is particularly difficult to evidence. The qualitative data, however, suggest that students see the potential for games to increase their ethical and social awareness via two means: by experiencing alternative perspectives through the games and by interacting with players from different backgrounds in the context of playing games together. There are clear connections with several of Gee's principles here, including the Cultural Models about the World Principle' and the Identity Principle. Participants' comments also recall points made in *The Civic Potential of Video Games* (Kahne et al. 2009, pp. 51–53) wherein the authors call for educators to help young people "reflectively engage with video games" to increase civic and political awareness. They also note that educational games such as *Real Lives* (Educational Simulations 2001) can "help foster empathy and understanding of the lives of others and teach about dynamics associated with different political systems, economic structures, cultural beliefs, and religions". This idea very closely mirrors what George Eliot had to say about novels, which she believed could offer an excellent understanding of moral sentiment: "The greatest benefit we owe to the artist, whether painter, poet or novelist, is the extension of our sympathies" (Eliot 1881). Eliot suggested that a good novel could provide insight into the true social, moral, and political beliefs of the 'social classes', noting that we "want to be taught to feel, not for the heroic artisan or the sentimental peasant, but for the peasant in all his coarse apathy, and the artisan in all his suspicious selfishness".[1] In assuming the role of, for example, the border official in *Papers, Please* (3909 LLC 2013), video games might well be considered "a mode of amplifying experience and extending our contact with our fellow-men beyond the bounds of our personal lot", as Eliot says of art more generally. There is also a potential connection with Francis Bacon's belief that

"Reading maketh a full man, conference [discussion] a ready man, and writing an exact man" (1625/1928). Games, as evidenced here, can certainly form the basis of useful discussion, so perhaps 'playing' could be substituted for 'reading' in Bacon's aphorism: playing maketh a full person.

Kahne et al. also cite the commercial title *Democracy* (Positech Games 2005) as an example of a game that might be of interest to educators tasked with developing students' social awareness. Rusnak et al. (2008) has shown that a purpose-built serious game can be used to support affective learning and change students' attitudes to social issues (in that case, homelessness). Based on interview responses given here and bearing in mind that the proportion of games selected for this study that were intended to relate directly to this attribute was small (two of eight), it may be that there is still untapped potential for commercial games to be used in this capacity.

However, it is important to recall the participant who rightfully decried the heteronormative homogeneity of game protagonists: diversity of representation is generally lacking in contemporary commercial video games. Female protagonists are seriously underrepresented in mainstream video games and people of colour or those from the LGBTQ (lesbian, gay, bisexual, transgender and queer or questioning) community are even less common as playable characters (Jayanth 2014). The study here did include games with female protagonists (*Borderlands 2*, *Portal 2*, and *Lara Croft and the Guardian of Light*) and depictions of LGBTQ characters (*Gone Home*), but it is notable that titles such as *Team Fortress 2* don't, by default, include any female player characters.

This is a potential issue to explore in any future work and it is likely that greater emphasis should be placed on games that represent more diverse characters, cultures, and identities. In order to avoid excluding or discouraging students for whom the stereotypical straight, male protagonist is not relevant or appealing, it would be important to include more diverse options in the games used in a higher education context. Furthermore, including such diversity can only help expose students to alternative perspectives and cultures where they might ordinarily choose to accept stereotypical player characters. This was the reasoning behind including a game such as *Gone Home*, and the comments of Participant N ("I'm not a lesbian, so ...") suggest that there is certainly potential for an exercise such as that described here to provide new perspectives for students to consider and new identities to explore. And, while mainstream games featuring LGBTQ characters are few—notable exceptions include *Dragon Age: Inquisition* (BioWare 2014) and *The Last of Us* (Naughty Dog 2013)—there are numerous smaller budget 'indie' games besides *Gone Home* that offer greater diversity, including *Undertale* (Toby Fox 2015) and *Night in the Woods* (Infinite Fall 2017). Indeed, while video games are not celebrated for their rich tapestry of representation, recent work by Adrienne Shaw has revealed LGBTQ game content exists in games various forms (Shaw and Friesem 2016). Shaw's LGBTQ Video Game Archive[2] includes hundreds of examples of 'non-normative' content in video games and work such as this may help reveal potential for games to help educate and inform players about LGBTQ culture. As noted by Participant O in Chap. 4, LGBTQ—or even female—characters rarely feature as the playable protagonist in mainstream games, but Shaw's work suggests that greater diversity may lie below the surface. The widespread occurrence of homophobia and transphobia (not to mention racism) in game culture is worrying but, if presented in suitable terms, such content might aid discussion and understanding of these problematic points of view—not least because, given the right game, players may experience the negative consequences of regressive attitudes for themselves. Such opportunities may, indeed, extend to issues such as racism: in common with good science fiction, games can use allegory to tackle weightier issues such as race. *The Elder Scrolls V: Skyrim* (Bethesda Game Studios 2011) is one example of a mainstream game that permits the player to observe the effects of racial discrimination 'firsthand', albeit in a limited sense (Simpson 2015). It may sound facile to suggest that a player may learn something by encountering tensions between fictional races in a game such as *Skyrim*. However, games not only offer the obvious benefit of an immersive and interactive environment where the player's actions can have consequences; when played collectively as a group, the shared nature of the experience can also provide an opportunity to discuss the issues encountered and to reflect on different players' actions and the consequences thereof.

Reflective Learners

Dewey (1933, p. 17) suggested that reflection "enables us to direct our actions with foresight. [...] It enables us to know what we are about when we act." In learning from their mistakes, it can certainly be argued that players are better able to direct subsequent actions, suggesting that reflective learning has taken place. However, as the range of responses documented in Chap. 4 indicates, some forms of reflection are more productive than others. Moore and Ash (2002) identified four types of 'reflective activity' in their study of trainee teachers:

- 'Ritualistic reflection', wherein reflection comprises little more than 'going through the motions' of reflection, to meet some requirement to reflect, that is, reflection may be performative in nature;
- 'Pseudo-reflection', where there is a genuine intention to reflect but no development or change results;
- 'Constructive', 'productive', or 'authentic' reflection, which actively seeks to problematise situations and to challenge existing views, perspectives, and beliefs, promoting or leading to development or change;
- 'Reflexivity', whereby reflection extends beyond the situation at hand, and includes considerations of previous experiences, and responses to these.

There are echoes of deep and surface learning here, with 'reflexivity' representing the deepest form of reflective learning. Based on interview responses, the forms of reflective learning that were most commonly observed in relation to these games might be the second and third forms identified by Moore and Ash. Where players have genuinely learned from their mistakes and altered their approach to solving an in-game problem, then the reflection might be described as 'constructive' or 'productive'. However, where players recognise the need to learn from their mistakes but fail to come up with an alternative approach to solving the problem, they might be said to be engaging in 'pseudo-reflection'. There is little impetus to engage in 'ritualistic reflection' when playing these games, aside from a desire to placate fellow players in a cooperative game by acting as though one cares enough about the game to reflect on their actions. And, since there was little agreement that reflections on gameplay were of utility beyond the games, it cannot be said that 'reflexivity' has occurred.

So, much of the reflection discussed here relates only to the games played. This is not to say, however, that the data are not interesting: the participants' comments clearly support several of the ideas put forward by Gee, for example, and if reflective learning—albeit about playing a game—is taking place, then the students involved are, at least, exercising this attribute. Perhaps the two most relevant of Gee's learning principles are the Probing Principle (2007, p. 105) and the "Psychosocial Moratorium" Principle (2007, p. 59). The participants here make numerous references to trial and error and imply that games provide a safe space in which to fail. Gee's principles, respectively, refer to carrying out some action, reflecting on the outcome, and acting again; and, learners being able to risk-taking certain actions without serious consequence. The data here provide evidence for the existence of these principles in commercial video games, even if the transferability or wider applicability of the gameplay experience is less obvious.

Additional Outcomes

Largely in response to the initial question, students perceived a range of potential benefits arising from playing games on campus, over and above the development of the stated graduate attributes. These benefits including games' utility as 'ice breakers':

> It's a very fun ice breaker … it's a very disguised ice breaker as well. It didn't seem like we were playing these games to get to know each other. It seemed like we were just playing the games and, by collateral damage, ended up having to talk to each other. (Participant T)

Related to this idea, several participants saw great potential for video games to form the basis of team-building exercises. One participant, for example, suggested that the lab sessions could be repurposed as such:

If it was a kind of like a team building workshop type thing, like a confidence building workshop, a team building workshop where you'd play games with people you'd never met before. (Participant R)

Ice breakers and team building are often associated with the corporate world, and individuals such as Sivasailam 'Thiagi' Thiagarajan and organisations such as the North American Simulation and Gaming Association have published on the use of non-digital games for such purposes (see Thiagarajan and Parker 2008; Blohm and Piltz 2012). However, the most broadly cited additional benefit was that of video games providing a means of 'de-stressing' or relaxing. The stress of university life was mentioned specifically by several participants:

For me, it's an outlet for adrenaline, stress, so I think it would be very beneficial to university students, especially those that are still getting accustomed to university life. (Participant H)

Because uni is stressful, it would be nice if students had somewhere they could go to just play some games. That way you're relaxing and getting some benefit out of it as well. (Participant L)

There's value in the sense that it was nice to come in for a couple of hours and de-stress. You just play something, and you don't have to think about your coursework for a little while. (Participant G)

Other participants expressed similar ideas in terms of the games offering an opportunity to relax, and welcomed the idea of being able to play games on campus:

I think it would be good because of it being kind of restful. It would be nice to be able to spend a very reasonable amount, an hour or so, just be in that setting and not need to go home. It would be nice to be able to go 'I'm going to go and play for an hour and then go back to studying'. (Participant C)

I remember one day, it was kind of the beginning of the study, maybe second or third week, and I was really upset. I can't remember why. Because of school I had, I think, some problem with lessons ... and I came here, and I played and it really helped me. ... I immediately felt better. (Participant S)

The contrast between study and play was thought to be beneficial, too, as Participant D noted: "I looked forward to coming into the labs because it was a nice change of pace from just studying and university work and stuff". Or, as Participant B suggests:

> *That would be really cool, if you could go and play games with some mates. Like, you have your mind in another thing for a while. So, you're not thinking all the time about the lectures, but you still have to think.*

The cathartic effects of playing video games have been debated and documented elsewhere. Bonus et al. (2015), for example, showed that playing violent games could reduce feelings of frustration and improve mood in players, although such improvements were also associated with a tendency to perceive the real world in more hostile terms. Furthermore, Bourgonjon et al. (2015), in their analysis of online discussion forums dedicated to games, found that one of the many benefits players associated with playing was stress relief, and identified mention of catharsis in 16.3% of the forum messages analysed. The potential for games to offer students an opportunity to relieve stress, however, was not explicitly explored in this study, which makes it striking that this idea has emerged from the interview data.

Challenges and Limitations

As described in Chap. 3, *Lara Croft and the Guardian of Light* is a cooperative game that requires two players. The case of *Lara Croft*, however, illustrates the challenges associated with running a drop-in gaming lab with multiplayer games: it is not always possible to guarantee the availability of the required number of players. Here, one participant has undoubtedly displayed a form of resourcefulness in progressing through the cooperative game on his own, by alternating his control of the two on-screen characters. That this opportunity for resourcefulness arose not by design of the game or the experiment is interesting in itself and arguably represents a particularly authentic example of this attribute being exercised. However, such unplanned opportunities to develop a skill do not further the case for using video games to do so.

The games' ease of access and breath of appeal must also be considered. In some respects, the RTS (real-time strategy) genre—which the *Warcraft* series (Blizzard Entertainment 1994–) helped define—is perhaps the least accessible of the genres employed here. Certain participants, specifically those who had played the game, or its sister series, *Starcraft* (Blizzard Entertainment 1998–), relished the opportunity to take part in Local Area Network (LAN)-based RTS skirmishes. For others, however, the game's amalgam of unique fantastical units and associated strategies proved initially baffling and the required two hours of gameplay was more of a chore than a pleasure. As such, *Warcraft III* was probably the most divisive of the titles used in the study and it may be that the RTS genre—despite its clear potential to develop certain skills—may not be well suited to a university-based intervention such as that described here. *Team Fortress 2* on the other hand, was selected in favour of other free-to-play team-based shooters, such as *Counter-Strike* (Valve Corporation 2000), on the basis of its broad appeal. The thinking here was that the game's cartoonish aesthetic and humorous presentation would appear more inviting than serious, overtly militaristic titles. However, inexperienced participants were occasionally observed to be somewhat bewildered by the game, struggling not only to operate their allocated weapon effectively but also failing to grasp the geography of the game's constantly changing maps: cries along the lines of "I don't even know where I am!" were not uncommon. For the most part, though, participants did appear to enjoy the game on the basis of its frenetic and often comedic tone, and as a result of the team-based structure. The range of roles afforded by the game's various character classes also encouraged players to find a niche in which they were comfortable. As indicated by several participants during their post-intervention interviews (see Chap. 4), it was possible to assume the role of a lowly grunt—responsible, perhaps, for pushing the payload in certain missions—and still gain satisfaction from being part of the team while other, more experienced players assumed more complex duties. In the case of *Team Fortress 2*, then, it appears that concerns around accessibility are largely offset by the advantages offered by the game's class-based, team-focused gameplay design.

Summary

This chapter has explored some implications of the interview data presented in Chap. 4 and highlighted the connections between student reflections on playing selected video games and established theories of learning and development. These empirical observations serve to vindicate the ideas presented by scholars such as Gee and suggest further connections between game-based learning and established theory. It's important to note, however, that these interview data refer to the circumstances under which specific, selected games were played: the participants make multiple references to the effects of being asked to play games with people other than their friends. Several of the attributes discussed here appear to be influenced by the fact that students played with strangers from differing cultural backgrounds and with varying gaming experience. So, while the interviews elucidated the factors that may be at play here, they also underline the fact that the effects on attribute attainment can only be said to be a consequence of playing these games under the specified conditions—we cannot say more about the effects of playing video games more generally.

Notes

1. Dr Steve Draper, whom the author must thank for making this connection between games and Eliot's remarks, maintains a set of notes and links to further reading at http://www.psy.gla.ac.uk/~steve/localed/eliot.html.
2. https://lgbtqgamearchive.com/.

References

3909 LLC. (2013). *Papers, Please.* 3909 LLC.

Abramo, G., D'Angelo, C. A., & Murgia, G. (2013). Gender Differences in Research Collaboration. *Journal of Informetrics, 7*(4), 811–822. https://doi.org/10.1016/j.joi.2013.07.002.

Anderson, J. R. (1993). Problem Solving and Learning. *American Psychologist, 48*(1), 35–44. https://doi.org/10.1037/0003-066X.48.1.35.

Assunção, C. (2016). No Girls on the Internet': The Experience of Female Gamers in the Masculine Space of Violent Gaming. *Press Start, 3*(1), 46–65.

Bacon, F. (1625/1928). *Of Studies* (pp. xii–3). Samuel T. Farquhar.

Barab, S. A., Scott, B., Siyahhan, S., Goldstone, R., Ingram-Goble, A., Zuiker, S. J., & Warren, S. (2009). Transformational Play as a Curricular Scaffold: Using Videogames to Support Science Education. *Journal of Science Education and Technology, 18*(4), 305–320.

Bethesda Game Studios. (2011). *The Elder Scrolls V: Skyrim.* Bethesda Softworks.

BioWare. (2014). *Dragon Age: Inquisition.* Electronic Arts.

Blizzard Entertainment. (1994–). *Warcraft Series.* Blizzard Entertainment.

Blizzard Entertainment. (1998). *Starcraft.* Blizzard Entertainment.

Blizzard Entertainment. (2002). *Warcraft III: Reign of Chaos.* Blizzard Entertainment.

Blohm, J. M., & Piltz, D. (Eds.). (2012). *NASAGA Training Activity Book.* Chichester: Wiley.

Bonus, J. A., Peebles, A., & Riddle, K. (2015). The Influence of Violent Video Game Enjoyment on Hostile Attributions. *Computers in Human Behavior, 52*, 472–483. https://doi.org/10.1016/j.chb.2015.05.044.

Bourgonjon, J., Vandermeersche, G., Wever, B. D., Soetaert, R., & Valcke, M. (2015). Players' Perspectives on the Positive Impact of Video Games: A Qualitative Content Analysis of Online Forum Discussions. *New Media & Society*, 1461444815569723. https://doi.org/10.1177/1461444815569723.

Brown, J. S. (2006). *New Learning Environments for the 21st Century.* Retrieved from http://www.johnseelybrown.com/newlearning.pdf.

Brown, J. S. (2012, August 7). How World of Warcraft Could Save Your Business and The Economy. *Big Think.* Retrieved August 1, 2018, https://bigthink.com/videos/how-world-of-warcraft-could-save-your-business-and-the-economy-2.

Canary, D. J., & Hause, K. S. (1993). Is There Any Reason to Research Sex Differences in Communication? *Communication Quarterly, 41*(2), 129–144. https://doi.org/10.1080/01463379309369874.

Coates, J. (2015). *Women, Men and Language: A Sociolinguistic Account of Gender Differences in Language* (3rd ed.). London: Routledge.

Connolly, T. M., Stansfield, M., Ramsay, J., & Sutherland, J. (2004). *Applying Computer Games Concepts to Teaching Database Analysis and Design.* Presented at the International Conference on Computer Games, AI, Design and Education, Reading, UK.

Crebert, G., Bates, M., Bell, B., Patrick, C.-J., & Cragnolini, V. (2004). Developing Generic Skills at University, During Work Placement and in Employment:

Graduates' Perceptions. *Higher Education Research & Development, 23*(2), 147–165. https://doi.org/10.1080/0729436042000206636.

Crystal Dynamics. (2010). *Lara Croft and the Guardian of Light*. Square Enix.

Dewey, J. (1933). *How We Think: A Restatement of the Relation of Reflective Thinking to the Educative Process*. D.C. Heath and Company.

Educational Simulations. (2001). *Real Lives*. Educational Simulations.

Eliot, G. (1881). *The works of George Eliot*. Standard Edition: Essays. Edinburgh: Blackwood.

Ennis, R. H. (2015). Critical Thinking: A Streamlined Conception. In M. Davies & R. Barnett (Eds.), *The Palgrave Handbook of Critical Thinking in Higher Education* (pp. 31–47). New York: Palgrave Macmillan US. https://doi.org/10.1007/978-1-137-37805-7_2.

Erikson, E. H. (1959). *Identity and the Life Cycle: Selected Papers*. Oxford, UK: International Universities Press.

Gearbox Software. (2012). *Borderlands 2*. 2K Games.

Gee, J. P. (2007). *What Video Games Have to Teach Us About Learning and Literacy* (2nd ed.). New York: Palgrave Macmillan.

Grice, H. P. (1969). Utterer's Meaning and Intention. *The Philosophical Review, 78*(2), 147–177. https://doi.org/10.2307/2184179.

Heller, P., Keith, R., & Anderson, S. (1992). Teaching Problem Solving Through Cooperative Grouping. Part 1: Group Versus Individual Problem Solving. *American Journal of Physics, 60*(7), 627–636. https://doi.org/10.1119/1.17117.

Infinite Fall. (2017). *Night in the Woods*. Finji.

Jayanth, M. (2014, September 18). 52% of Gamers Are Women – But the Industry Doesn't Know It. *The Guardian*. Retrieved September 30, 2016 from https://www.theguardian.com/commentisfree/2014/sep/18/52-percent-people-playing-games-women-industry-doesnt-know.

Kahne, J., Middaugh, E., & Evans, C. (2009). *The Civic Potential of Video Games*. The MIT Press.

Kuhn, P., & Villeval, M. C. (2014). Are Women More Attracted to Co-operation Than Men? *The Economic Journal, 125*(582), 115–140. https://doi.org/10.1111/ecoj.12122.

Lord, R. G., & Smith, W. G. (1999). Leadership and the Changing Nature of Performance. In E. D. Pulakos & D. R. Ilgen (Eds.), *The Changing Nature of Performance: Implications for Staffing, Motivation, and Development*. San Francisco: John Wiley & Sons.

Maltz, D. N., & Borker, R. A. (1982). A Cultural Approach to Male–Female Miscommunication. In J. J. Gumperz (Ed.), *Language and Social Identity* (pp. 196–216). Cambridge: Cambridge University Press.

Marton, F., & Säljö, R. (1997). Approaches to Learning. In F. Marton, D. Hounsell, & N. J. Entwistle (Eds.), *The Experience of Learning: Implications for Teaching and Studying in Higher Education*. Edinburgh: Scottish Academic Press.

Matsouka, K., & Mihail, D. M. (2016). Graduates' Employability: What Do Graduates and Employers Think? *Industry and Higher Education, 30*(5), 321–326. https://doi.org/10.1177/0950422216663719.

Mojang. (2011). *Minecraft*. Mojang.

Moore, A., & Ash, A. (2002). *Reflective Practice in Beginning Teachers: Helps, Hindrances and the Role of the Critical Other*. Presented at the Annual Conference of the British Educational Research Association, University of Exeter, England.

Naughty Dog. (2013). *The Last of Us*. Sony Interactive Entertainment.

Nicol, D. J. (2010). *The Foundation for Graduate Attributes: Developing Self-Regulation Through Self and Peer-Assessment*. Glasgow: The Quality Assurance Agency for Higher Education.

Norris, S. P., & Ennis, R. H. (1989). *Evaluating Critical Thinking*. Midwest Publications.

Nuangjumnong, T. (2016). The Influences of Online Gaming on Leadership Development. In M. L. Gavrilova, C. J. K. Tan, A. Iglesias, M. Shinya, A. Galvez, & A. Sourin (Eds.), *Transactions on Computational Science XXVI: Special Issue on Cyberworlds and Cybersecurity* (pp. 142–160). Berlin, Heidelberg: Springer Berlin Heidelberg. https://doi.org/10.1007/978-3-662-49247-5_9.

Ployhart, Robert E., & Bliese, Paul D. (2006). Individual Adaptability (I-ADAPT) Theory: Conceptualizing the Antecedents, Consequences, and Measurement of Individual Differences in Adaptability. In *Understanding Adaptability: A Prerequisite for Effective Performance within Complex Environments* (Vols. 1-0, Vol. 6, pp. 3–39). Emerald Group Publishing Limited.

Positech Games. (2005). *Democracy*. Positech Games.

Pulakos, E. D., Arad, S., Donovan, M. A., & Plamondon, K. E. (2000). Adaptability in the Workplace: Development of a Taxonomy of Adaptive Performance. *Journal of Applied Psychology, 85*(4), 612–624. https://doi.org/10.1037/0021-9010.85.4.612.

Reeder, H. M. (1996). A Critical Look at Gender Difference in Communication Research. *Communication Studies, 47*(4), 318–330. https://doi.org/10.1080/10510979609368486.

Rusnak, P., Dobson, T., & Boskic, N. (2008). *Articulation of Ecological Values in Alternate Reality Gaming: A Case Study of World Without Oil*. Presented at the 2nd European Conference on Games Based Learning, Univesitat Oberta de Catalunya, Spain.

Schwabe, G., Goth, C., & Frohberg, D. (2005). Does Team Size Matter in Mobile Learning? In *International Conference on Mobile Business (ICMB'05)* (pp. 227–234). Presented at the International Conference on Mobile Business (ICMB'05). https://doi.org/10.1109/ICMB.2005.35.

Shaw, A., & Friesem, E. (2016). Where Is the Queerness in Games?: Types of Lesbian, Gay, Bisexual, Transgender, and Queer Content in Digital Games. *International Journal of Communication, 10*(0), 13.

Simpson, C. M. (2015, July 31). *In Another Time with (an)other Race: Representations of Race and National Narratives in Elder Scrolls V: Skyrim And Fallout 3*. Arlington: University of Texas at Arlington.

Smith, E. M., Ford, J. K., & Kozlowski, S. W. J. (1997). Building Adaptive Expertise: Implications for Training Design Strategies. In M. A. Quiñones & A. Ehrenstein (Eds.), *Training for a Rapidly Changing Workplace: Applications of Psychological Research* (pp. 89–118). Washington, DC: American Psychological Association.

Stajkovic, A. D. (2006). Development of a Core Confidence-Higher Order Construct. *Journal of Applied Psychology, 91*(6), 1208–1224. https://doi.org/10.1037/0021-9010.91.6.1208.

Stojanović-Prelević, I. (2011). On Communicative Intention and Saying/Implicating Distinction. *Facta Universitatis, 9*(2), 107–114.

Tempone, I. (2012). Desirable Generic Attributes for Accounting Graduates into the Twenty-First Century: The Views of Employers. *Accounting Research Journal, 25*(1), 41–55. https://doi.org/10.1108/10309611211244519.

The Fullbright Company. (2013). *Gone Home*. The Fullbright Company.

Thiagarajan, S., & Parker, G. (2008). *Teamwork and Teamplay: Games and Activities for Building and Training Teams* (1st ed.). Pfeiffer.

Toby Fox. (2015). *Undertale*. Toby Fox.

Toups, Z. O., Kerne, A., & Hamilton, W. A. (2011). The Team Coordination Game: Zero-fidelity Simulation Abstracted from Fire Emergency Response Practice. *ACM Transactions on Computer-Human Interaction, 18*(4), 23:1–23:37. https://doi.org/10.1145/2063231.2063237.

Valve Corporation. (2000). *Counter-Strike*. Valve Corporation.

Valve Corporation. (2007). *Team Fortress 2*. Valve Corporation.

Valve Corporation. (2011). *Portal 2*. Valve Corporation.

Van Lier, L. (2004). *The Ecology of Language Learning: Practice to Theory, Theory to Practice*. Presented at the UC Language Consortium Conference on Theoretical and Pedagogical Perspectives, University of California, Santa Cruz.

White, S. S., Mueller-Hanson, R. A., Dorsey, D. W., Pulakos, E. D., Wisecarver, M. M., Deagle, E. A., & Mendini, K. G. (2005). *Developing Adaptive Proficiency in Special Forces Officers*. Arlington, VA: U.S. Army Research Institute for the Behavioral and Social Sciences.

Williams, B. (2001). Developing Critical Reflection for Professional Practice Through Problem-Based Learning. *Journal of Advanced Nursing, 34*(1), 27–34. https://doi.org/10.1046/j.1365-2648.2001.3411737.x.

Xanthopoulou, D., & Papagiannidis, S. (2012). Play Online, Work Better? Examining the Spillover of Active Learning and Transformational Leadership. *Technological Forecasting and Social Change, 79*(7), 1328–1339. https://doi.org/10.1016/j.techfore.2012.03.006.

Zauszniewski, J. A., Lai, C.-Y., & Tithiphontumrong, S. (2006). Development and Testing of the Resourcefulness Scale for Older Adults. *Journal of Nursing Measurement, 14*(1), 57–68. https://doi.org/10.1891/jnum.14.1.57.

6

The Educator Perspective

This book has largely focused on one particular application of game-based learning in higher education, concerning the use of commercial video games to develop graduate skills or attributes. However, games are used in a multitude of ways throughout higher education, and this chapter draws on interviews with educators to provide examples of the novel ways in which games and gamification are being used to teach or otherwise develop university students.

The Practice of Game-Based Learning

Video games are not widely used with the intention of developing graduate skills—at least, not yet—but they are utilised by some educators to support the teaching of subject-related material. Using games in such a manner does not preclude skills development, however, and those educators who leverage video games to develop students' disciplinary knowledge are aware of the potential for these games to develop skills and competencies in their students.

© The Author(s) 2019
M. Barr, *Graduate Skills and Game-Based Learning*, Digital Education and Learning,
https://doi.org/10.1007/978-3-030-27786-4_6

Steve Connelly is a Senior Lecturer in the Department of Urban Studies and Planning at the University of Sheffield in the UK. Connelly delivers a module titled "Sustainable Development: A Critical Perspective" to an increasingly international cohort of students. Remarking that he has "never been one for standing up in front of the class and lecturing for two hours", Connelly describes how his approach to teaching the module incorporated short lectures augmented by student exercises and discussion, with students presenting material based on, for example, their home town. However, despite this enlightened approach to delivering the module, Connelly began to observe a fall in student participation. Furthermore, students were struggling to understand sustainable development as "a political and very contested idea" with complicated underlying policy processes. And so, drawing on his knowledge of problem-based and experiential learning, Connelly decided to try something different:

> I took the crazy idea of seeing whether getting people to do something that was supposed to be sustainable, in real time in the class, would actually be a better way of doing these things. The idea of using Cities: Skylines was born, which to me was insane, because I don't do computer games.

Acknowledging this dearth of gaming experience, Connelly approached learning technologist Bryony Olney for support. Now Higher Education Training Consultant for Pearson Education, Olney immediately thought of the *SimCity* series (Maxis 1989–), which might offer opportunities to examine sustainability as applied in a city context. However, after some investigation, it emerged that *Cities: Skylines* (Colossal Order 2015) had been used by urban planners in the US for consultation exercises and planning competitions. So, as Olney puts it, "if it was favoured amongst the urban planning and design fraternity, I thought that was probably quite a good place to start". With no previous experience of playing *Cities: Skylines*, the learning technologist was forced to spend many long hours with the game: "a hardship, as you can imagine". Olney's goal was to determine if *Cities* could be used to illustrate the model underpinning Connelly's module: the 'Connelly Triangle', which considers sustainability in terms of economic, environmental, and social concerns (Connelly 2007). And, while certain social factors were absent—the game lacks any representation of religion or ethnicity, for example—the financial and environmental aspects of the Connelly Triangle were better served by the game's mechanics. Olney and Connelly remained concerned, however, about "what black box coding, what assumptions the game had made"; for example, the assumption that renewable energy sources, while ecologically clean, are always very expensive. A great many more such assumptions are built into the game's logic, and often not made explicit to the player. Furthermore, aside from the absence of religion and ethnicity, the game necessarily eschews numerous other factors and processes that influence the planning and sustainability of a city, such as gentrification.

However, the limitations of the game as a system—echoing Kurt Squire's early experiences with *Civilization III* (Firaxis Games 2001)—became a focus of the learning. Instead of accepting the version of the world that *Cities: Skylines* presented, the students were encouraged to critically reflect on and discuss how the game differed from reality. Olney summarises the role of the game as follows:

So, really, the use of the game was a lever, it wasn't the be all and end all, it wasn't the thing that everything hinged on, it was kind of a pivot point for them to reflect on some of the theoretical concepts that they were exploring in the sessions.

What is interesting to note here is that while *Cities: Skylines* enhanced the students' understanding of subject-specific material, the game also allowed them to exercise their critical thinking and reflective learning. This was exactly what Connelly had hoped to achieve: in addition to the 'substantive content', he also intended that students developed "the political and the critical understanding of how contested the concept was".

While Connelly and Olney found *Cities: Skylines* better suited to their needs, the venerable *SimCity* continues to enjoy widespread use in education. Vanessa Haddad, Assistant Professor and chair of Liberal Arts, General Studies at the State University of New York (SUNY) Erie in New York, US, has used the game to teach an introductory sociology course, for example. While her experience was marred somewhat by technical challenges—discussed below—Haddad describes the exercise as 'semi-successful'. With the aim of helping students understand how factors including law, health care, economics, and politics intersect in relation to sociological theory, Haddad observed that students did gain something from playing the game:

> *Students were able to make connections between very basic functional perspectives—conflict theory, that kind of thing—and seeing what the interplay between social structure looked like in a stimulated environment. And then they had to make decisions about those things. So, it was a good starting exercise.*

Heinrich Söbke, of Bauhaus-Universität Weimar in Germany, uses *SimCity 4* (Maxis 2003) in delivering a technical infrastructure management course (Arnold and Söbke 2019). Just as Haddad's goal was to illuminate the intersections between myriad factors, the aim here is to help students understand the many interdependencies in a complex system. Using the game, Söbke can demonstrate that controlling technical infrastructure systems "requires the observation of the effects of these interdependencies and immediate reaction to system changes". Students play the game in groups, with each group's screen projected on to the wall, allowing everyone in the room to monitor everyone else's progress. Söbke runs three supervised sessions: an introductory play session, intended to familiarise students with the game; a session based on a given scenario, where the city zones are already laid out; and, a free play session where students must develop their own scenario from scratch, according to a given specification and assessment scheme. At the end of this session, students are debriefed, and the game status assessed. Söbke is satisfied that the students come away with an understanding of infrastructure planning and the need to "react immediately to an imbalanced development".

Söbke highlights the time pressure under which the students must operate—simulating real-world conditions—while emphasising that teamwork is essential to achieving a positive outcome. One member of the group might deal with the moment-to-moment micromanagement of the city, while another identifies the measures required to keep the system in balance, while still another monitors and reports back on the other groups' progress. Thus, playing the ostensibly single-player *SimCity* in this configuration exercises collaborative and communicative skills in addition to the critical thinking and reflection that playing the game normally demands.

Aside from *SimCity*, Vanessa Haddad uses a number of indie games in her teaching, including *Two Interviewees* (Mauro Vanetti 2016) and *Every Day the Same Dream* (Paolo Pedercini 2009).[1] *Two Interviewees* is intended to expose the often hidden gender bias that is embedded in the recruitment process, as Haddad explains:

> *It shows gender bias in interviewing a male and a female character. You have to make the same decisions for both of them and it shows through empirical research what the outcomes of those decisions would be for both the male and the female character. It's a really great discussion point for students, for showing what they might be up against in the future and of thinking about how they present themselves in the marketplace.*

Haddad has used the game to teach rhetoric, for example, in relation to existentialism. As part of her sociology class, she also uses *Two Interviewees* to help students develop an 'empathetic understanding' of concepts such as labour alienation. She believes that in higher education, much of our time is spent talking about terms and concepts, as presented in books, and that students want something more:

> *Often, I have found students are looking for more of a connection beyond just what's in our books and what we are trying to present in a lecture. So, I bridge the gap with that game into an emotional understanding of something that's very Marxist but also a reality that students might themselves face, should they not make decisions that are in line with who they are and their identity.*

Tom Boylston, Lecturer in Social Anthropology at the University of Edinburgh in the UK, also sees value in the capacity for games to elicit empathy in his students, describing his use of the text-based title, *The Long Day of Young Peng* (Andrea E. Pia n.d.). The creation of a team led by anthropologist Andrea E. Pia, *Peng* allows the player to experience what it is like to migrate from rural China to Beijing, based on Pia's ethnographic work in the region. Boylston is enthusiastic about the game's impact, observing that students became more confident in their understanding of the material and associated readings:

It's really realistic fantastic and it's experimenting with a different way of communicating ethnographic experience, getting students to empathise in different ways or to see field sites from a different perspective and it's something you couldn't do without a game.

Johansen Quijano is Assistant Professor of English at Tarrant County College, Texas, US, and has long argued in favour of using games in the teaching of English as a second language (ESL). More recently, he has used games to introduce students to literature and composition, where, like Haddad, he uses the medium to illustrate rhetorical concepts. Quijano describes the purpose of his game-based ESL classes as "to help students develop their reading and listening skills during play and then practice their spoken and written skills via in-class discussion and short written assignments". In Quijano (2007), role-playing games (RPGs) are identified as the ideal genre for teaching ESL, due to the games' typically voluminous quantities of spoken dialogue and written text. In particular, Quijano points to the *Final Fantasy* and *Tales Of* series, including entries *Final Fantasy XIII* (*Square Enix 1st Production Department* 2009) and *Tales of Vesperia* (Namco Tales Studio 2008).

Quijano is broadly positive about using these games to teach English as a second language, noting that "the students did practice and improve their language skills and the results showed that students improved more than students from sections where only print texts were used". However, he did not observe any significant difference in learning outcomes when comparing the game-based approach to using short stories supplemented with recorded readings. Furthermore, Quijano "noticed that while students who already played video games were more engaged in class discussions than average students, students who didn't care much for video games were apprehensive". This observation extends to the composition and literature classes that Quijano delivers using games: the student response is mostly positive, but, "there are always a handful of students who claim to hate video games and thus refuse to participate in class discussions and procrastinate in their written assignments".

The composition classes are intended to "help students think critically about texts, media, and society" and to "master basic rhetorical concepts", including logos, ethos, pathos, and rhetorical situation. The games used here include *Every Day the Same Dream* and *The Republia Times* (Lucas Pope 2012), the latter of which is set in one of the fictional nations that feature in *Papers, Please* (3909 LLC 2013)—another of Lucas Pope's titles, used in the study described in previous chapters to exercise critical thinking. Indeed, while he has not empirically measured the impact of *The Republia Times* on students' critical thinking ability, this is one of Quijano's intended learning outcomes for the composition classes. Usefully, Quijano has conducted an A/B study to determine the impact of using such games to teach rhetoric and initial analysis of these data suggests that the games "have a strong positive impact on students' knowledge of rhetorical concepts". He also suspects that students are developing a deeper systemic understanding of the world:

I have also observed that students in the sections where I use games have a more thorough understanding of the systems that shape our society—legal, education, media, et cetera—and are more willing to dig deeper when trying to understand how we are influenced by our surroundings than students who don't discuss these games in class.

Quijano uses a wide range of games to teach literature, with the intention to help his students "better understand character development and narrative structures, specifically focusing on time and narrative, and setting and narrative", while also helping them to learn to think critically about a text. Drawing out concepts such as setting, plot structure, and character development, Quijano has used games as varied as *Portal* (Valve Corporation 2007a), *Super Mario Bros.* (Nintendo Creative Department 1985), *Beyond: Two Souls* (Quantic Dream 2013), *Life Is Strange* (Dontnod Entertainment 2015), *The Last of Us* (Naughty Dog 2013), and *Chrono Trigger* (Square 1995). He has also used *Second Life* (Linden Lab 2003) to introduce students to literature (Quijano 2016), although, in this author's opinion, *Second Life* does not constitute a game. Again, aside from a minority of students for whom games held zero appeal, Quijano observed positive outcomes from the literature classes:

Students had a stronger grasp of character development and narrative structures as concepts. Perhaps unsurprisingly, students who played games like Beyond:

Two Souls had an especially strong grasp of time in narratives, while students who played Portal *had a stronger grasp of spatial storytelling than average students.*

In a vein similar to Vanessa Haddad's use of games to develop students' 'empathetic understanding', Debra Ramsay, Lecturer in Film at University of Exeter, UK, uses games in delivering a module on affect. Here, Ramsay has the class play *Battlefield 1* (EA DICE 2016) together in a room, taking turns with the controls, to illustrate how the medium can elicit an affective response:

One of the things that interests me is the kind of affective shifts that happen during game play. So, you can go from those moments of intense excitement, to moments of different kinds of emotions within seconds. And there's no contradiction there, necessarily.

Ramsay found that, while the students might need such affective shifts pointed out to them, "once they start clocking it, then it's really exciting to see them starting to think about how that's working, and why it might be working the way it is". Naturally, some students were unfamiliar with video games and struggled somewhat with the controls, but Ramsay uses this as an opportunity to show that the affective experience that a medium can provide is mediated by its interface:

It's not necessarily all about a smooth, narrative experience. It can, sometimes, just be about, oh, my God, I'm stuck in a trench and I don't know how to get out.

Sherry Jones is a subject matter expert and instructor at Rocky Mountain College of Art and Design, Colorado, US, who has utilised everything from MOOCs (Massive Open Online Courses) to escape rooms in her teaching and has made extensive use of games. Back in 2013, Jones obtained a grant to develop and deliver a MOOC that taught rhetoric and composition. What was different about her approach was that, while there was a supplementary textbook for the course, it was not required reading. Instead, Jones suggested over 50 games from which students should choose to play in order to learn about rhetoric and composition. Each week, students were asked a series of questions about their selected game, related to how the rhetoric of the game was expressed. The approach builds upon Ian Bogost's work on the procedural rhetoric of games (Bogost 2010):

> *We put* [Bogost's procedural rhetoric] *into action but we made it full-scale, so we said, 'if you examine what this game is doing, considering what the narrative is doing and concerning the specific mechanics that are implemented, what kind of political message is this game expressing, what kind of social message is this game expressing?'*

Jones now uses games to teach moral philosophy and cites *Fallout Shelter* (Bethesda Game Studios 2015) as an example of one of the many games she incorporates into her classes. Inspired by the McCarthyism of 1950s US politics, and the anti-Communist paranoia that fuelled fears of nuclear Armageddon, *Fallout Shelter* provided Jones' students with an opportunity to study the theory of egoism, which suggests any action is morally justified if it serves self-interest. In the world presented by the *Fallout* series, egoism—and its capitalist and corporatist manifestations— has apparently led to the destruction of civilisation and, yet, still governs the actions of the surviving few.

Over time, Jones' approach has evolved from treating games as texts to be studied, to using them as a form of assessment. As Jones remarks, "no teacher should think, yes, I'll just give a game to a student and they'll just learn something. Well, they play games on their own, they don't learn anything." Instead, Jones teaches her students the relevant theory in a more conventional manner, through lectures, readings, and discussion, then asks the students to play a particular game without any specific direction. The students make notes and take screenshots as they play, assembling a corpus of data about the game. Then, Jones asks the students to identify which of the taught theories is manifested in the game, using the materials they have gathered to produce a report that demonstrates how, for example, the game illustrated a specific virtue. Jones elaborates:

> *So, we do very deep analysis of the game, but the point of this exercise is that the students were already taught theory before they were getting to play the game. I never tell the students, 'hey this is a theory you're supposed to get from the game'. I just tell them, you need to play the game, with a scholarly mind.*

Nudging her students towards the upper reaches of Bloom's taxonomy, Jones finally asks them to redesign their game so that it either represents an alternative philosophical position, or reinforces the philosophy already present in the game by incorporating additional elements. Such elements might include a new narrative, additional characters, or modified game mechanics.

Responses to Game-Based Learning

While some educators enjoyed a uniformly positive response from students—Tom Boylston, for example, "found it universally a positive experience and something students wanted more of"—others encountered variability in their students' enthusiasm for game-based learning. As noted above, Johansen Quijano reports that most of his ESL, composition, and literature students—around 90–95%, by his estimate—were positive about the game-based classes. However, it is useful to understand the attitudes of those students who were less open to playing games in class and Quijano suggests that such students believe that "games are for losers" or "they're just pointless activities". These are attitudes that several other educators have encountered, as Sherry Jones remarks, "their parents and other people tell them games are frivolous, games are low-brow". Jones goes so far as to reveal that she has "lost a couple of students because they want the old school, me lecture, lecture and they write, write, write and they take a test". More astonishingly, perhaps, Jones has encountered student resistance to games that feature LGBTQ themes or characters, despite such themes being included in the syllabus.

Steve Connelly reports no such push back from his urban planning students, although his colleague Bryony Olney observed that "inevitably we had some students that were more adept and interested in using the game". Meanwhile, both Connelly and Olney report that no real improvement in the quality of students' submitted work was observed. However, Connelly remains confident that, as a pilot of something new, the game-based approach was successful enough to warrant another attempt—not least because the pilot coincided with industrial action across the UK, meaning that the module was not delivered in quite the fashion he would have preferred. Connelly summarises the student response as follows:

Some of the feedback was absolutely wonderful. You know, people saying things like, 'it's helped me understand sustainable development in a much deeper and richer way than I would possibly have done just by being lectured at'. You know, bang on exactly what I was trying to get across.

In addition to using games to look at affect, Debra Ramsay includes games in her module on media and war, "in an attempt to get [the students] to understand, not just different representations of war, but the profound relationships between various media industries and the military". Ramsay notes that she, too, encounters a degree of scepticism from some students, but this quickly evaporates:

There's a bit of a snobbery about games. You always have a number of them going, 'this is nonsense', or 'I don't like violent games'. And within seconds of starting to play it's like, oh, my God, I shot him in the head. And there's a lot of excitement and competitiveness there, which is exactly what I'm teaching them about.

Many interviewees described supportive institutional environments that enabled—or, at least, did not obstruct—their use of games in higher education. Steve Connelly, for example, enjoyed the support of a dedicated and enthusiastic learning technologist in Bryony Olney. Andrew Peterson runs a game-based learning institute at Ferris State University, which exists to support faculty staff in their efforts to gamify or introduce game-based learning into curricula. Vanessa Haddad highlights that she's had two separate grants to support her use of *SimCity*, although some colleagues don't quite understand what she is trying to achieve with that game. Scout Blum describes a similar experience at Troy University, New York, US, where the response has been, for the most part, very positive:

You get some professors who think that if you're playing games it's not really serious or academic, and I think that mainly just stems from them not knowing what we're doing, in the classroom. And once they see what I'm doing, they do understand better, that it is very rigorous, or it can be, anyway.

While at the Rochester Institute of Technology, New York, US, Andy Phelps also noted the effect that receiving a grant to do game-based work can have on institutional reception. He recalls the increase in 'buy-in' that resulted from receiving funds from Microsoft Research: "The minute that you get outside funding, people are like, oh, well, this must be good."

So, a picture begins to emerge of shifting attitudes to game-based learning at universities, where the idea is more widely embraced. But this support is still far from universal and, in some cases, institutional attitudes might be better described as tolerant of, or even oblivious to, game-based activities on campus. Clara O'Shea, for example, describes the relatively privileged position she and her colleagues enjoy at the University of Edinburgh's Moray House School of Education. Here, several senior figures at the university have a personal interest in the programme that O'Shea delivers, affording her tacit approval of her game-based efforts. However, even in this case, O'Shea notes that they are able to do what they do partly by virtue of the fact that the university "doesn't really know what we're up to". Heinrich Söbke similarly describes how his use of *SimCity* flies under the radar: "there is no institutional resistance as the usage of *SimCity* is not stated in any curricula or course description which has to be approved". Indeed, while Söbke notes that there are some lecturers and students who appreciate the "enormous potential" of game-based learning in higher education, "often games are not considered as a kind of serious learning".

In some cases, the challenge of using games in higher education is technical in nature rather than attitudinal. The issue may be as simple as lacking access to a computer lab where digital games may be installed, as Sky LaRell Anderson has experienced at Denison University, Ohio, US, while more complex challenges are associated with the installation and licencing of games in a shared, institutional IT environment. The digital platforms on which PC games are typically distributed require individual log-in credentials for each student. Bryony Olney describes the administrative effort required to manage Steam accounts and individual students' game saves as a "ball ache of epic proportions"—a stance with which this author can empathise. Vanessa Haddad describes similar challenges with using EA's Origin—a rival platform to Steam—to get even a single game on a restricted university machine:

When I planned the exercise, what I didn't anticipate were all the technical challenges that I was going to face and that was very naive on my part. It's one thing to open an indie game on a projector and we all play it together and it's another to purchase licences and set up Origin and get students oriented to a very complex game.

Debra Ramsay highlights the simple but important difference between games and other forms of media that may be used in teaching: "you have to play them". This throws up both logistical challenges ("[students] find it difficult to get hold of the equipment they need to play") and attitudinal ("the ones who don't turn up for that gaming session don't necessarily understand why it's important to play, not to watch a walk-through"). Ramsay encountered both "bureaucratic and technical" challenges when attempting to use her institution's shiny new digital humanities lab. The lab was equipped with a "massive, high resolution screen", ideal for playing games, but

Oh, my God, to sort it all out, I'm not joking, it took me three years. And it's three years of talking to people about things like, whose budget do the games console's come out of? Who keeps the games consoles, who's responsible for them? Who keeps the games, how do we make sure that the students can have access to the consoles and the games? How do we set up the games room? All of that kind of thing.

Playing Games at University

It is perhaps no surprise that, despite the inherent challenges, this group of interviewees was positive about the idea of using video games to develop graduate skills. Indeed, as we have seen, even where educators have used games to teach subject-specific material, a common ancillary outcome—intended or otherwise—has been to develop skills including collaboration and critical thinking. When asked if the results of the study described in previous chapters were unexpected, the answer was almost invariably 'no', with interviewees offering their own reflections on why they believed this to be the case.

Andrew Peterson, instructional technology coordinator at Ferris State University, Michigan, US, suggests that to be successful in gaming requires the 'exact same' skills as those measured in our graduates. He highlights the growth of eSports on campus,

> *Competitively playing* Overwatch *is probably one of our biggest digital games and it's the same type of thing: it's leadership, it's communication, it's practice, it's rigour, it's research. The only thing different about that conversation is that it's focused on a game and game play, rather than focused on research methods in … pick your discipline.*

Overwatch (Blizzard Entertainment 2016), of course, is another team-based shooter that builds directly on the success of titles such as *Team Fortress 2* (Valve Corporation 2007b), as used in the study described here. Peterson goes on to suggest that supporting the development of eSports clubs at universities could have positive effects on student transitions and retention, but stresses that further research would be required before asking the university administration to invest in such an initiative. Andy Phelps agrees that the results of this study make 'perfect sense' and also connects the findings with campus-based eSports, noting the role that traditional varsity teams already play in the US. He also highlights the benefits of students taking part in more casual, non-competitive games clubs on campus:

> *What you find is that those students typically develop these really deep friend-ships, they develop a support network, they develop communication skills because they're working in teams to solve problems, all that kind of stuff. So, it doesn't surprise me in the slightest that that's one of the findings there.*

However, Phelps is very clear that professional, competitive eSports and casual games clubs are not to be confused: "let's just understand that there are many varied forms of play and that each of them have value". Peterson suggests that some of the value of more casual gaming on campus may lie in the attendant opportunities for socialising:

> *We've seen success with it, even just playing socially, building up those social circles. At the previous institution I worked at, West Shore Community College,*

we would regularly have a LAN party [wherein multiplayer games are played over a local area network] *and you would see the friendships that came out of that, would last their entire career there.*

Like Peterson and Phelps, many of the educators interviewed here were supportive of the idea that playing video games on campus can develop students' communication skills. As Sherry Jones, who serves on the Steering Committee Board of the International Game Developers Association (IGDA)'s Learning, Education and Games (LEG) Special Interest Group, says, "of course I would totally buy the premise that games improve communication because [players] need to communicate to finish levels and reflect". For Jones, communication is promoted by virtue of the fact that her students are experiencing something together. This applies even if they are playing at separate tables or machines; when they next regroup, they have a shared experience that they can discuss and debate. Of course, in a multiplayer game, such discussion and debate can happen in real time, as Heinrich Söbke notes, "games require students to reach game-defined goals and these goals can be reached more effectively when students collaborate or communicate about possible strategies and solutions". Vanessa Haddad makes a similar observation:

I found whenever I run a game activity or exercise in the classroom, students tend to become much more engaged. They become more talkative. They communicate with each other a lot more and they also communicate more with me and they support each other to problem solve.

The University of Edinburgh's Tom Boylson suggests that the findings described in this book seem 'intuitively correct', and draws parallels with his experience of running tabletop *Dungeons & Dragons* sessions on campus:

It fostered a different way for them to interact with each other. And, they started bringing in ideas that we'd used in the readings in different ways. So, they were using the space differently, they were able to express themselves differently.

Indeed, many of the educators interviewed here make use of a range of analogue games in their teaching, from tabletop games like *D&D* to LARP (live action role-play). Andrew Peterson, for example, describes how he has used board games such as *Pandemic* in a variety of educational contexts, including a communication class. And non-digital games are used to support the teaching of subject-specific material, including Sky LaRell Anderson's incorporation of *Monopoly* into his classes:

> *I was teaching about how interactive, or procedural, rhetoric interacts with other rhetorics: the rules of* Monopoly *present a rhetoric that is quite critical of capitalism, but the experience of playing the game, the colorful money, the social interaction, et cetera, all speak to the fun or excitement of capitalistic competition.*

Scout Blum describes how she uses board game *Settlers of Catan* to supplement her teaching on the origins of civilisation. Following a lecture on the subject, Blum's students are asked to play the game and reflect on the fact that it does not include any representation of warfare. This leads to a discussion of how the game codifies certain cultural beliefs and how these beliefs relate to the historical context in which the game was designed. Both Blum and Peterson refer to the Reacting to the Past (RTTP) series of role-playing games that run out of Barnard College at Columbia University in the US. Blum describes the games as follows:

> *Their games are role-playing games where the students are put into historical situations and they're given a role to play as a real person in history. They have to manage their way through a certain situation, looking at documents from the time period and figure how they would make those decisions based on the character they are.*

Peterson, who has written about the use of LARP in education (Vanek and Peterson 2016), describes one RTTP scenario, based on the Democratic National Convention in Chicago in 1968:

There's all sorts of very US-centric politics that are involved with the civil rights, Vietnam, there's some racism overtones, a lot of your typical politics, lobbyists, journalists, senators, all trying to figure out where the national Democratic Party is going to head, at that time. So, you end up having a lot of personalities debating major points of national politics.

For Peterson, the incorporation of role-playing gives students "something meaningful to debate and so you're actually trying to persuade someone that your character is passionate about, rather than just a fluff piece". And this is what makes the RTTP series so relevant here: it is not delivered as part of a History class, but, rather, as a means of developing the students' communication and debating skills. As Peterson explains:

We've never actually run a Reacting to the Past scenario in a history course. So, all of the history, it's not a primary focus of the game itself. We want the student to be able to give a decent speech and so the whole class, leading up to this game, they've been learning about how to give a good speech. This is just their way to showcase that skill, so that we can assess that, and anything that they would have learned about history or politics, really becomes secondary.

Blum sees how the role-playing game could develop other graduate skills, too, noting that as the students played, they would have to determine how their character would have reacted. As she explains, "that really pushes them to listen and to be adaptable and to be able to apply knowledge and to be resourceful. We definitely see that with the students of the role-playing games, absolutely."

Returning to video games, and looking beyond communication and collaboration, interviewees suggested that games might help develop other of the graduate skills examined here, including those which are not always explicitly taught or measured. Heinrich Söbke, for example, suggests that because players are tasked with determining the most efficient strategies for reaching in-game goals, limited only by the formal rules of the game, both adaptability and resourcefulness are fostered. Stephen Connelly, noting that such skills acquisition isn't directly assessed, says he would expect that "critical thinking, being able to extract ideas into practice and then being reflective about that, those raw skills, gaming would be very good at teaching". Debra Ramsay, drawing parallels with the military, suggests a range of skills that games could hone: "it can be things like teamwork, the ability to process a great deal of information very quickly, and make snap decisions about that information, which is exactly the kind of skills that soldiers need". In short, there was little resistance to the idea that video games could be used to enhance graduate skills.

However, while he is not surprised by the findings in this book, Sky LaRell Anderson argues that "any well-applied learning activity can aid students in learning those skills". Perhaps, then, games are simply another tool we can use to support the development of our students' skills and competencies, albeit a potentially powerful tool. Bryony Olney, recalling how Arnseth et al. (2018) used a game to "to spark conversation and reflection and dialogue", rather than making the game 'the thing', suggests that this is the role the games have played here: that of a 'great tool' for developing communication, adaptability, and resourcefulness.

And, as Clara O'Shea suggests, more traditional learning activities may be enhanced by incorporating game-like components into their design. Perhaps the most widely accepted definition of gamification is that offered by Sebastian Deterding and colleagues: "the use of game design elements in nongame contexts" (Deterding et al. 2011), and that is just what O'Shea describes in relation to her 'course cup', where students are rewarded with points for engaging with the course:

I don't think it necessarily has to be a game; I think a playful approach can be quite fun. I wouldn't necessarily class the course cup as a game, but it's certainly playful, and so I think there's space for that. I think there is a huge amount about the way the games work that could be really useful, particularly in terms of motivation and immersion and flow, and the ability to fail and it not be the end of the world.

While the gamification of learning is not the focus of this book, it is important to acknowledge that efforts are underway to gamify higher education, primarily "to improve student engagement, motivation, and performance" (Subhash and Cudney 2018). It is also useful to differentiate between gamification and game-based learning, where the former concerns the use of elements such as points, leaderboards, or role-playing in a real-world scenario, and the latter refers to the use of actual video games in a learning environment. It may seem pedantic, but the terms are frequently confused, with game-based learning interventions such as that described in this book often referred to as 'gamification'. This, in turn, creates a muddied picture of current practice in higher education and beyond. Returning to O'Shea's course cup, this is an example of what Kapp et al. (2014) refer to as "structural gamification", or "the application of game elements to propel a learner through content with no alteration or changes to the content". This is by far the most common implementation of gamification in higher education, and it may be used to improve student engagement with specific taught material, such as an undergraduate course (Dias 2017), or with university services, such as the library (Barr et al. 2016) and other facilities (Martinez et al. 2012). Less common is the form of gamification that Kapp et al. term "content gamification", or "the application of game elements, game mechanics and game thinking to alter content to make it more game-like". However, the LARP-based classes that both Peterson and Blum describe above are a strong example of such content gamification in higher education: here, the game *is* the class.

Vanessa Haddad believes that "there's so much to be gained from incorporating various types of games in and outside of the classroom, whether it's teamwork, problem-solving, collaboration, improving communication skills, empathy development, or learning content". For Haddad, to ignore video games in higher education is a "hugely missed opportunity". Debra Ramsay sees similar potential in games and observes that only recently has the medium of television been accepted into higher education. She is emphatic about games' inclusion in the curriculum:

Absolutely. Every single one of my students will have played a game of some kind. And the fact that we're just ignoring this massive medium, well it's not a medium really, it's a series of enabling technologies, but the fact that we're just ignoring it, and pretending it's not there, does my head in.

Indeed, while it is notable that any such validation is required, this is how Sherry Jones justifies her use of games in the classroom, by saying "it's just another medium". Sky LaRell Anderson makes a similar point, suggesting that "all forms of popular culture should be standard experiences for students, including literature, films, television, et cetera. They need to become literate in the media that surrounds them, including games." For Scout Blum, this requires educators to be able to adapt to using a range of media, including games, to engage learners:

We need to utilise different methods to get to our students. A lecture-only based class may work very well for some students, but it doesn't work well for all of them. And so, we need to be able to use different methods and to use things that are engaging, to get students into different topics in the classroom.

Heinrich Söbke agrees that games, as a medium, should be included in higher education curricula, suggesting that they "connect to the personal experiences" of students for whom such digital media are a familiar means of engaging with the world. Meanwhile, for Andrew Peterson, playing video games with students—demonstrating that we are familiar with the medium, too—helps bolster the teaching staff's 'social credibility'. This, in turn, eliminates the stigma that many students feel exists around coming to their professors for help:

Being able to frag [blow up] your professor, all of a sudden, there's no concern, there's no barrier for them coming to see me during office hours because they've gamed with me, they've killed me in the game, many, many, many times.

So, should video games be played at university? These educators certainly believe that games have a role to play in higher education, although some caveats apply. Heinrich Söbke, for example, believes that there remains untapped potential for using games but observes that "an appropriate didactical context has to be ensured"; the game must be presented in such a way as to support learning, without lessening its inherent appeal. Söbke notes that when playing a game is framed as a mandatory exercise, any sense of playfulness is diminished, and the experience may be perceived as work. This observation, of course, recalls classic definitions of play, such as those offered by Huizinga and Caillois, which invariably state that play must be a voluntary activity. Sherry Jones similarly stresses the importance of scaffolding the gaming experience such that the student may learn from it; it is not enough to "throw it at them and go, 'figure it out'". Jones refers to this scaffolding process as priming: "you've got to prime their brain, so they know what they're looking for, otherwise what are we doing? Just throwing cookies at them, and that doesn't make any sense."

There are other concerns about incorporating video games into university provision, too. Related to his comments above about observing the separation between different forms of play, Andy Phelps is uneasy about the boundaries between playing games for academic purposes and playing games for leisure becoming blurred. Phelps advocates for 'thoughtful' use of games within higher education, acknowledging that to not have games played on campus would be to "censor a form of our culture", while also being wary of positioning games as another domain of academia. Finally, Bryony Olney voices concerns about assuming video games will appeal to all students, as was touched upon in the discussion of Gee's learning principles in Chap. 1:

I'm mindful of those students that aren't game players and making sure that there are enough activities to draw them in and keep them engaged, and that they know the value of what they're doing.

As Olney indicates, a student's interest in playing a game at university will quickly wane if they fail to see how it is relevant to their studies, a problem that can only be exacerbated where the student is already apathetic towards the medium. A lack of interest in video games can be a result of factors other than personal preference, too: as Olney highlights, there exists a digital divide that sees a portion of the population entirely alienated by digital technology, including games. When underlying factors such as age and socioeconomic background are taken into consideration, the fact that video games may seem wholly uninviting to some students starts to become an issue of accessibility. This is a concern that will most likely pale into insignificance with time, but, for now, educators must be cognizant of the risk of excluding a minority of their students if they opt to embrace game-based learning in higher education.

Summary

In this chapter, we have seen how a selection of educators from different disciplines are using video games in higher education. Their experiences have been almost uniformly positive, although concern about excluding a small proportion of the class, for whom games are unappealing, was raised by several interviewees. In most cases, game-based learning activities are tied to the delivery of subject material, but educators are well aware that video games may also exercise a range of valuable skills and competencies. Interviewees here referred to ancillary outcomes that include the development of their students' communication and collaboration skills, their critical thinking ability, and their capacity to empathise and reflect. Of course, the transmission of disciplinary knowledge and understanding is not divorced from the development of such abilities—these are 'graduate skills', after all—and being able to think critically and reflect upon the learning experience is often crucial to a student's mastery of their subject. What we might surmise from the examples above, however, is that video games are particularly well suited to nurturing those skills in our students. As Andrew Peterson remarks, "once you see it and you're in that environment, it seems obvious".

Note

1. Haddad's use of *Every Day the Same Dream* is documented in *100 Games to Use in the Classroom & Beyond* (2019), edited by Karen Schrier.

References

3909 LLC. (2013). *Papers, Please*. 3909 LLC.
Andrea E. Pia. (n.d.). *The Long Day of Young Peng*. Andrea E. Pia.
Arnold, U., & Söbke, H. (2019). SimCity 4. In *100 Games to Use in the Classroom & Beyond* (Vol. 3). Halifax, NS: ETC Press.
Arnseth, H. C., Hanghøj, T., & Silseth, K. (2018). Games as Tools for Dialogic Teaching and Learning: Outlining a Pedagogical Model for Researching and

Designing Game-Based Learning Environments. *Games and Education: Designs in and for Learning*, 123–139. https://doi.org/10.1163/978900 4388826_008.

Barr, M., Munro, K., & Hopfgartner, F. (2016). Increasing Engagement with the Library via Gamification. In *Proceedings of the GamifIR 2016 Workshop*, Pisa, Italy. Retrieved January 7, 2017.

Bethesda Game Studios. (2015). *Fallout Shelter*. Bethesda Softworks.

Blizzard Entertainment. (2016). *Overwatch*. Blizzard Entertainment.

Bogost, I. (2010). *Persuasive Games: The Expressive Power of Videogames*. Cambridge, MA: MIT Press.

Colossal Order. (2015). *Cities: Skylines*. Paradox Interactive.

Connelly, S. (2007). Mapping Sustainable Development as a Contested Concept. *Local Environment, 12*(3), 259–278. https://doi.org/10.1080/13549830601183289.

Deterding, S., Khaled, R., Nacke, L. E., & Dixon, D. (2011). Gamification: Toward a definition. In *Proceedings of CHI 2011 Gamification Workshop* (pp. 1–4). Vancouver, BC, Canada. Retrieved February 4, 2016.

Dias, J. (2017). Teaching Operations Research to Undergraduate Management Students: The Role of Gamification. *The International Journal of Management Education, 15*(1), 98–111. https://doi.org/10.1016/j.ijme.2017.01.002.

Dontnod Entertainment. (2015). *Life Is Strange*. Square Enix.

EA DICE. (2016). *Battlefield 1*. Electronic Arts.

Firaxis Games. (2001). *Civilization III*. Infogrames.

Kapp, K. M., Blair, L., & Mesch, R. (2014). *The Gamification of Learning and Instruction Fieldbook: Ideas into Practice*. San Francisco, CA: Wiley. Retrieved February 4, 2016.

Linden Lab. (2003). *Second Life*. Linden Lab.

Lucas Pope. (2012). *The Republia Times*. Lucas Pope.

Martinez, R., Martin, C., Harris, S., Squire, K., Lawley, E., & Phelps, A. (2012). Just Press Play: Design Implications for Gamifying the Undergraduate Experience. In *Proceedings GLS 8.0* (pp. 9–13). Presented at the Games + Learning + Society Conference, Madison, Wisconsin, USA: ETC Press.

Mauro Vanetti. (2016). *Two Interviewees*. Mauro Vanetti.

Maxis. (1989–). *SimCity Series*. Maxis.

Maxis. (2003). *SimCity 4*. EA Games.

Namco Tales Studio. (2008). *Tales of Vesperia*. Namco Bandai Games.

Naughty Dog. (2013). *The Last of Us*. Sony Interactive Entertainment.

Nintendo Creative Department. (1985). *Super Mario Bros*. Nintendo.

Paolo Pedercini. (2009). *Every Day the Same Dream*. Molleindustria.

Quantic Dream. (2013). *Beyond: Two Souls*. Sony Computer Entertainment.

Quijano, J. (2007). Video Games and the ESL Classroom. *The Internet TESL Journal, 13*, 2. Retrieved May 19, 2019.

Quijano, J. (2016). Engaging Students with Literature in Virtual Spaces: Second Life. In *Teaching Literature with Digital Technology: Assignments*. New York: Bedford/St. Martin's. Retrieved May 19, 2019.

Square. (1995). *Chrono Trigger*. Square Enix.

Square Enix 1st Production Department. (2009). *Final Fantasy XIII*. Square Enix.

Subhash, S., & Cudney, E. A. (2018). Gamified Learning in Higher Education: A Systematic Review of the Literature. *Computers in Human Behavior, 87*, 192–206. https://doi.org/10.1016/j.chb.2018.05.028.

Valve Corporation. (2007a). *Portal*. Valve Corporation.

Valve Corporation. (2007b). *Team Fortress 2*. Valve Corporation.

Vanek, A., & Peterson, A. (2016). Live Action Role-Playing (LARP): Insight into an Underutilized Educational Tool. In *Bringing Games into Educational Contexts* (Vol. 2, pp. 219–240). ETC Press.

7

The Games Industry Perspective

When considering the use of commercial video games in education, it is common to focus on the students and educators engaged in playing the games or designing learning activities around them. Less well documented is how those responsible for producing commercial video games view the educational potential of the medium. Specifically, do commercial game developers think of their games as having the capacity to develop useful skills in those who play them? Or, do they believe video games present players with opportunities to learn something about the world, or about themselves? Might developers consciously include such opportunities in their games, despite their remit to entertain and—in most cases—generate revenue? To explore some of these questions, games industry personnel responsible for developing the games used in the previously described study were interviewed. The interviews began by asking developers if they had considered that their respective games might develop useful skills or experience in players.

Paul Hellquist, Creative Director and Lead Designer on *Borderlands 2* (Gearbox Software 2012), is clear that the development of such skills was not a goal on that game. However, in retrospect, Hellquist identifies how the player's application of critical thinking is embedded in the game's design:

© The Author(s) 2019
M. Barr, *Graduate Skills and Game-Based Learning*, Digital Education and Learning,
https://doi.org/10.1007/978-3-030-27786-4_7

That was certainly not a goal, to make a game that encourages people and helps them learn how to collaborate or whatever. But I definitely can see how the game could help with that. Certainly, critical thinking was important to me. My goal wasn't to teach or to train, but from my game design standpoint, critical thinking was important to me.

Hellquist describes how forcing the player to think critically about the weapons and other loot that they obtain in the game is actually part of the fun. During the development of *Borderlands 2*, this philosophy led to an internal debate about just how much information players should be given about each item they encounter. For weapons, in particular, there was an argument in favour of reducing their on-screen statistics to a single 'damage per second' figure, in a manner similar to *Diablo* (Blizzard North 1996). Hellquist resisted such a move, explaining that because attacks on an enemy in *Diablo* requires nothing more than a click of a mouse, it makes sense to reduce such a transaction down to a simple 'damage per second' calculation. In a shooter like *Borderlands 2*, the outcome of an enemy encounter is affected not only by weapon statistics but also by factors related to player skill. So, from a game design perspective, reducing weapon statistics down to a single 'damage per second' stat made little sense. Instead, players were to be presented with a number of different stats for each weapon, requiring a degree of critical judgement to determine their relative merits:

What I thought was a really important and core element of the fun of looting in Borderlands *was forcing the players to actually look at two weapons and say, 'Hmm, is it more important for me to have a faster reload time or a higher rate of fire? How do I compare those two things? Which one do I think, as a player, will result in a higher damage per second?' I wanted those questions to be unknown, so that players could do that critical thinking and make their own decisions.*

One of the intended side effects of obfuscating the absolute merits of in-game items was to encourage online debate within the player community, which Hellquist feels paid off. Certainly, the game has inspired innumerable online forum posts, player guides, and wiki entries which address—in significant detail—the strengths, weaknesses, and strategies associated with the weapons, characters, enemies, and maps featured in the game.[1] Such collaborative efforts are not uncommon in online gaming communities, of course, and discussion around the more opaque titles is particularly lively. What is notable, perhaps, is the quality of the debate and subsequent documentation that games can inspire. Barr (2014), for example, examines the wikis that players have produced in relation to *Dark Souls* (FromSoftware 2011)—perhaps one of the most opaque mainstream games of recent years. Such wikis, it may be argued, demonstrate significant 'academic' proficiency on the part of the players that construct them, as they critically examine and debate the game's complex inner workings.

Karla Zimonja, Director on *Gone Home* (The Fullbright Company 2013), also connects that game with critical thinking. Here, players are provided with incomplete—and perhaps conflicting—information, which also forces them to think critically:

I feel as if there should be a certain amount of critical thinking that Gone Home *could help develop, sure. We definitely tried to not fill in all the blanks, fictionally, but instead to allow room for the player to make the mental leaps themselves. This investment of mental work is much more enjoyable and interesting than just giving the information would have been. Learning is fun and working to understand a thing is super rewarding and satisfying when you succeed.*

For Matt Charles, Producer on *Borderlands 2*, having players develop new skills was a personal goal, although, like his colleague Hellquist, this goal was closely coupled with a desire to make the best possible game.

I believed that I had noticed that really great games challenge you in a new way, and a challenge is really just an opportunity to learn something new. Or, it's a mechanic presented in a new way or maybe it's a recurring mechanic from another game presented in a creative way, in an unexpected way. But either way you're learning, right? You're being challenged by it; it feels fresh and new.

So, for Charles—echoing a sentiment expressed by the likes of James Paul Gee and Raph Koster—part of what makes a game fun is the learning it is designed to elicit. This also chimes with what Zimonja says above in relation to *Gone Home*: learning is fun. As Charles goes on to suggest, if a game feels stale, "that probably means that, well, we're not really engaging the player, they're not having fun, they're not learning anything new". In line with Hellquist's comments above, Charles acknowledges that teaching players anything that might be applicable beyond the game was not the objective on *Borderlands 2*:

> *The mission for* Borderlands 2 *was pretty much more, better* Borderlands. *We're trying to expand the audience, we're trying to gratify more people to a greater degree than we did with the first one, and we're going to do that by refining the things that worked, adding new things to keep people entertained and maybe grow the audience a little bit, and honestly cut the stuff that doesn't work.*

However, Charles is optimistic that some of the design decisions made on *Borderlands 2* might have facilitated personal growth in those who played the game:

> *Maybe they related to a particular character that had a struggle that was represented in a light that they had never considered before. You know, some way of empathising with somebody struggling with something that had never really occurred to them. That's what I'd consider a useful experience, that they might take with them out of the game.*

The empathetic learning potential of games to which Charles alludes here is a phenomenon that has already generated interest amongst academics and is touched on elsewhere in this book. In Chap. 4, for example, participants involved in the study on which this book is based discussed how playing games such as *Gone Home* had presented opportunities to explore new perspectives. Gee's Identity Principle, which states that "learning involves taking on and playing with identities in such a way that the learner has real choices (in developing the virtual identity) and ample opportunity to meditate on the relationship between new identities and old ones" (Gee 2007, p. 67) is also relevant here, as is the growing body of research on games' potential to develop empathy (Bachen et al. 2012; Belman and Flanagan 2010; Harrington and O'Connell 2016). What is interesting to note here is that game developers are aware of such potential.

Mike Ambinder is Principal Experimental Psychologist at Valve, creators of both *Portal 2* (Valve Corporation 2011) and *Team Fortress 2* (Valve Corporation 2007). Ambinder's role involves applying knowledge and methods drawn from the discipline of Psychology to game design; for example, "to foster cooperation or communication among players or to manipulate visual attention on screen or to design experiments for in-game economy". However, like Hellquist and Charles, Ambinder's focus is entirely on making the best possible game, rather than creating an experience that will develop skills:

The underlying goal is always to make something that is entertaining to our customers. Make something they enjoy playing. And that's a nebulous description, but it ends up being something that players will come back to and continue to play over time.

That said, Ambinder can also see potential for exercising skills such as cooperation in Valve's games, citing the acclaimed zombie-themed multiplayer titles in the *Left 4 Dead* series (Valve Corporation 2008–):

Left 4 Dead *and* Left 4 Dead 2 *were specifically designed to enforce cooperation. That was a very specific part of the game design where we did not want to encourage players to go off on their own, so there are consequences for doing that. And we wanted to encourage players to work together, so there are game mechanics that are implemented that directly work to that end. So, when a player is incapacitated, some other player has to save them. You get higher bonuses for getting your entire team to the end of the level as opposed to just one person surviving, for example.*

So, for Ambinder, it comes down to "what kind of game we're making and what kind of behaviours we want to foster", citing a King of the Hill type scenario as an example where encouraging cooperative behaviours would be counter to the goals of the game: "your game mechanics would not encourage that and then you wouldn't get to see those benefits". In general, though, Ambinder suggests it may be *possible* for games to develop useful behaviours in players:

But I think that with games, they are interactive and dynamic and adaptive and constantly changing. So, you do have the ability to elicit certain forms of behaviour that are ancillary to playing the game, but actually end up having better benefits outside the game.

However, Ambinder is very clear that neither he nor Valve would make any such claims about their games' potential to develop useful player behaviours without investigating them thoroughly, citing an "innate scepticism about claims I haven't directly investigated". Ambinder continues:

It's possible, and you know, it'd be great for Valve if that were the case. But the honest answer is I'm not actually sure if that's the case. I think you could walk through logical trains of reasoning, where you're trying to teach problem-solving or critical thinking. Problem-solving is maybe the fundamental tenant of intelligence, and useful across almost every domain of cognition that exists. And, you know, Portal is absolutely a series of problems, and so you have to learn how to solve a series of increasingly more complex challenges. The notion that some of your learnings there could be transferable to other domains is very appealing, but we know transfer of ability or knowledge is difficult and hard to show.

Speaking to Daniel Bryner and Jeff Wajcs, level designers on *Lara Croft and the Guardian of Light* (Crystal Dynamics 2010), a similar picture emerges: while the game was not designed with the intention of developing useful skills in players, the application of certain skills is central to the game's design. Bryner explains that the game was built "from the ground up for couch co-op", meaning that players must communicate constantly in order to succeed—as was observed and commented upon by participants in the experimental study. Wajcs also highlights the cooperative nature of the game:

The Guardian of Light is a cooperative game that encourages players to work together to solve its puzzles and working cooperatively is another valuable skill in the real world.

Wajcs is clear that *The Guardian of Light* was not intended to develop attributes like communication skill, resourcefulness, or adaptability, expressing surprise that this may be the case. He can, however, see the potential for the transfer of related skills, such as problem-solving:

Certainly, using a bomb to knock a boulder onto a pressure plate is not a skill that has many real-world applications, but problem-solving and 'thinking outside the box' are two very valuable skills in a wide range of fields. Perhaps in solving these puzzles, the players are waking up and exercising specific problem-solving muscles in their brains that they could then apply in other contexts.

However, while the developers "worked very hard to add plenty of moments of player cooperation" to the game, Wajcs notes that the potential to subvert this spirit of cooperation might result in a life lesson of a rather different sort:

At the same time, The Guardian of Light *also encouraged players to 'grief' each other relentlessly. My favorite moments in that game have been using bombs to knock my partner into a pit of spikes or letting go of the rope and letting my partner fall into lava. Hopefully, learning to never trust another human being ever again was not a lesson that players were taking away from our game!*

Minecraft (Mojang 2011) is a game that has, unlike the titles discussed thus far, become closely associated with learning, to the extent that Microsoft have released a modified version of the game, *Minecraft: Education Edition*, for use in formal learning environments such as schools. While the original manifestation of the game may not have been intended to develop useful skills in its players, there is little doubt that this is the intention of the team behind its educational incarnation. When asked if *Minecraft* can develop skills like communication, resourcefulness and adaptability, Deirdre Quarnstrom, General Manager for *Minecraft: Education Edition*, is very confident that it can:

Yeah, definitely. Those are some of the top skills that we hear from educators who bring Minecraft *into their classroom. And often what we've seen is, they have brought it in for a specific subject area. But what the teachers report out is they actually see much bigger gains and opportunities in areas like adaptability, communication, collaboration, problem-solving.*

Neal Manegold, former Director on *Minecraft: Education Edition*, reflects on his use of *Minecraft* in the classroom, noting that the game excels at developing otherwise nebulous skills and experience in students:

As a teacher, we always struggle: how do you teach creativity, how do you teach collaboration? And what I've seen with Minecraft *since I think the very first class that I did three years ago, is those kinds of skills are being built alongside the game. All of them, but especially the collaboration between students; debating and discussing and having conversations in ways that we know will benefit them for both college and career.*

Quarnstrom goes on to describe her first trip to Stockholm to meet some of the original Mojang team to ask them about their educational ambitions for the game. She was initially taken aback when Lydia Winters, brand director for the *Minecraft* franchise, replied, "well, we want to change the world". However, as the conversation progressed, Winters expanded on this ambition:

She explained that we have people who are playing Minecraft *that are learning about consequences and rules of society. The next generation of world leaders are growing up playing online video games like* Minecraft. *And really, exploring collaboration and virtual spaces, which describes how so many of us work together so much.*

So, it seems that those involved in the development of *Minecraft* do see the game playing a role in shaping its players, particularly where the development of key '21st century skills' such as virtual collaboration and communication are concerned.

Considering titles beyond those on which they had worked, the developers consulted here were asked if they thought video games might present players with opportunities to learn something about the world, or about themselves. Valve's Mike Ambinder sees such potential but again stresses that the actuality of such potential remains untested. Ambinder, noting that "games are very useful tools for delivering practice", describes how a player might learn some new skill through the experience of playing a game:

For example, resource allocation in an RTS [real-time strategy] game. Maybe you haven't had much experience in saying, 'I have a fixed number of constraints, a fixed number of resources that will lead to a certain set of outputs. That will have some sort of production, or some sort of measurable impact on the world.' And saying, 'okay, how do I allocate those resources sufficiently to achieve my goals?' It makes sense, anyway, that you'd be able to acquire a skill, a general skill, like resource allocation, or will come across it and then be able to apply that in other domains.

However, while acknowledging that practicing a skill is likely to develop it, Ambinder retains a healthy scepticism about the transferability of such skills, stating that "these notions are more based on the potential of games, as opposed to actually showing the direct impacts of these effects". Indeed, Ambinder is not alone in raising questions about the transferability of skills developed in-game, as discussed below.

Putting *Borderlands 2* to one side, Matt Charles also believes that there is potential for learning from most games, given a suitably reflective player:

Yeah. I think I'd be hard pressed to name a game that doesn't [support learning], *because I think if you're introspective or perhaps open to learning or just engaged with whatever you, as a person, happen to be experiencing at the time, that's always an opportunity to learn something about the world.*

Charles goes on to highlight another Gearbox-developed title, *Brothers in Arms: Hell's Highway* (Gearbox Software 2008), a World War II shooter that draws heavily on historical accounts of the conflict to inform its story and setting. He suggests the game might help develop "emotional maturity or empathy, rather than a particular skill":

It makes you think about the situation that the soldiers were up against and constantly being stuck between a rock and a hard place. It should teach you about the world, it should teach you a little bit about yourself. I think if you're paying a little bit of attention, you come away from that sort of game with a sense of gratitude for all the people that came before you in your life.

However, Charles notes that this is a highly individual response to the game, which is influenced by his personal circumstances—not least the fact that members of his own family had previously served in the military.

As was touched upon by educators in the previous chapter, participation in team sports at university or college is often suggested as a means of developing students' ability to collaborate and communicate. Asked whether multiplayer video games could develop some of the same skills and attributes that team sports are believed to develop, Charles immediately names collaborative pirate adventure, *Sea of Thieves* (Rare 2018), and the indomitable MMORPG (massively multiplayer online role-playing game), *World of Warcraft* (Blizzard Entertainment 2004), noting that many games "teach people how to be social in different ways and be collaborative". Charles also makes the point that board games can exercise the same skills:

> *If this question is applicable to video games it should also be applicable to board games and tabletop games because it's the same sort of interactions in terms of, 'let's all pick out a role and figure out how to collectively—collaboratively, most of the time—solve a particular problem'.*

Minecraft's Neal Manegold agrees, and highlights his previous experience of using board games as an educator before he joined the *Minecraft: Education Edition* team:

> *We did loads of board games, and not only students playing board games and understanding the rules behind them, but also trying to develop their own. I think it was great for them to understand game theory, great for them to understand probability. It's also great for students who, oftentimes, are very rulebound to understand how we might change the rules of this game to have it be more equitable or to have them take some kind of a leadership role.*

The educational and developmental utility of board games and other forms of non-digital gaming is discussed by several educators in the previous chapter. Here, it is interesting to consider the parallels between multiplayer video games and team-based sports, of the sort that students are encouraged to play at university. Fellow *Borderlands 2* alumnus, Paul Hellquist, agrees with Charles on this, noting that for some people, traditional sports lack appeal. However, his views are not coloured by any personal dislike of more athletic pursuits ("sports were, to me, just another type of game"). Hellquist elaborates:

> *In today's world there's so many great multiplayer games that require cooperation if you want to succeed. I think, especially in the club realm, it's definitely just as good as your athletics in terms of helping people. Just meeting people and*

collaborating and coordinating, and all those kinds of skills, for sure. It would
be great to have some more of those kinds of things be a little more recognised by
the universities, as a way to give their students those same sorts of skills.

Lara Croft's Daniel Bryner similarly highlights the communication that underpins many online games, suggesting that *Journey* (Thatgamecompany 2012) should be "top of the list" because it requires players to communicate non-verbally and thus evades the toxicity that unfortunately characterises so many online interactions. Valve's Mike Ambinder also sees potential in multiplayer games, while insisting that we must "operationalise whatever concept it is we're discussing, and then measure it in some fashion" before we can understand any direct benefits. Ambinder points to *DOTA 2* (Valve Corporation 2013), a Multiplayer Online Battle Arena (MOBA) title, wherein a player may have to coordinate a team of five people against an equivalent opposing team, while determining the most efficient path to the enemy base and deploying their hero characters to maximise impact. Ambinder then goes on to describe what is expected of a *World of Warcraft* player, again highlighting the complexity involved in leading a team in that game:

planning raids and getting certain people to coordinate to take down a boss and
understanding exactly what your role is and how to do online problem-solving
in real-time. You have to go through the fight and make sure that you're per-
forming your role and you have situational awareness about what is happening.

While studies suggest that playing team sports may have positive effects on young people's self-esteem and social interaction (Eime et al. 2013), the evidence for sports' capacity to develop the broader set of skills that many assume to be exercised by team play is limited. Extejt and Smith (2009), for example, found no correlation between prior team sports participation at school or college and subsequent leadership skills. Holt et al. (2009), on the other hand, suggest that the attendant peer interaction, not the sports *per se*, was the most important factor in developing players' 'life skills'. As with research into the effects of playing video games, the data on the effects of participating in team sports are too sparse to support any convincing conclusions. Despite this lack of evidence, sports enjoy a rarefied position at college and university, where the benefits—over and above the obvious and real effects on health—are *assumed* to include the development of skills such as leadership, resilience, and communication.

Perhaps the most prevalent theme to emerge from talking to developers about the educational and developmental potential of video games concerned the idea of games providing a safe space to experiment and experience failure. This is an oft-cited idea in the game-based learning literature and, naturally, Gee has identified an associated tenet, the 'Psychosocial Moratorium' Principle, which states that "learners can take risks in a space where real-world consequences are lowered" (Gee 2007, p. 62). Gee's take on this idea is particularly thoughtful: he does not state that the consequences of in-game actions are nil, only that they are lowered. This formulation acknowledges that in-game experiences can, and do, have real-world effects, for example on a player's mood. This is an obvious criticism of Huizinga's 'magic circle' (Huizinga 1949, p. 10) which seems to imply that there is an impermeable boundary that insulates a game from the outside world. The tediousness of the discussion around the magic circle is second only to that which surrounds the 'ludology versus narratology' debate that similarly haunts games scholars, however. The concept will not, therefore, be considered further here but, for an entertaining and enlightening overview of the magic circle discourse, see Zimmerman (2012). The point is, leading a raid that results in the wholesale slaughter of one's party is a bad outcome, yes, but nobody was actually hurt. There is the opportunity to make another attempt, to experiment with another strategy, based on what was learned from the first attempt.

For *Borderlands 2* producer, Matt Charles, this is an important aspect of games' potential to support learning:

> *I feel pretty biased but, yeah, I strongly believe games teach people things. You've got to have play so you can have a safe space to experiment with new thoughts and new ideas, and games allow the space to have safe play.*

Minecraft's Neal Manegold observed the benefits of providing an "empathetic safe space to explore" while working in special education and with gifted students. He noticed that students who were "reticent about

making mistakes with paper and pencil" had no qualms about acknowledging they had made a mistake while building something in *Minecraft*,
flattening their flawed creation and starting over. Manegold elaborates on
what he believes makes games different:

> *I think the closest we've come to understanding that from our side is that ability
> for students to feel like there isn't somebody looking over their shoulder and it
> really is kind of an emotionally safe place for them to keep doing the things that
> they did when they were younger: the risk-taking, the hammering at the same
> problem time and time again until they get it right, and also exploring the soft
> problems in different ways.*

Taking a more pragmatic stance, Valve's Mike Ambinder suggests that
games might provide an opportunity to gain experience of operating
under conditions that are otherwise rare, while noting that we simply
don't know for sure if such in-game practice translates into real-
world gains:

> *Games seem to be very useful devices to practice certain aspects of cognition that
> maybe we don't get to work at as much in the real world. Like real time
> problem-solving: how often are you under a time pressure, where in the next five
> minutes you have to do 13 things absolutely correctly?*

Lara Croft level designer Jeff Wajcs picks up on the fact that games
can be very challenging, describing how he will spend his first play
through of a game "dying a whole lot and clawing my way past each
stage". On his second play through, however, that determination in the
face of repeated failure has paid off: "suddenly I am effortlessly completing stages that kicked my butt the first time through. It's a great feeling
to have mastered a game." However, Wajcs shares Mike Ambinder's
scepticism about the transferability of what he gained from this
experience:

> *Do those skills translate back in to the real world? Was the game teaching me
> determination as it killed me over and over again, or was it simply testing what
> determination I already had? I don't think I can say.*

Others are more certain that games can usefully develop resilience and resourcefulness. Reflecting on her childhood efforts to complete *Super Mario Bros.* (Nintendo Creative Department 1985), *Minecraft's* Deirdre Quarnstrom suggests that "games are really great at encouraging players to embrace failure and try and try again" and that "encouraging that kind of skill in a game helps build the muscle that teachers want to see in the classroom". Quarnstrom maintains that *Super Mario Bros.* not only taught her to be more resilient but improved her confidence when she completed it:

> *For me,* Super Mario Bros. *definitely became a point of pride and something that gave me confidence as well. I'd worked so hard at it and tackled it, and could go talk to all my friends at school, the boys and the girls. So, I think there is something in that, that developing mastery in an area, games can be great equalisers across physical limitations, gender differences, and really a place where people can celebrate something that they feel confident in.*

Confidence is another attribute that employers seek, and that many universities—including this author's institution—aim to instil in their graduates. And, as documented in Chap. 4, confidence is an attribute that most students involved in the study described here felt they had developed through playing the selected games. Quarnstrom's *Minecraft* colleague, Neal Manegold, also notes the capacity for video games to develop a player's confidence, with particular reference to leadership. Referring to students who have previously not participated in class, Manegold describes the transformative effect that being part of an 'affinity space' around a game like *Minecraft* can produce:

> *All of a sudden, they're the group leader and all of a sudden, they're raising their hand and wanting to go 'present'. And for me as an educator and a parent, there's nothing more powerful than seeing a student who didn't feel like they had a leadership voice, be able to use this game to develop that.*

The idea that games may nurture players' confidence and resilience is related to the wider notion that games may facilitate personal growth, as discussed above. Such personal growth might, in part, be ascribed to the fact that games permit players to explore alternative identities, providing a mechanism by which the player may learn something about themselves. Paul Hellquist observes that indie games increasingly encourage self-reflection—titles such as *Undertale* (Toby Fox 2015) and *Night in the Woods* (Infinite Fall 2017) immediately come to mind—but he also points to triple-A stalwart, *BioShock* (2K Boston 2007), on which he served as lead designer. He describes how a friend, who had always enjoyed playing the bad guy in games—embracing the dark side in *Star Wars* titles, for example—responded to *BioShock*. *BioShock*, of course, features characters referred to as Little Sisters, genetically modified and psychologically conditioned children that roam the sunken city of Rapture, each protected by an imposing Big Daddy figure. The concept of the Little Sisters is horrifying in itself, but the player is offered a particularly harrowing choice when they defeat a Little Sister's accompanying Big Daddy: to harvest or rescue the child. Harvesting the Little Sister rewards the player with a stock of ADAM, the in-game resource used to upgrade the player's abilities. While saving the child opens up the possibility of other, less immediate rewards, choosing to harvest their ADAM is what anyone playing the game as a bad guy would choose to do. However, Hellquist's friend couldn't do it. Having recently become a father, being confronted with a terrified, unprotected Little Sister forced him to choose "his true self", as Hellquist puts it; "he learned a little bit about who he truly is, from that decision in that game".

According to Hellquist, this potential for self-reflection is a function of the game's design:

> *One of the reasons the main character in* BioShock *was just a cypher and didn't really talk, is we wanted you to become that person in that situation and have you think about 'how would I actually deal with this situation?' And, so, some people that connects with, and they have those experiences, and others just continue to think of it as entertainment, and that's fine as well. But I definitely think that games can connect to people and help them get to the heart of their soul.*

Finally, Hellquist suggests that a player's agency, their ability to affect the world their in-game character inhabits, means that "games have a better chance of connecting with people and helping them learn more about themselves, than just from watching a movie or reading a book". This statement recalls what George Eliot and Francis Bacon had to say about the relationship between art—specifically novels, in Eliot's case—and learning about the human condition (discussed in Chap. 5). The contention here, however, is that the agency afforded by video games enhances the learning experience; "play maketh the man", to paraphrase Bacon. Indeed, this idea has previously been discussed in the literature, with Begg et al. (2005) suggesting that player agency, combined with self-reflection, provides excellent potential for constructivist learning:

> *Through personal experience and critical reflection on* [players'] *beliefs about the world in which they live and the domains in which they hold affective agency, learners come to* know *themselves and what they are* becoming.

Naturally, the work of James Paul Gee is also relevant here. In addition to the Identity Principle, discussed above, the Cultural Models about the World Principle (2007, p. 166) states that "learning is set up in such a way that learners come to think consciously and reflectively about some of their cultural models regarding the world". According to Gee, players are exposed to new or potentially conflicting ideas about the world which, in turn, cause the player to reconsider their own interpretations of familiar concepts; Gee, for example, cites *Operation Flashpoint: Cold War Crisis* (Bohemia Interactive Studio 2001) as having caused him to rethink his conception of warfare. Games offer opportunities to learn about ourselves, the world, and our place in it.

When asked if games should be played at university, the developers of the games used here are perhaps surprisingly reticent in their responses. *Lara Croft* level designer Daniel Bryner is quick to say yes to games being played at university but is equally quick to point out that as a life-long gamer, he is somewhat biased. Fellow *Lara Croft* designer Jeff Wajcs describes the idea of using games in a college curriculum as very exciting but is unsure about how exactly the games would be incorporated, playfully suggesting that "maybe we will start seeing RPGs [role-playing games] that incorporate calculus into their battle systems!"

Borderlands 2 lead Paul Hellquist agrees that integration with the curriculum would be the challenge:

I definitely think you guys in academia could come up with a curriculum around playing certain games; I don't think any old game is going to do it. I think you would have to be very careful and very thoughtful about which games you wanted to expose your students to, and how you could build a lesson and a curriculum around those games.

While Hellquist notes that he had not previously considered the potential relevance of games to the teaching of Philosophy, he recalls being asked to watch a range of films when he studied the subject, including popular titles such as *Total Recall* (Verhoeven 1990) and *A Clockwork Orange* (Kubrick 1971).

The professor used those to talk about philosophical topics like, 'what is reality?' was Total Recall's *whole thing, you know, because that movie's so much about him trying to figure out what was real and what isn't real. And then that got us into the discussion using the movie as, sort of, a back drop for the philosophical discussion, of what makes reality.*

Games could be used in a similar fashion, Hellquist suggests, before recounting a story from the development of *BioShock*. The option to save or harvest the game's Little Sisters presents a stark moral choice, and Hellquist recalls discussing the ethical implications of the child-like characters' inclusion with his wife and family. Ultimately, given that the player is presented with a choice, rather than being forced to perform an immoral or unethical act, Hellquist concluded that the presence of this mechanic was justified. Indeed, his goal was not only to instil terror in the player, but to force them to think critically about the moral implications of their choice. It follows, then, that asking students to play the game and reflect on their actions might provide an excellent starting point for some philosophical discussion. As Hellquist notes:

I could totally see using particular games, where you can potentially have players experience some of these sorts of things, that you could create curriculums that utilise the games as examples for larger concepts that you want to explore, and whatever topic or class, you're trying to do.

BioShock has, indeed, been used to teach philosophical concepts. Just as renowned as the horrifying Little Sisters is the fact that the game is informed by the Objectivism of Ayn Rand, writ large in the actions and beliefs of the game's protagonist, Andrew Ryan. This overt representation of a particular school of philosophical thought, coupled with complex moral choices, and questions about free will and what it means to be oppressed, results in a game that is ripe for inclusion in a Philosophy class. In fact, games *are* used to teach Philosophy, as described by Sherry Jones in the previous chapter, while Karen Schrier's edited volume *Ethics and Game Design: Teaching Values Through Play* (2010) provides an excellent primer on the application of games to encourage ethical thinking and moral development in learners. Indeed, this volume includes a close reading of *BioShock* by Roger Travis (2010, pp. 86–101), intended to illustrate how the game can be used to teach ethics, with reference to Plato's allegory of the cave (*Republic* 514a).

So, while the focus of this book has been on the development of students' skills and competencies, it is clear that developers—like the educators featured in the previous chapter—see potential for games to develop students' understanding of subject-specific material. Such potential is alluded to by Valve's Mike Ambinder:

> *There are historical games that can give you declarative knowledge about the world and the way things worked. Knowledge you didn't have before. So, that was the game providing you with some sort of benefit that has applicability outside the game, because now you know more about the Roman Empire because you were playing* Civilization *or whatnot.*

Paul Hellquist also suggests that historically themed games such as *Crusader Kings* (Paradox Interactive 2004–) could be useful for developing an understanding of the underlying subject matter, proposing that homework might be more popular if the task was to "play the *Crusader* games for four or five hours and explain how Medieval England worked". Such an approach, Hellquist suggests, "would be a lot more engaging for a lot of people than reading some stuffy academic book".

Kurt Squire's work with *Civilization III* (Firaxis Games 2001) was a direct influence on the study underpinning this book, and there is little doubt that a skilled educator can make use of games such as *Civ* to teach

History (Squire and Barab 2004). Indeed, many educators have gone on to use games, including titles in the *Civ*, *Total War* (Creative Assembly 2000–), and *Assassin's Creed* (Ubisoft Montreal 2007–) series, to teach History at various levels—see McCall (2016) for an excellent overview. A common theme, however, is that the games are rarely used to facilitate the learning of historical facts alone. There is certainly scope for historical video games to teach "declarative knowledge": the best such games are meticulously researched pieces of work featuring carefully reconstructed representations of historically significant artefacts, locations, and people. However, games' real strength, it may be argued, lies in their ability to convey the shifting context in which history unfolds. Understanding the interplay between politics, geography, and economics—not to mention the human factors that dictated how actual historical events played out— requires the application of critical thinking and an ability to understand complex systems. These are transferable skills that any graduate entering the jobs market might be expected to possess, regardless of their degree discipline.

Lara Croft level designer, Jeff Wajcs, makes a slightly different point, suggesting that games may provide the inspiration for subsequent learning, rather than forming the basis of the learning *per se*:

> A game with a historical or mythological setting may spark an interest in History and other cultures. A physics puzzler may inspire someone to learn more about Physics. I myself have played enough RPGs that I was motivated to take classes in Japanese. These games do not actually have to teach the player anything about these subjects—it is enough that they inspire the player to learn more about them on their own.

Anecdotally, this is an idea that students frequently cite when quizzed about the influence of video games on their academic development. Indeed, early focus groups, intended to inform the design of the work described in this book, provided multiple examples of students connecting their choice of university subject with prior gaming experience. These ranged from playing *Age of Empires* (Ensemble Studios 1997) or *Age of Mythology* (Ensemble Studios 2002) as a child resulting in a desire to study Classics, to making an explicit connection between early experiences of basic games programming (via the use of POKE commands) and choosing to study Computing Science at university. Indeed, this author has often suggested that playing the original *SimCity* (Maxis 1989) and its immediate sequel, *SimCity 2000* (Maxis 1993) resulted in an interest in Geography and Computing Science that extended to taking both subjects at university. This is pure speculation, however: it is not possible to disentangle the myriad influences on our academic choices, years after the fact. Recollection bias and the generally tricky nature of memory mean that we cannot isolate the influence of, for example, an inspirational teacher or engaged parent. Even in the moment, it may be difficult to pinpoint exactly why we chose particular subjects.

Returning to the broader question of whether games have a place in higher education, *Minecraft's* Neal Manegold reflects on his own teaching experience, highlighting the mismatch between students' experiences inside and outside of the classroom. For today's students, a game such as *Minecraft* is a familiar and natural medium through which their understanding of the world may be mediated. So, for Manegold, using games in the classroom is about more than simply hitting the intended learning outcomes:

> *so much of classroom teaching is about connecting with the students in front of me and beside me as individuals and understanding what they have that's interesting and what's going on in pop culture and what's relevant to them and speaking their language.*

A game such as *Minecraft* provides a mechanism for engaging with students in a meaningful way—echoing comments made by several educators in the previous chapter—while offering the flexibility to address a wide range of learning outcomes, as Manegold suggests:

> *Students are running in the door to get started with the work that they're up to in my classroom, and I know I can engage in some really deep learning around the game itself.*

Of course, the things that interest and engage students evolve over time. Manegold, for example, recalls that while his own interests reflected those of his students at the beginning of his career, their interests began to diverge as the years passed. The students were no longer playing the same games as their teacher, for one thing. This raises a broader concern about game-based learning. If the games used by educators are perceived as being out of date, is their capacity to 'connect' with the students diminished? Particularly for more gaming-literate students, this seems likely to be the case: if the games they are asked to play at university appear archaic, there is the risk that they will disengage. This is particularly troubling when considered in light of the student responses discussed in Chap. 5, where the authenticity of the gaming experience—the fact that they are being asked to play games they might themselves choose to play—is part of what makes the campus-based gaming palatable. Perhaps using anachronistic games runs the risk of damaging this notion of authenticity, of exposing the broccoli that is surreptitiously encased in chocolate, to use Habgood's (2009) analogy. The implication, then, is that educators must keep abreast of gaming developments, such that they may select the most relevant titles from the current crop of games and ensure that their game-based class or activity continues to connect with students.

Summary

Based on these interviews, it is apparent that game developers see educational or developmental potential in the games they create. The potential identified by developers aligns with much of the research and academic writing on game-based learning, including the study on which this book is based, and the theories put forth by Gee. This alignment of views is reflected both in terms of the kinds of skills that may be exercised, including critical thinking, collaboration, and confidence, and in terms of the affordances of games that facilitate learning, such as the provision of a safe space in which to experiment and fail. Equally apparent, however, is the fact that commercial game developers are reluctant to make claims about such potential that they cannot verify. A final word from Valve's Mike Ambinder summarises this position:

> If we could show that games improve communication or teamwork dynamics or problem-solving or whatnot then, yeah, it's valuable. Whatever tools we have at our disposal, to teach students how to think more adaptively, or creatively, or to

work better together, or to solve more difficult problems, we should absolutely take advantage of them. And games could be useful there, but we don't know. We'd like to figure that out.

Indeed, it is hoped that the work described in the book represents a first step towards figuring it out.

Note

1. See, for example, the official Gearbox Software *Borderlands 2* discussion forum at https://forums.gearboxsoftware.com/c/borderlands-2.

References

2K Boston. (2007). *BioShock*. 2K Games.

Bachen, C. M., Hernández-Ramos, P. F., & Raphael, C. (2012). Simulating REAL LIVES: Promoting Global Empathy and Interest in Learning Through Simulation Games. *Simulation & Gaming, 43*(4), 437–460. https://doi.org/10.1177/1046878111432108.

Barr, M. (2014). Learning Through Collaboration: Video Game Wikis. *International Journal of Social Media and Interactive Learning Environments, 2*(2), 119–133. https://doi.org/10.1504/IJSMILE.2014.063385.

Begg, M., Dewhurst, D., & Macleod, H. (2005). Game-Informed Learning: Applying Computer Game Processes to Higher Education. *Innovate: Journal of Online Education, 1*, 6. Retrieved April 8, 2019.

Belman, J., & Flanagan, M. (2010). Designing Games to Foster Empathy. *International Journal of Cognitive Technology, 15*(1), 11.

Blizzard Entertainment. (2004). *World of Warcraft*. Blizzard Entertainment.

Blizzard North. (1996). *Diablo*. Blizzard Entertainment.

Bohemia Interactive Studio. (2001). *Operation Flashpoint: Cold War Crisis*. Codemasters.

Creative Assembly. (2000). *Total War*. Electronic Arts.

Crystal Dynamics. (2010). *Lara Croft and the Guardian of Light*. Square Enix.

Eime, R. M., Young, J. A., Harvey, J. T., Charity, M. J., & Payne, W. R. (2013). A Systematic Review of the Psychological and Social Benefits of Participation in Sport for Children and Adolescents: Informing Development of a

Conceptual Model of Health Through Sport. *International Journal of Behavioral Nutrition and Physical Activity,* *10*(1), 98. https://doi.org/10.1186/1479-5868-10-98.

Ensemble Studios. (1997). *Age of Empires*. Microsoft.

Ensemble Studios. (2002). *Age of Mythology*. Microsoft Game Studios.

Extejt, M. M., & Smith, J. E. (2009). Leadership Development through Sports Team Participation. *Journal of Leadership Education, 8*(2), 224–237.

Firaxis Games. (2001). *Civilization III*. Infogrames.

FromSoftware. (2011). *Dark Souls*. Namco Bandai Games.

Gearbox Software. (2008). *Brothers in Arms: Hell's Highway*. Ubisoft.

Gearbox Software. (2012). In 2K Games (Ed.), *Borderlands 2*.

Gee, J. P. (2007). *What Video Games Have to Teach Us About Learning and Literacy* (2nd ed.). Basingstoke: Palgrave Macmillan.

Habgood, J. (2009). Wii Don't Do Edutainment. In *Proceedings of Game-based Learning 2009*. London, UK. Retrieved from http://www.gamelearning.co.uk/share/Outnumb3r3d.pdf.

Harrington, B., & O'Connell, M. (2016). Video Games as Virtual Teachers: Prosocial Video Game Use by Children and Adolescents from Different Socioeconomic Groups Is Associated with Increased Empathy and Prosocial Behaviour. *Computers in Human Behavior, 63*, 650–658. https://doi.org/10.1016/j.chb.2016.05.062.

Holt, N. L., Tamminen, K. A., Tink, L. N., & Black, D. E. (2009). An Interpretive Analysis of Life Skills Associated with Sport Participation. *Qualitative Research in Sport and Exercise, 1*(2), 160–175. https://doi.org/10.1080/19398440902909017.

Huizinga, J. (1949). *Homo Ludens*. London, Boston and Henley: Routledge and Kegan Paul.

Infinite Fall. (2017). *Night in the Woods*. Finji.

Karen, S. (Ed.). (2010). *Ethics and Game Design: Teaching Values through Play*. Hershey, PA: IGI Global.

Kubrick, S. (1971). *A Clockwork Orange*. Burbank, CA: Warner Bros.

Maxis. (1989). *SimCity*. Maxis.

Maxis. (1993). *SimCity 2000*. Maxis.

McCall, J. (2016). Teaching History with Digital Historical Games: An Introduction to the Field and Best Practices. *Simulation & Gaming, 47*(4), 517–542. https://doi.org/10.1177/1046878116646693.

Mojang. (2011). *Minecraft*. Mojang.

Nintendo Creative Department. (1985). *Super Mario Bros*. Nintendo.

Paradox Development Studio. (2004). *Crusader Kings*. Paradox Interactive.

Plato. (n.d.). *Republic* (Vol. VI).

Rare. (2018). *Sea of Thieves*. Microsoft Game Studios.

Squire, K., & Barab, S. (2004). Replaying History: Engaging Urban Underserved Students in Learning World History Through Computer Simulation Games. In *Proceedings of the 6th International Conference on Learning Sciences* (pp. 505–512). International Society of the Learning Sciences.

Thatgamecompany. (2012). *Journey*. Sony Computer Entertainment.

The Fullbright Company. (2013). *Gone Home*. The Fullbright Company.

Toby Fox. (2015). *Undertale*. Toby Fox.

Travis, R. (2010). Bioshock in the Cave: Ethical Education in Plato and in Video Games. In *Ethics and Game Design: Teaching Values Through Play* (pp. 86–101). Hershey, PA: IGI Global. Retrieved April 10, 2019.

Ubisoft Montreal. (2007). *Assassin's Creed*. Ubisoft.

Valve Corporation. (2007). *Team Fortress 2*. Valve Corporation.

Valve Corporation. (2008). *Left 4 Dead*. Valve South.

Valve Corporation. (2011). *Portal 2*. Valve Corporation.

Valve Corporation. (2013). *Dota 2*. Valve Corporation.

Verhoeven, P. (1990). *Total Recall*. Culver City, CA: TriStar Pictures.

Zimmerman, E. (2012, February 7). Jerked Around by the Magic Circle – Clearing the Air Ten Years Later. *Gamasutra*. Retrieved April 9, 2019, from http://www.gamasutra.com/view/feature/135063/jerked_around_by_the_magic_circle_.php.

8

Gaming for Graduates

This book has expanded upon the findings of a randomised study that suggested playing selected video games on campus could develop certain graduate attributes: the skills and competencies that students are said to develop at university, in readiness for employment. Interviews with students revealed how participants in the study felt that the games might have developed these attributes, and a number of ancillary benefits—particularly the potential for campus-based video games to offer relief from stress—were uncovered. Interviews with educators revealed the breadth of uses of games in higher education, from the inclusion of video games that complement taught material, to the gamification of courses, and the incorporation of board games and LARP (live action role-play). Finally, interviews with game developers suggested that while the industry is aware of the potential for their games to exercise useful skills, this is not their aim, and they make no claims about such potential. It is simply the case that many games are designed to elicit players' critical thinking ability, communication skill, and capacity for collaboration in order to engage and entertain. It was also shown that games exhibit clear links with theories of learning, including elements of constructivism, experiential learning, mastery, and scaffolding—echoing the ideas put forth by

© The Author(s) 2019
M. Barr, *Graduate Skills and Game-Based Learning*, Digital Education and Learning,
https://doi.org/10.1007/978-3-030-27786-4_8

James Paul Gee. Here, these theories have been applied to the development of skills that graduates will be expected to demonstrate in the workplace, arguably enhancing their employability, in a manner similar to that suggested by John Seely Brown. It was nonetheless striking that an intervention of such short duration—just 14 hours of gameplay over a period of around eight weeks—was apparently able to produce significant gains in attribute attainment.

While the constraints of a controlled experiment are one of this approach's greatest advantages (all participants play the same games under the same conditions, allowing for results that are more comparable), there is little doubt that playing games under such circumstances is not representative those under which they are normally played. However, this does not necessarily reflect poorly on the use of such experiments if the intention is to ascertain the utility of video games in a university environment. Certainly, the controlled experiment design, in this context, seems less problematic than it might, for example, if the object was to determine the behavioural effects that playing violent video games could have on children. In that case, the laboratory environment and ethical considerations mean the experimental setting is entirely divorced from the reality of games being played by children in their own homes. And yet, claims are made about the effects of games on players more generally. For the purposes of this study, then, the advantages of an experiment in terms of controlling for certain variables outweigh concerns about the authenticity of the environment in which the games are played. But perhaps more importantly, the drop-in lab configuration in which the study operated is just the sort of facility that might be created by a university wishing to offer game-based skills development opportunities on campus.

That said, no experimental design is perfect, and the study described here is certainly not without its limitations. Randomisation controlled for many variables, and statistical analysis suggested that, in terms of the factors considered (such as age, gender, and existing exposure to video games), the intervention and control groups were suitably similar in composition. However, a more robust design might introduce a third group—an active control—that was asked to convene under circumstances similar to those under which the intervention group played video games. Participants in the active control group would not play games, but would engage in some broadly comparable activity, such as watching television box sets together, on an equivalent timescale. If the study were to be repeated, the inclusion of an active control might add further weight to any statistical analysis or subsequent claims about the efficacy of games for developing graduate attributes. However, statistics are only part of the picture: just as important as the statistical analysis presented in Chap. 3 is the qualitative material described in subsequent chapters. Fixating on quantifiable outcomes and their statistical significance risks failing to recognise the personal and social contexts in which we learn and develop. Thus, alternatives to the quantitative self-report measures used here might be sought, should the study be repeated. Given sufficient resources, an observational approach, wherein suitably qualified experts gauge students' development, might offer a more nuanced understanding of any gains in communication skill or ability to collaborate. Employers, too, might be called upon to help determine if the game-based intervention appeared to produce more employable graduates. In addition, the study could—and, really, should—be extended to include participants other than the relatively privileged undergraduate students involved here. The term 'graduate attributes' is something of a misnomer, after all: these skills are developed in myriad ways and by individuals who have never set foot in a university. They are not the exclusive domain of university graduates. With this in mind, a subsequent study might include further education students, unemployed people, or existing employees; if the game-based approach works, it could function as a form of training or continued professional development well beyond the confines of academia. These are all avenues to be explored in future research, and this author would welcome the opportunity to do so, should a suitably enlightened funding body be minded to support such work.

There are other issues to consider, too. A point that has been made repeatedly in this book relates to video games' appeal: not everybody enjoys video games or sees their educational potential. In Chap. 1, the idea that students can get a lot out of a game for relatively little input was queried, while the educators interviewed in Chap. 6 almost invariably reported that a small proportion of their students were sceptical about the use of games at university. It is to be expected, then, that some students will not engage with video games in the classroom and may be left behind by efforts to incorporate game-based learning into the curriculum. Of course, this has clear implications for student satisfaction and retention, but it is worth noting that not everybody enjoys lectures, either. Gee and others remind us that learning is supposed to be enjoyable—'deeply pleasurable' in fact—but this is not necessarily how students describe their university experience. This author, for one, has yet to have his lectures pronounced 'deeply pleasurable'. So, while games are absolutely not the panacea for higher education that some may proselytise, it's important to remember that no single existing pedagogical approach—including lectures, labs, tutorials, and other, more active forms of learning—has been revealed as a silver bullet for student engagement, either.

However, while games bring with them an abundance of unique advantages for learning and the development of graduate attributes, they do also present some unique challenges. Asking students to play video games as part of their university course—or encouraging games' use as a valuable extracurricular activity—assumes that everyone is able to do so. As with all digital technology, games' accessibility must be considered: if a student requires assistive technology in order to use a computer, they will require similar support to play computer games. And, while developers are increasingly cognizant of the need to provide accessibility options in their games, there is little doubt that enabling a student with certain disabilities to play a fast-paced team shooter may require some serious thought. To be clear: accessibility features such as the Assist Mode in *Celeste* (Matt Makes Games 2018) or the suite of options in *Uncharted 4* (Naughty Dog 2016) that allow the player to adjust on-screen colours and control mechanisms are incredibly welcome. Indeed, the availability of such options might become a prerequisite for a game's inclusion in a university-based initiative.

The selection and appraisal of games to be used in such an intervention is obviously important and, while the games chosen for this study appeared well suited to developing the relevant attributes, further refinement of the selection criteria may be warranted. The team-based multiplayer games used here were generally well received and students saw value in their cooperative nature, but a minority of participants remained unconvinced of their relevance and baffled by their interfaces. On the other hand, *Portal 2* (Valve Corporation 2011)—which employs a similar control scheme—was universally praised by students for its potential to exercise a host of attributes while engaging and entertaining even the least experienced players. Easily the most polarising title deployed here was the real-time strategy game, *Warcraft III* (Blizzard Entertainment 2002), which proved somewhat impenetrable for some participants, even if they could be persuaded of its developmental merits. Meanwhile, the inclusion of smaller independent titles, *Gone Home* (The Fullbright Company 2013) and *Papers, Please* (3909 LLC 2013), was welcomed by participants, who connected these games with the development of ethical and social awareness—perhaps one of the most difficult graduate attributes to 'teach'.

If a game-based approach to graduate attribute development were to be adopted by universities, a number of recommendations regarding the selection of games can be made. First, it is suggested that an exercise to map potential game titles to the desired attributes is undertaken, in a fashion similar to that taken here. This process must include games experts, even if those tasked with establishing the gaming facility are familiar with video games. A more diverse set of suggestions can only improve the variety of games selected and thus help ensure that there is diversity of representation in the titles chosen. Involving the student body in the selection process might be especially productive, and it should be borne in mind that an assortment of games is thought to be important for developing adaptability and resourcefulness. Then, these suggestions must be filtered through practical concerns, including cost and hardware or network infrastructure requirements: early engagement with technical support personnel is recommended. As noted previously in this book, the quality of the games must also be considered, and well-received games prioritised over low-quality titles that students may find less engaging. Finally, this process should be repeated, probably on an annual basis, to ensure currency and relevance of the selected titles. This is not to say that the selection of games must include the very latest releases—none of the games used in the study described here were exactly cutting edge—but it is important to keep abreast of gaming developments, should an especially germane title be released or a previously selected title become obsolete in the eyes of more avid players. As noted by educators in Chap. 6, the right games can connect with students, but if a title is judged to be outdated, its authenticity and appeal will begin to wane.

Across interviews with students, educators, and game developers, a substantial degree of agreement on games' potential to develop useful skills was observed. It is interesting to note that in this triangulation of views many of the same ideas put forward by Gee and other advocates of game-based learning have emerged quite spontaneously. This is not surprising, perhaps, but, to this author's knowledge, the perspectives of all three parties have not previously been brought to bear on the issue of games being used in such a fashion at university level.

It was clear from the interviews documented in Chap. 6 that video games are currently used to complement teaching provision in higher education, but they are not typically the focal point of a course. Instead, they are used to elucidate taught material. However, a game may also be positioned as an object of study in and of itself, if students are prompted to interrogate the limitations of the game's representation of theoretical concepts. Such an approach encourages mastery of the taught material, but also exercises students' critical thinking and evaluative judgement. The educators here articulate how they use games to offer students different perspectives on the world and to explore taught concepts from different points of view. And, in addition to using games to support the teaching of subject material, these educators see potential for the experience to simultaneously develop graduate attributes. This is not to suggest that games have a place in every university class, however—far from it. The real potential for using games in higher education lies in their capacity to develop skills and competencies, not to deliver course content. Where games can be integrated into the curriculum—as many of the educators interviewed in this book have done with success—then the experience is rendered all the more valuable by the fact that a range of attributes are also nurtured. To shoehorn games into every class, without a clear and meaningful articulation between game and subject matter, would be ultimately counterproductive. At the same time, stand-alone 'graduate attribute classes' are known to be ineffective, if only as a result of their unpopularity with students. However, if such classes were genuinely fun and engaging, and their efficacy supported by research, student attitudes might be swayed. Certainly, the students involved in this study were able to express the benefits they perceived in playing video games at university. While the students interviewed here were those who persisted with the study, and are thus not representative of the larger student body, their responses to the games offer clues as to how others may be persuaded of their value.

Amongst the students' reflections was an aspect of video games that is often overlooked: their capacity to facilitate learning about the world by assuming alternative identities. Of course, it has been some time since James Paul Gee first made this point, but the popular discourse around games has yet to catch up. Nonetheless, it is obvious to a group of undergraduate students—some of whom have played games for only a few hours—that this potential exists. We have seen that developers and educators, too, are aware of the capacity for games to elicit empathic responses from students, to learn something by placing themselves in the shoes of another. Social aspects of learning are also frequently overlooked, as commentators perpetuate the ludicrous notion that games are inherently antisocial. Of course, phenomena such as *Fortnite* (Epic Games 2017)— popular at time of writing—and stalwarts like *World of Warcraft* (Blizzard Entertainment 2004) are fundamentally social in nature. Here, students talked at length about teamwork and playing with people of differing experience or from differing backgrounds. This is where Gee's Affinity Group Principle (Gee 2007) is manifest: in the social interactions that are predicated on players' shared appreciation of the games they play together.

Multiplayer titles, then, are of specific utility, as players collaborate in order to understand the game and progress as a group—a point made by several students in Chap. 4 and subsequently echoed by both educators and developers. All parties—students, educators, and developers— referred to the communication required to support in-game cooperation, and, in particular, the need to communicate efficiently under pressure. Cooperation, underpinned by effective communication, was almost unanimously identified as being essential to succeeding in the multiplayer titles played here. However, it was observed that cooperation also arose from single-player games being tackled simultaneously in the lab, as players pooled their knowledge of the games and helped guide one another through the abandoned environs of *Gone Home* (The Fullbright Company 2013). Perhaps with this game-based camaraderie in mind, several students suggested that a similar set-up be used for team-building purposes, in place of the awkwardly artificial exercises to which employers—and universities—typically resort. What video games apparently offer would-be teams is a mixture of authenticity (commercial video games are intended to be fun, rather than consolidate teams) and complexity (in terms of the variety of roles and experiences afforded by modern games) that is usually absent from team-building exercises.

However, it is important to remember that the data here refer to the specific circumstances under which carefully selected games were played. In interviews, participants make multiple references to the effects of being asked to play games with people other than their friends, and several of the attributes discussed here appear to be influenced by the fact that students played with strangers from quite different backgrounds. As such, claims cannot be made about the effects of playing games outside of the lab and that is not the intention of this book. There is no reason to suggest, however, that an equivalent campus-based gaming lab could not offer comparable benefits.

While it might have been expected that students, educators, and developers could agree that especially multiplayer games might offer opportunities to exercise collaboration and communication, it was interesting to note the prevalence of the less obvious notion that games offer a space in which to experiment. Across all three sets of interviews, references are made to experimentation, or trial and error, alongside the ideas of safety, second chances, and failure. This relates to Gee's "Psychosocial Moratorium" Principle, which suggests that the consequences of a player's in-game actions are lowered, allowing experimentation with new strategies at little personal cost. Given that several of the more sceptical interviewees expressed doubts about the transferability or general applicability of their gaming experience, it is perhaps surprising that being allowed to fail in a game is considered valuable. But several players made a connection between the experience of trying, failing, and trying again with an increase in their confidence. They have 'practiced failure', and it no longer holds the power over their real-world actions that it once did. Indeed, practice was another common theme, with the prevailing wisdom that practice is how we improve not only our ability to deal with failure but also a host of skills and competencies, from leadership—also associated with confidence—to communication. Game developer Raph Koster has previously made exactly this point:

> *If games are essentially models of reality, then the things that games teach us must reflect on reality. The very phrase 'it's just a game' implies that playing a game is a form of PRACTICE for a real-life challenge. From playing cops and robber to playing house, play is about learning life skills.* (Koster 2005, pp. 52–53)

If any ability can be practiced, then this idea may be extended to how we develop critical thinking; indeed, this was another attribute on which there was agreement from students, educators, and developers. Nicol (2010) has suggested that something like critical thinking—what he terms "critical evaluative experience"—may underpin a range of what we currently think of as discrete graduate attributes. Another way of looking at critical thinking, then, is that it is about critical evaluation, or judgement. And, as one student interview suggested, games are "all about judgement". Developers indicated that requiring players to think critically, or make evaluative judgements, was integral to many games' design. Be it filling in the blanks of a story that's told through incomplete or conflicting scraps of information or making sense of deliberately ambiguous in-game item descriptions, critical thinking is an often-crucial aspect of gameplay. Problem-solving—or puzzle solving—was highlighted by many students and developers in relation to games' capacity to exercise critical thinking, in line with the host university's definition of this attribute. Related to critical thinking, students also referred to the need for strategic thinking in many of the games, reflecting John Seely Brown's assertion that multiplayer titles require players to strategise, as well as manage team members and resources (Brown and Thomas 2006).

From speaking to developers, it is clear that the opportunities afforded by games to develop such skills do not occur by accident: in striving to make the best game possible, many developers work to ensure that their games require critical thinking and adaptability, or promote communication and collaboration, because exercising these attributes is *fun*. But perhaps fun in itself is an important aspect of student development: certainly, this is one interpretation of the students' numerous references to the stress-relieving benefits of playing games on campus. As perhaps the most commonly cited such benefit to emerge—unprompted—during student interviews, the potential de-stressing effects of play surely demand further exploration. Such effects might stem from the afore-mentioned idea that failure is an option in games, when it is not, ideally, an option at university. This idea is one of several related features of video games that both Gee (2007) and Squire (2011) identify in relation to learning. They also note that, in a video game, the player receives immediate feedback on their actions, and progress can often be made on a variety of fronts, even while a particular challenge currently appears insurmountable. These features may position games in stark contrast to some students' experience at university and offer beneficial respite from the occasional but unavoidable challenges of university life. Whatever the underlying cause, many of the students interviewed here certainly hold the belief that playing games can reduce stress. If this is the case, then it is even possible that the stress-reducing effects of playing games is—to some unknown extent—responsible for the marked differences in the control and intervention groups' attribute scores in this study. Any future work in this area should attempt to gauge stress levels in partici-pants, to ascertain if playing games on campus might reduce stress. This would allow us to explore the question of whether reduced stress levels are related to gains in attribute scores made by the intervention group, and possibly help explain the loss of function observed in control group scores. It might also be significant that the games are played on univer-sity premises, with the tacit approval of the institution, as this might ameliorate stress-inducing concerns that playing games is frowned upon by the university, and at odds with academic success.

This work has also offered an opportunity to reflect on the notion of graduate attributes more generally. Graduate attributes are multifaceted phenomena and there is a danger that they are reduced to items on a checklist, without considering their complex and interconnected nature. Indeed, work such as this, which necessarily seeks to operationalise and quantify attribute attainment, arguably increases the risk of such a reduc-tive approach. Games, however, are also complex, multifaceted phenom-ena. They provide rich opportunities to exercise the skills and competencies that graduates are expected to possess, and each of the games described in this book exercises a variegated blend of interrelated skills. As in the workplace, and life more generally, the demands placed on players are variable and unpredictable, and these demands arise naturally from the games' design: in order to progress, a player must communicate, collaborate, think critically, and adapt. Thus, the development of these attributes is an authentic aspect of the game experience, rather than some tacked on, inherently artificial exercise designed solely to develop a particular skill.

Attributes are not routinely measured at university, although they are often implicit in our assessment of student work: writing an essay in History must exercise critical thinking, for example, while a programming assignment in Computer Science demonstrates problem-solving ability. However, it might be argued that, as a sector, we are making somewhat unsubstantiated claims about the extent to which we develop our students' graduate attributes. As discussed in Chap. 2, measuring the attainment of graduate attributes—or any such 'soft skills'—is challenging, but universities must do more to assess students' skills development. And, if we do so, we may discover that more needs to be done to develop our graduates, which is where new approaches such as that described in this book may have value.

Conclusion

Ask any reasonably experienced player if they believe video games might help develop useful skills and competencies in those who play them, and the answer is likely to be yes. This is especially likely if the player has experience of multiplayer games that quite demonstrably require communication skills and an ability to collaborate, if not also lead. Fans of single-player games will also likely be able to point to the problem-solving or strategic thinking that their favourite pastime demands. To those familiar with modern video games, the entire premise of this book makes intuitive sense, even if they had not previously considered that games may be harnessed by universities to develop our students. Neither will the findings discussed in this book come as a surprise to scholars such as James Paul Gee and John Seely Brown, whose ideas this work sought to test by investigating the utility of commercial video games in an educational context. And, bearing in mind the limitations outlined above, the work has demonstrated that games *can* play a role in developing our students' graduate attributes.

But this is a small first step. No book, thesis, or paper, it seems, can conclude without suggesting that further research is required, and this is very much the case here. The empirical evidence for using video games to develop graduate attributes or, indeed, for using video games in higher education at all, has hitherto been rather slight. There are pockets of excellent work, some of which have been touched upon in this book, and a number of respected scholars, eminently more learned than this author, have espoused the potential of game-based learning. But the data, both quantitative and qualitative, are lacking. This work has made a contribution, but larger, still more rigorous studies are required, and it is important that disproportionate claims are not made about the relatively small (but reasonably well-formed) study on which this book is partly based. If readers remain unconvinced by the statistics presented in Chap. 3, then they should at least consider the evidence presented by students, educators, and game developers in support of the idea that games have a potential role to play in higher education. On the other hand, if the empirical data presented here have persuaded readers that games do deserve greater prominence at university, then some recommendations follow.

First, games should be integrated into higher education curricula where appropriate, but *only* where appropriate. The material presented in Chap. 6 provides some examples of what appropriate incorporation of game-based learning might look like. If integrated thoughtfully, games can provide students with opportunities not only to develop their understanding of taught material but also, simultaneously, to exercise a range of attributes that will stand them in good stead for the workplace.

Second, universities should afford video games at least the same status as sports and other such worthy pursuits currently enjoy. This means making games available on campus, perhaps in a form similar to the lab described here, such that students may engage with gaming as they would any other university-sanctioned extracurricular endeavours.

Third, while we know that the provision of 'bolt-on' graduate attribute training has not always proven successful, or popular with students, there is sufficient evidence here to suggest that we should consider offering more formal game-based opportunities for attribute development. This may be especially relevant where existing teaching provision does not address such development, perhaps due to the characteristics of a particular discipline. Many educators are at a loss as to how they are expected to nurture the full range of graduate attributes within their subject area, and this is a perfectly reasonable position: the sooner we acknowledge that not all subjects are comparable in terms of their affinity with employability-focused attributes, the sooner we can start to take seriously the need for some alternative provision.

Finally, we must challenge the prevailing negative portrayal of games. Video games continue to be vilified in numerous quarters, from the rabid sensationalism of the tabloid press to the ill-considered pronouncements of bodies such as the World Health Organization. While this mischaracterisation of the medium endures, games can never fulfil their considerable potential in higher education and beyond.

References

Blizzard Entertainment. (2002). *Warcraft III: Reign of Chaos*. Blizzard Entertainment.

Blizzard Entertainment. (2004). *World of Warcraft*. Blizzard Entertainment.

Brown, J. S., & Thomas, D. (2006, April 1). You Play World of Warcraft? You're Hired! *Wired*. Retrieved June 16, 2019, from https://www.wired.com/2006/04/learn/.

Epic Games. (2017). *Fortnite*. Epic Games.

Gee, J. P. (2007). *What Video Games Have to Teach Us About Learning and Literacy* (2nd ed.). Basingstoke: Palgrave Macmillan.

Koster, R. (2005). *A Theory of Fun for Game Design* (1st ed.). Scottsdale, AZ: Paraglyph Press.

Matt Makes Games. (2018). *Celeste*. Matt Makes Games.

Naughty Dog. (2016). *Uncharted 4*. Sony Computer Entertainment.

Nicol, D. J. (2010). *The Foundation for Graduate Attributes: Developing Self-Regulation Through Self and Peer-Assessment*. The Quality Assurance Agency for Higher Education.

Squire, K. (2011). *Video Games and Learning: Teaching Participatory Culture in the Digital Age*. London: Teachers' College Press.
The Fullbright Company. (2013). *Gone Home*. The Fullbright Company.
Valve Corporation. (2011). *Portal 2*. Valve Corporation.

Index[1]

---

[1] Note: Page numbers followed by 'n' refer to notes.

© The Author(s) 2019
M. Barr, *Graduate Skills and Game-Based Learning*, Digital Education and Learning,
https://doi.org/10.1007/978-3-030-27786-4